CRICKET'S EXILES

CRICKET'S EXILES

The Saga of South African Cricket

Brian Crowley

Angus & Robertson Publishers

ANGUS & ROBERTSON PUBLISHERS
London • Sydney • Melbourne

First published in South Africa
by Don Nelson Publishers in 1983
First published in Australia
by Angus & Robertson Publishers in 1984
First published in the United Kingdom
by Angus & Robertson (UK) Ltd in 1984

ISBN 0 207 14909 7

Typeset in 10pt Times Roman
Printed in Hong Kong

CONTENTS

Dedicated to a truly united South Africa, on the cricket field and off.

INTRODUCTION

The following pages will hopefully become the final attempt at compiling a divided history of South African cricket. This work deals in the main with cricket on the international level and cannot therefore be described as a comprehensive history of South African cricket.

A reader searching for fuller information relating to domestic cricket is directed to the fine work done by M.W. Luckin in his two monumental volumes covering the years 1875 to 1927, by Louis Duffus, who chronicled the events from 1927 to 1947, and, in more recent times, by Geoffrey Chettle and the meticulous Denys Heesom in the 'South African Cricket Annual', and the 'Protea Cricket Annual of South Africa' which, combined, have now reached their 29th edition thanks to the efforts of Peter Sichel, Michael Owen-Smith and Eric Litchfield over the past couple of years.

Andre Odendaal's exhaustive work entitled 'Cricket in Isolation — the Politics of Race and Cricket in South Africa' has also been an invaluable source reference and the chapter relating to the history of Black Cricket in the present volume would have been impossible to compile without reference to the works of S.J. Reddy and D.N. Bansda who were virtually the only historians of cricket on "the other side of the fence". Other reference works are fully listed in a bibliography at the end of this book.

The approach to this book was such that it was felt that full justice could not always be done to outstanding individual players without disturbing the flow of the text. To overcome this the Publisher and I have decided to include special panels devoted to such giants as Faulkner, Taylor, Nourse, Pollock and others. I have selected pieces written which have impressed me and which I felt gave the best picture of the man and his achievements.These have not been specially written for this book but have been taken from a variety of publications over the years. The name of the author,the publication and the date of publication are given at the end of each panel.

The many notable contributors to this attempt at presenting the story of South African cricket are well known to cricket enthusiasts: Peter Pollock, Chris Greyvenstein, Tom Reddick, Charles Fortune, Jackie McGlew, A.C. Parker, C.O. Medworth, Peter Walker, Arthur Goldman, Jimmy Hattle and Dick Whittington represent as fine a selection of cricket writers as will be found anywhere.

Lay-out design and production was handled by Peter Ibbotson in his customary sensitive and professional style and Chris Greyvenstein made the invaluable contribution of his vast experience in the creating of major sports publications. The final accolade is reserved for publisher Don Nelson whose firm guiding hand was always in evidence.

BRIAN CROWLEY
Cape Town, 1st August, 1983

Aubrey Faulkner — one of the six greatest all-rounders the world has seen

CHAPTER ONE

THE EARLY YEARS AND THE FIRST GOLDEN AGE

When the crowd of almost 18 000 of all races rose as one man to greet the West Indian opening batsmen as they stepped onto the Newlands turf on that historic day of 15th January 1983, few present would have been aware that this was not in fact the first occasion on which a match had been arranged between a team of cricketers from the veld and an eleven from the Caribbean.

At the height of the Anglo/Boer War in the year 1900 a South African team was scheduled to visit Britain, a trip which eventually took place the following season. The postponement of this tour removed all possibility of what would have been an intriguing fixture scheduled to start at the legendary Lord's ground on July 25th 1900.

A West Indies team under the captaincy of the famous Sir Pelham Warner's brother, R.S.A. Warner, and including in its ranks Lebrun S. Constantine, father of the incomparable Learie Constantine, was also due to play in England that year and the two countries had been matched in a fixture entitled "West Indians versus South Africans".

Neither country was then of course regarded as of test match calibre and the encounter would not have been labelled "international" but it would certainly have been an interesting precedent to say the least. South Africa was awarded test status seven years later but the West Indies had to wait until their 1928 tour of England to gain recognition.

And, strangely enough, the cancellation of a proposed Indian tour in 1904 to coincide with another South African venture in the same year saw the removal from the fixture list of a match entitled "South Africans versus Indians"! Hopefully this also indicates some good portent for South Africa in the near future.

Eighty three long years were to elapse before a South African eleven would be matched with one from the West Indies but, during this period, South African international cricket, based on selection solely from the white population group, was to flower and flourish, and grow to unprecendented stature before being so brusquely cut down whilst in full bloom during the fateful 1970's.

In all probability cricket arrived at the Cape when the first British garrison troops appeared in 1795 and the first recorded reference to a match being played in South Africa appeared in the *Cape Town Gazette and African Advertiser,* the only newspaper then published : "A grand match at cricket will be played for one thousand dollars a side on Tuesday, January 5, 1808, between Officers of the Artillery Mess, having Colonel Austen of the 60th Regiment and the Officers of the Colony, with General Clavering. The wickets to be pitched at 10 o'clock."

So professional cricket of a kind appeared in the Cape some 170 odd years before Graham Gooch's S.A. Breweries "rebels" took the stage to break South Africa's ten-year international isolation.

Although what is now regarded as South Africa's first official test match commenced at St George's Park in Port Elizabeth, home of South Africa's oldest cricket club, on 12th March 1889, the home eleven was nowhere near test class and the legitimacy of the 1888/89 series must always remain in some doubt.

The famous "Golden Age" South African XI of 1905/06
Standing: Mr Malraison (scorer) A.W. Nourse, S.J. Snooke, A.E. Vogler Seated: L.J. Tancred, J.H. Sinclair, R.O. Schwarz, P.W. Sherwell (captain), W.A. Shalders, C.M.H. Hathorn In front: G.A. Faulkner, G.C. White

The visitors, captained by the colourful C. Aubrey Smith (a famous Hollywood actor in his later years who was knighted at the age of eighty-one and was once described as the "world ambassador of the English gentleman") included one or two leading England players, notably "Bobby" Abel, George Ulyett and Johnny Briggs, but were themselves far from being regarded as of test status.

England won both "test matches" (the second was played at Newlands) by overwhelming margins and to the diminuitive Surrey batsman Abel went the distinction of scoring the first hundred in Anglo/South African games. Left-hander Johnny Briggs, a man known for his grand sense of fun but who was to die tragically, had the South African batsmen in a spin and gathered 21 wickets in the two encounters for under five runs apiece.

Aubrey Smith and another member of the party, M.P. Bowden, actually set up a stock-broking firm on the Rand after the tour and both played in the inaugural Currie Cup clash between Kimberley and Transvaal at Kimberley in April 1890. Bowden's shares were particularly bullish and he contributed 63 and 126 not out when Transvaal took the honours in the first match of what has become one of the toughest domestic competitions in the world.

Another illustrious member of the England X1 was Frank Hearne, member of a famous cricketing family which produced five test and county players, and who was so pleased with his first trip to South Africa that he stayed on at the Cape to become one of the best coaches the country has seen and to actually represent his adopted land in the only test match played during W.W. Read's next English tour in 1891/92.

England won the single test that season (at Cape Town) by an innings thanks to a hundred by wicket-keeper Wood and 13 wickets from former Australian player J.J. Ferris. Two of Frank Hearne's brothers, George and Alec, plus his cousin John were in the England team to make it a cosy family affair.

The energetic Lord Hawke captained the next England side to tour south in 1895/96 and such "giants" of the day as George Lohmann, Tom Hayward and C.B. Fry were present in the English ranks. An ever-struggling South African eleven could find no answer to the superb bowling of Lohmann and the stylish Hayward graced the first test at the Old Wanderers ground in Johannesburg with a fine innings of 122.

However, one nineteen-year-old South African hero of the future in the sizable form of Jimmy Sinclair, had his first taste of test cricket and aquitted himself admirably in the Wanderers' game with scores of 40 and 29, whilst his team companions crashed on all sides during a rout which ended in a massive innings defeat for the home side.

Of classic build and proportion, Sinclair had actually appeared against the previous England team in 1892 whilst still a fifteen-year-old pupil at Marist Brothers' School. Going in last man in a team of eighteen players he immediately gave notice of future intentions by smacking the first ball he received for four (he was caught in the deep off the next delivery).

The sight of this six-foot-four giant of a man was always greeted with delight by the spectators wherever he played in South Africa, England and Australia and his outstanding record includes the unbeatable honour of having scored his country's first-ever test century.

His record-creating 106 was scored in exceptionally quick time out of just 150 runs added whilst he was in occupation against a strong attack at Newlands. During the previous game at the Wanderers Sinclair had notched South Africa's first test match fifty to give him a unique record of achievement. Then, against Joe Darling's first Australian team in 1902/03, the mighty hitter excelled himself with an innings of a lifetime.

Darling's team had come to South Africa after a thrilling series in England, eleven years after the first aborted attempt to persuade the 1890 Australian X1 to come to the Cape. The Australians came up against unexpectedly strong opposition in the first test clash at Johannesburg where the visitors were actually compelled to follow-on and only a fine 142 from the classic left-hander Clem Hill held pending ignominy at bay. With Sinclair, W.A. Shalders, Louis Tancred, Charles Llewllyn, Maitland Hathorn and the indomitable A.W. "Dave" Nourse in their line-up, the South African "Golden Age" X1 of the 1900's was beginning to take shape.

As a prelude to his finest hour of achievement Sinclair smashed a breathtaking two-hour hundred to give South Africa a welcome 65-run first innings lead during the second match at the Wanderers. This grand effort was to no avail as a dogged 159 not out from the broad bat of the even broader Warwick Armstrong (surely the heaviest man ever to play test cricket) and some clever bowling by left-hand medium-pacer J.V. Saunders gave Australia a 1-0 lead in the series.

So the stage was set for a crucial final performance at Cape Town. And drama there was aplenty when a dismal South African collapse saw Darling invite the home side to follow-on. More distress for South Africa followed but an incredible solo effort from the mighty Jimmy Sinclair dispelled the gloom, albeit for a short eighty minutes of thundering glory.

Dave Nourse once related an amusing story concerning the nervous behaviour of popular former South African manager W.V. "Billy" Simkins during the ensuing six-hitting effort by the giant South African. Simkins hastily arranged for the pavilion waiter to supply him with a long whisky-and-soda each time Sinclair smacked one over the ropes so that he could fill the time in comfortably whilst the ball was being retrieved. After three such hits in one over Simkins was lagging drastically behind in his off-the-field performance but breathed a sigh of relief when the next big hit landed in an adjoining field which was occupied by a ferocious young bull and it took some five minutes to get the ball back into play.

Sinclair reached his fifty in 35 minutes (the world test record is 28 minutes by J.T. Brown for England vs Australia in 1894/95) and, with eight fours and six glorious sixes (by today's rules a couple of his fours would have been registered as sixes as well) he completed his hundred in only eighty minutes, just five minutes short of the time set by Gilbert Jessop of England at the Oval two months earlier, a record which may well have been the South African's were it not for Simkin's bull!

During one eight ball sequence of his amazing innings Sinclair slammed 34 runs and in a gesture typical if his approach to the game, be it test match or club knock-about, he was out stumped in the final over of the day.

Sinclair was also a fine medium-paced bowler who used his great height effectively to extract life from the deadest pitch and his first test hundred at the Wanderers was preceded by a bowling effort of six wickets for 26 thus making him the first test player to take six wickets *and* score a hundred in the first innings of a test match, and the only one to do so for South Africa.

This genial man was possibly the most popular and loved South African sportsman of his time (his death at the early age of 37 came as a great shock and thousands attended his funeral) and it is difficult to accept the allegations made by English writer Rowland Bowen that Sinclair was one of the South Africans who so cruelly taunted the allegedly coloured Springbok all-rounder Charles "Buck" Llewellyn about his skin colour during the South Africans' 1910/11 tour of Australia that the latter was forced to seek refuge from his tormentors in hotel lavatories.

Llewellyn's daughter, resident in England, denies vehemently that her father was in actual fact a coloured man and there must therefore be some doubt about the whole story. In a letter to *Cricketer International* she refutes all claims to her father being called "South Africa's first coloured cricketer" and points out that her parents *and* grandparents were of pure British stock.

In any event the only important fact of the matter was that G.C.B. Llewellyn was undoubtedly one of South Africa's finest cricketers of the first "Golden Age". He played so well as an all-rounder for Hampshire that he was even once chosen in the England squad for a test match against Australia (to be omitted on the morning of the match) and achieved the honour of inclusion as one of Wisden's "Five Cricketers of the Year" in 1911. Dave Nourse incidentally always considered him as the best left-hander of his time.

A game played on the billiard table and which delights in the peculiar name "twisty grab" provided the first link in a chain of events which led to the bowling innovation that provided the South African eleven with its most notable and potent weapon during the early part of the century and led to South Africa's first ever test match and series triumph over England in 1905/06.

Bernard Bosenquet, a versatile games player at Oxford, first developed the "googly" whilst fooling around with a billiard ball. The "off-break bowled with a leg-break action" is still known in Australia as the "bosie", in honour of its inventor, and this novel form of attack soon became the trade -mark of several successive South African combinations.

Reggie Schwarz, who had played for Middlesex, first tried it out during the second Oxford innings when South Africa were in England in 1904. His initial chance at a bowl on the tour was at first considered as something of a joke by his colleagues, but five cheap wickets soon gave Schwarz the last laugh and he actually ended the season at the head of the bowling table.

The South African change bowler's

success with the new type of delivery prompted three others, Ernest Vogler, Aubrey Faulkner and Gordon White, to emulate his style (although Schwarz was somewhat unique in that he bowled the googly as his stock ball and did not bowl leg-breaks at all).

Of the quartet, Vogler was probably the most dangerous and he was described in Wisden as "the best bowler in the world during 1907". His "wrong-un" was extremely difficult to detect and few contemporary batsmen could "read" his hand at the moment of delivery. Vogler, who was born in Queenstown, varied his pace and flight expertly and included a deadly slow yorker in his repertoire. He was even considered, when at his best, to be as good as England's world-beater Sydney Barnes. The spinner's ten wickets for 26 effort for Eastern Province versus Griqualand West in 1906/07 remains the only instance of a South African achieving the bowlers' grand-slam.

In his obituary notice in *The Times* of London, September 11th, 1930, Major George Aubrey Faulkner was described as "not only one of the dominating figures in South African cricket, but also one of the finest all-round cricketers in the game". His dominating batsmanship and magnificent fielding were but two aspects of the complete all-rounder (rated by that impeccable statistician the late Denys Heesom as the most succesful South African all-rounder in history).

Faulkner even rivalled Ernest

THE FIRST-EVER TEST MATCH VICTORY

It's a full toss on the leg side and the burly man with the soup strainer moustache heaves the ball hard and true to the boundary.

"Plum" Warner, England's captain and still destined to become Sir Pelham Warner, allows his well-bred self control to show the tiniest of cracks as he mutters a reproachful "good heavens, Bert" to the erring bowler and then he and all the other players on the field are swallowed up in a seething crowd of 10 000 men and women suddenly gone stark-staring crazy with sheer delight.

This was the scene on Johannesburg's old Wanderers Ground when South Africa gained its first-ever international victory in cricket.

There are many golden days in the long history of Springbok cricket but none with a more enduring glitter than January 4, 1906. It marked the emergence of the "Colonials" as worthy foes for any cricketing country, but it was the manner in which the win was achieved rather than victory itself, that made it one of the truly great moments of South African sport.

"A match I will remember to my dying day", was how the sporting Warner described it in his memoirs many years later, and considering that South Africa only won by one wicket after a nail-chewing last wicket partnership, it is certain that Warner's words found an echo in the hearts of all who were there on that immortal day.

Cricketers, like retired generals, are keen starters when it comes to committing their memories to paper, and as a result we have got a lot more than just the dusty record books to tell us the story of South Africa's maiden Test win. Two of the central figures in the drama, "Plum" Warner and Dave Nourse, have perhaps told it best of all and it is through their eyes that we are able to roll back the years to relive that famous victory.

The MCC won the toss and took first strike on the matting wicket and they were soon in trouble against South Africa's leg-break attack. This type of bowler can be murderous on matting where the ball turns very quickly and they are usually much more dangerous than fast bowlers. In addition, the England batsmen could not adapt their footwork to matting with the result that they floundered badly against bowlers like Reggie Schwarz and Aubrey Faulkner and could only scratch together a paltry 184 in their first innings.

The South Africans fared even worse, and Lees, Blythe and Crawford had eight of them out for only 71 runs by the time stumps were drawn. The next day the South African innings crumbled completely and they were all out for only 91. The only batsman who came out of the mess with his reputation intact, was Dave Nourse, big and stolid with hands so huge that it was said that he could pick up a soccer ball with one hand and let it dangle from his fingers. Nourse carried his bat for 18, after batting for nearly one and a half hours.

England's second innings started with a bang and at one stage they were leading by 205 runs with five wickets still in hand, but the tail failed to wag effectively and they were all out for a total of 190, leaving South Africa with the formidable task of scoring 284 runs for victory. At the end of the day's play, the South African score stood at 68 for the loss of two wickets and the stage was set for the final act of the drama.

And what a drama it turned out to be.

A crowd of 10 000 people lined the Old Wanderers that morning of January 4, 1906, and the cycle track surrounding the cricket field was reduced to a ribbon of red dust by the shuffling of so many nervous feet. Soon, in their excitement, the crowd encroached on the playing area and the boundary became a

Vogler very closely for the title of leading googly bowler and was, at times, possibly even more dangerous that his counterpart, because of his ability to bowl, in addition, a yorker almost as fast as anyone else around at the time.

Although the great man's batting style could never be described as free or forcing and conveyed in fact an impression of awkwardness, he always made his runs with a firm assurance which was based on the soundest of techniques.

His *Faulkner School of Cricket* at Walham Green was opened amidst much carping criticism but his sound and ever patient methods visibly assisted the careers of such notables as K.S. Duleepsinhji and the two fine English googly merchants R.W.V. Robins and Ian Peebles. The latter worked for some time as Faulkner's secretary and in a piece on his former employer in his autobiographical *Spinner's Yarn* states that "despite the abundance of talent the game has produced in the fifty years since last he played, Faulkner has strong claim to be numbered amongst the six greatest all-rounders the game has yet seen".

Peebles goes on to state firmly that in his opinion only Sir Garfield Sobers would seem to eclipse Faulkner in playing capability. Aubrey Faulkner the cricketer was well defined but Faulkner the man remained an enigma and his tragic suicide by gassing in 1930 remains a mystery unsolved. He was a life-long tee-totaller and, according to

swaying mass of people.

Within minutes after the restart of the match, South African hopes were about as low as they could get. Shalders was run out, Lees trapped Snooke leg before wicket and it was Lees again who tempted Jimmy Sinclair, tall and rangy but with magnificent shoulders and forearms, to pick the wrong ball to clobber. Fane snapped up the magnificent catch and now the South Africans were well and truly in the soup.

Aubrey Faulkner, later to die so tragically by his own hand and certainly one of the greatest all-rounders in the long annals of cricket, was next man in and there was not a person in that anxious crowd who did not feel that here was the last hope of the South African team.

But this was not to be Aubrey Faulkner's day. With only six runs behind his name on the board, he tried a short run and Board, snatching up the ball like a hawk scooping up a chicken, threw down the stumps to catch him yards out of his crease.

Six of South Africa's most valuable batsmen were back in the pavilion, and if ever a team appeared to be in a hopeless situation it was this one. The spectators were now standing quietly in the sun reconciled to seeing their team being humiliated but still hoping for the miracle that could turn the tables.

Dave Nourse and Gordon White were together, and painstakingly they toiled to rebuild the shattered South African image. A single here, a boundary there and slowly but surely they began to grind the energy out of the MCC bowlers. White was the senior partner (he went in second wicket down and had held up his end while wicket after wicket had fallen around him) and few batsmen have ever played a more responsible innings than this member of the Pirates Club.

Nourse was content to keep his end up and this he did with a single-minded concentration almost painful to watch. Anything slightly off the wicket was left strictly alone and he presented the broadest of bats to any ball threatening his stumps. Runs he regarded as secondary at this stage — it was his job, so he felt, to stay in and to allow Gordon White to bring the team nearer to that goal so slowly coming within reach.

Soon the crowd — ever hopeful in the tradition of sports spectators the world over — began to regain their confidence and every run scored, every ball blocked safely, reaped wild cheers from all sides of the field.

Finally, after four hours of brave defiance, White lost his wicket and a moan of despair went up from the crowd. He and Nourse had scored 121 runs in their partnership but now, so the spectators had felt, the end had finally come. With only Vogler, Schwarz and skipper Percy Sherwell to bat, it was surely too much to ask of Nourse to steer the team to victory.

Vogler and Schwarz lasted until only 45 runs were needed and then Percy Sherwell, last man in, strode purposefully to the wicket.

This is how Dave Nourse, many years later, described his captain walking towards the pitch:

"It must have been a terrific strain on him, being skipper and having to come in at a time like that. If it were so, then he certainly concealed it well for he came in, as usual, laughing and full of confidence."

He may have been laughing and not nervous at all, but there was no mistaking his determination. His huge moustache bristling and his shoulders set for anything the slightest bit off target, Sherwell settled down to play the sort of innings authors used to dream up for *Boy's Own Paper* and other publications designed for a more gullible generation.

The first ball he received, he hit for four and soon the crowd began to realise that the miracle could happen after all. With Nourse in complete command and Sherwell as steady as any opening bat, the South African score slowly crept along until it stood at his young wife's evidence at the coroner's inquest, he had no pressing financial problems, although she reported that he had been rather depressed for some time and had even threatened to take his own life on a few occasions. One fact was evident, he was a highly-strung personality and his temperament was not assisted by his tendency to overwork.

The fourth member of South Africa's eminent googly force , Gordon White, was better known for his batting talents and did not get to bowl as frequently as his counterparts. Sir Pelham Warner, who captained the 1905/06 M.C.C. team in South Africa (the first side sent out under the appellation of the famous Marylebone club), regarded the left-hander as the finest of his opponents' batsmen and the form of this elegant stroke-player certainly proved instrumental in guiding his country to its first-ever test victory.

A dogged 121-run partnership with another left-hander, the nuggety Nourse, paved the way for a thrilling win in this most famous of all games played at the Old Wanderers ground during the years before it was bulldozed out of existence to make way for the present Johanesburg Railway Station.

In a contemporary report of that stirring encounter it was stated that "the excited spectators applauded every stroke" and that when South Africa's captain and wicket-keeper Percy Sherwell swept the last ball away to the ropes for four and a nail-biting one-wicket victory "hats and canes were hurled into the air as the huge crowd gave vent to their joy". Nourse, who hit 93 not out, and Sherwell were carried shoulder high to the pavilion and

eight runs behind the goal that had seemed so unattainable a few hours earlier.

Then Sherwell snicked a lucky four and Nourse scored an easy three and the scores were lying level.

The MCC captain now brought all his fielders to within a few yards of the bat and Bert Relf came pounding down to deliver to Sherwell. Two balls were pushed back to the bowler and a third, off the line of the stumps, severely left alone. The tension was unbearable and, strangely enough, it was the bowler who was affected most of all.

His fourth ball was a slow full toss on the leg side and Sherwell grabbed his opportunity with all the strength in his wide shoulders. He cracked it high and straight into the milling spectators on the boundary for four runs. Even as the MCC captain uttered his mild reprimand to Relf, the crowd burst on to the field to carry Nourse and Sherwell off in triumph.

"Men and women were screaming hysterically, some were even crying, and hats and sticks were flying everywhere", Warner wrote later. "The crowd simply flung themselves at Nourse and Sherwell and carried them into the pavilion. For some time afterwards, thousands lingered on . . . "

Several of the wealthy patrons of cricket, thrust gold coins at Sherwell and Nourse as they were being carried off, and by the time they reached the safety of the dressing-room, the two players had £87 between them.

The crowd kept milling around in front of the dressing-room until Warner, Sherwell and finally, Nourse had made speeches.

Harold Strange, then chairman of the Wanderers Club, grabbed hold of Nourse's bat (the bat with which he had scored 18 and 93, both times not out, in the match) and promptly bought it for an undisclosed sum. He later presented it to the club and to this day it is on display in the Clubhouse. So is the ball which Percy Sherwell hit for that historic boundary which gave South Africa her first-ever win in a cricket Test.

Chris Greyvenstein

The scoreboard at the end of the first test in 1906 tells the exciting story of the Nourse-Sherwell partnership which carried the day for South Africa

Victor Trumper — the incomparable Australian master who was the scourge of the famed South African googly bowlers in 1910/11

James H. Sinclair — Six-hitter supreme

the entire South African eleven appeared on the balcony to receive their supporters' ovation.

"Dave" Nourse, who was christened Arthur William but preferred to use his nickname of unknown origin, is described in *Barclays World of Cricket* (edited by that most eminent of modern cricket writers, E.W. Swanton and current *Wisden* editor John Woodcock, and surely one of the best half-dozen books on cricket ever produced) as "a left-hander of rock-like stability and nerve, South Africa's first great batsman".

And almost like the fabled "rock of ages" Nourse endured in top-class cricket for a remarkable career which commenced with his first Currie Cup appearance for Natal in 1897 (he hit 61 off Eastern Province) and finally ended four decades later in 1936 when, 58 years-old and playing with men young enough to be his grandsons, the "Grand Old Man of South African Cricket" proceeded to take a highly competent 55 off the Australian "terrible twins" Grimmett and O'Reilly. This was in the same year as that famous son of a famous father, Arthur Dudley Nourse decimated the Australian spin attack to the tune of a brilliantly executed 231 at the Wanderers.

There was never any thought of leaving Nourse senior out of the Springbok team and, starting with his international debut against Joe Darling's Australians in 1902, he made no fewer than 45 consecutive test appearances, with his final selection coming against England in 1924.

After the breathtaking first test win the 1905/06 South Africans, who played the same eleven men through the entire series, went on to totally overwhelm a fairly competent England side four matches to one, the only setback coming at Newlands where no answer could be found to the tantalising spin of "Charlie" Blythe.

Gordon White enjoyed a particularly succesful year with a top score of 147 in the third game (Maitland Hathorn scored a patient 102 in the first innings of the same match at Wanderers) and S.J. "Tip" Snooke excelled with a match bowling analysis of 12 wickets for 127 with eight of his victims falling in an England second innings collapse. Snooke was destined to be yet another

R.O. Schwartz — The first South African to try bowling the googly

long-lived cricketer who forced his way back into the South African X1 as late as 1923 after a ten-year absence.

The all-conquering Springbok team of 1905/06 certainly merits mentioning in full: (in batting order) — *Louis Tancred,* who hit 97 in his first test innings, the closest a South African has got to a debut hundred, unless Jimmy Cook's 114 against the SAB England Xl is taken into account (Kepler Wessels has achieved the feat for his adopted country Australia); *W.A. Shalders; Gordon White; Dave Nourse; Maitland Hathorn; Jimmy Sinclair; Aubrey Faulkner* (not yet a force in this series — his greatest triumphs were still to come); *S.J. Snooke; Reggie Schwarz; Ernest Vogler;* and the captain, and one of the first in a long line of outstanding South African wicket-keepers, *Percy Sherwell.*

The fact that Sherwell came in at number eleven was indicative of the great batting power of this eleven. During the very next series, in England

AUBREY FAULKNER

We all had our boyhood heroes. Mine was rather different, for over the span of years he still holds a pride of place in both my memory and affections. After living 23 years in South Africa I am amazed how little is known of one of her greatest cricketing sons — the peerless all-rounder Aubrey Faulkner.

Jack Hobbs, the prince of England's batsmen, acclaimed him as the one all-rounder who stood high above all others. No one could surely have known this man better, for these two faced each other both on the homespun mats of South Africa as well as on the varying turf pitches of Old Trafford and Lords.

In South Africa against England in 1909, Faulkner and Vogler took 65 of the 85 wickets that fell in that season. In 1907 at Leeds, on a sooty, damp wicket, Faulkner's googlies and leg-breaks, quick through the air and knife-like off the pitch hastily despatched England's Hayward, Johnny Tyldesley, Braund, Jessop, Arnold and Lilley for 17 runs.

Later, on the hard pitches of Australia, Faulkner scored 2 000 runs including a double century at Melbourne to average 73 in the five Tests of 1910/11. Australians are not inclined to cast their most fragrant bouquets at the feet of strangers, yet their brilliant left handed betsman Clem Hill described Faulkner as the most effective batsman ever to visit the Antipodes. Faulkner told me that on this tour, whenever possible, he went straight into the practice nets as the Springbok opening batsman left the dressingroom. When a genuine Aussie roar went up — signifying the fall of a wicket — he would walk out of the net, through the pavilion and proceed to the middle, where, as a rule, he continued to bat from where he had just left off.

Little is known of his boyhood days, though Doug Thomson, when writing a history of Wynberg Boys High School in the Cape, discovered in the school archives that Faulkner was a pupil there.

Though unheralded, his entry into the Transvaal cricket arena was sensational — Reggie Schwarz, after studying the methods of Bosanquet, the inventor of the googly, introduced this phenomenon to the trio Gordon White, Faulkner and Vogler. It was not long before the latter pair outstripped their mentor and wreaked havoc among batsmen on the responsive matting pitches.

Vogler later became the greatest of the three jugglers, but Faulkner was always hard in 1907, the Springbok captain actually opened and played a match-saving innings of 115 not out to rescue an imminently lost cause during the first test match at Lord's.

Although England revenged their 1905/06 defeat succesfully during 1907 there was much exciting cricket to be seen. Sherwell's match and face-saving effort at Lord's has been mentioned and, at Headingly in the second leg of a three-match rubber, only a dreadful second innings collapse by South Africa gave England a 53 run advantage.

Aubrey Faulkner had earlier turned in what can be recorded as his finest test bowling effort when he lured six England batsmen to destruction for a paltry 17 runs to put the home side out for an incredibly low tally of 76. On a devil of a pitch South Africa in turn struggled against the artful Blythe (8 for 59) but managed to gain a slender 34-run first innings lead.

The ever-elegant C.B. Fry then battled through on the dreadful wicket to hit top score in the match before falling leg-before-wicket to a Gordon White googly for 54. South Africa was left with the seemingly simple task of scoring 129 runs to win.

But it was not to be — the graceful left-hander "Charlie" Blythe, a man as devoted to his violin as to his art with a cricket ball, spun yet another web of deception to become the only bowler to take fifteen South African wickets in a test match in England.

A draw in the final game at The Oval was notable for another classical display from the imperious Charles Fry, whose style and manner so closely epitomised the Victorian Age.

An almost super-human all-round effort from the apparently tireless Aubrey Faulkner balanced the books again for South Africa when an M.C.C. side under H.D.G. "Shrimp" Leveson-Gower came to South Africa in 1909/10.

The result of this clash with a team

Colin Blythe — The only England bowler to take 15 South African wickets in a test in England

on his heels, His artistry and control of the leg-break, googly and top spinner, coupled with his outstanding ability with the bat, made him one of the most feared opponents of the day.

Harry Altham in his *History of Cricket* wrote: "Faulkner was a magnificent batsman. Though rather cramped at the start of an innings, he was a master of footwork and one of the greatest exponents of the hook stroke."

Though Australia was the scene of greatest batting triumphs, he was a failure there with the ball. The change from mat to the unresponsive shirt front was too much for him. The Australian Victor Trumper, in his most incredible form, was another persistent fly in the linseed oil on this tour. Such was his confidence and nerve, that in Test matches he would nonchalantly flick the fast yorker between his legs for four with what is vulgarly referred to as the "dog-shot".

Faulkner considered Trumper the greatest batsman he had ever seen or played against, yet when asked what episode during his career produced the supreme hallmark of cricket, he said without hesitation, "Herby Taylor playing Sidney Barnes on a matting wicket."

In the first World War he fought with distinction with the Royal Artillery. Such was his character and personality that he surprised no one when he achieved the rank of major and won the D.S.O. for his services at Gallipoli. With trepidation, I once asked him what feat of gallantry earned him his high award. "I was never quite sure," he answered, "but whenever an order was received to fire, I insisted on immediate response from my battery. I never found out how many Turkish wickets we took, but our enthusiasm certainly pleased the colonel!"

After demobilisation, Faulkner's big cricket days were numbered. He was yet to play at Eastbourne — the scene perhaps of his greatest triumph. The magnificent 1921 Australian side under Warwick Armstrong had contemptuously swept aside England and her counties. If undefeated, each player was promised a cash bonus on his return. They looked home and dry.

Their last match was to be played at Eastbourne against a side selected and captained by the ageing Archie McLaren, who had viewed over his ample hawk-like nose the English cricket season with a certain contempt and disapproval. He announced he would at last select a side to beat the invader and asked Faulkner to play.

In the first innings the all-conquering Australia attack, led by that country's greatest and fastest opening pair of bowlers, Gregory and McDonald, scythed their way through the opposing batsmen who could muster a bare 40 odd runs. Early on the third day victory looked certain for Australia and many pressmen shut up their typewriters and made tracks for home. They reckoned, however, without

Robert Abel who was a prolific scorer of runs for England against South Africa

that included such personages as Jack Hobbs (who must rank alongside the best half-dozen batsmen of all time), the ubiquitous left-hander Wilfred Rhodes (he enjoyed three separate careers for England — first as a left-arm spinner of guile and good length, then as an opening partner for Hobbs, and finally returning to the England team at the age of 48, once again as a cunning slow bowler, to assist his country in regaining the ashes from Australia) and the left-handed genius Frank Woolley (who has only been matched in recent years by South Africa's own champion Graeme Pollock), was a 3-2 victory for the Springboks.

Hobbs adjusted his style of play fluently to the unfamiliar matting wickets and tallied 539 runs in the five tests to delight the South African crowds with his wonderful stroke-play. Apart from the last of a fast-disappearing breed, the under-arm lob-bowler G.H. Simpson-Hayward, no one else really impressed and the season belonged to the South Africans. And none more so than the magnificent Faulkner who registered 545 runs and claimed 29 wickets in an unforgetable exhibition of all-round skill.

The England tour was a dress rehearsal for South Africa's most ambitious venture to date: the trip to Australia in 1910/11, an undertaking which sadly signalled the completion of the brief but glorious first "Golden Age". Apart from a minor resurgence in the mid-1930's and again under Jack Cheetham in the 1950's, South Africa's position in cricket's heirarchy remained inferior to that of their traditional opponents Australia and England until the heady days of the Pollocks, Barlow, van der Merwe, Bacher and company in the late 1960's and early 1970's.

The Australian odyssey of 1910/11

Faulkner who then joined one of the Ashton brothers at the wicket. This was his finest hour. First he parried the onslaught, then thrashed the might of Australia to amass a score of just over 150. It was enough. McLaren's side won by 28 runs. Faulkner also took 6 wickets in the match.

His feat was all the more remarkable for he had had no prior match play and very little practice. When asked how all this was achieved he answered, "I coached myself as I went along — the Aussies must have thought I was mad". An amazing performance when you consider how small the margin of error was with the thunderbolts of McDonald and Gregory descending upon him at the rate of 80 to 90 miles an hour.

Later the South African accepted a business appointment in Nottingham and played cricket for the millionaire sportsman Sir Julien Cahn.

He was most successful, but one day he failed to turn up to a match. On investigation it was discovered that Faulkner had vanished from his hotel. He was traced later to a Preparatory School in Surrey, happily teaching irregular verbs and the straight bat to freckly-faced little boys.

Faulkner had now entered the second phase of his cricketing life. An idealist, he wished to do something for the game he loved and so embellished. The idea of a Cricket School was already germinating in his mind, so before long he rented for this purpose a disused garage in Richmond. A year later he moved to a vacant bus garage in Walham Green where there was room for five nets with differing types of pitches, dressingrooms, offices and a restaurant. Here schoolboys, university, club, county and test cricketers came in their hoards.

Among the most successful were Duleepsinghi, Freddie Brown, R.W.V. Robins, Bob Wyatt who like most of his young disciples worshipped him and responded to his driving methods. Faulkner never spared himself and one never saw him standing outside the net merely offering advice; he was always in the thick of it and insisted on bowling himself. To relieve the strain he learnt to bowl accurately with either arm.

His approach always varied with each pupil. Some he goaded on with almost parade ground methods; the more timid he encouraged and led with a much lighter rein, and no change or correction was ever suggested to a pupil unless accompanied with a sound explanation as to the whys and wherefores.

Faulkner's judgement of a cricketer was uncanny. He watched Bradman play his first innings on his initial tour of England in 1928 at Worcester. When the "Don" reached 80 not out the South African wrote in the press that he had never seen such mastery from a batsman so young and predicted that here was a star that would make cricket history.

Before this a young bank clerk from Edinburgh spent a week of his annual holiday with Faulkner at Richmond School. On the second day Faulkner said to the young Scot, "Stay with me and you will bowl for England." At 19 Ian Peebles accompanied the M.C.C. team to South Africa.

His one mistake concerned myself. When I was sixteen he

was an arduous one by any standards. The South African party was virtually reduced to fourteen players through the indisposition of one of the main Springbok batsmen Maitland Hathorn, who played in only two first-class games, and the more succesful players had little rest. There was of course no air travel and dusty, uncomfortable coach and train excursions were frequently followed almost immediately by encounters with tough opposition, often against odds.

Added to South Africa's agony was the scintillating form of Australia's Victor Trumper. This majestic batsman accumulated 662 runs in nine test innings in his own inimitably dashing and domineering manner.

His aggregate of runs was, however, exceeded by South Africa's own hero, Aubrey Faulkner, who set a record which stands to this day by compiling a massive 732 runs in his ten visits to the crease. Nourse gave Faulkner most support in the big games, excelling particulalrly during a knock of 201 against South Australia at Adelaide. It was during this marathon innings that he heard of the birth of his son in far off South Africa and Dudley Nourse owes his name to the then Governor of South Australia, Lord Dudley. Apart from a dogged 92 not out at Melbourne, Dave Nourse failed in the test matches and, although the persevering J.W. "Billy" Zulch hit hundreds at Adelaide and Sydney, Faulkner rarely received much support.

The touring team's much vaunted googly attack came apart at the seams on the shirt-front Australian pitches and the lack of a truly fast bowler of the class and pace of the recently retired J.J. Kotze was sorely felt. Reggie Schwarz, surprisingly, proved to be the most consistently succesful performer with the ball, claiming 25 test wickets

Percy Sherwell — South Africa's first great captain and a fine batsman/wicket-keeper

said I would play for my country — mind you, he probably knew I was born in China!

My first contact with Faulkner was at the age of 14, when I won a scholarship to his school and was personally coached by the master. At 16 I joined his staff as Assistant Secretary and coach for 30 shillings a week and my lunch. We worked from morning till night, but it was a wonderful experience for a youngster living continually in the atmosphere of cricket and rubbing shoulders with many of the great players of that time. Lunch was the get-together time when starry eyed I listened to such as Douglas Jardine, Wally Hammond, Warren Bardsley, Plum Warner, and yes, our own Tuppy Owen Smith who was then at Oxford. Faulkner was then at his happiest and there were no signs portending the sad clouding over of his mind that came later.

Towards the end of my second year at the school I began to notice a change in him for he looked tired and began to worry over things that never disturbed him before. The school had been successful in every way except from the financial angle. Perhaps some of the high and mighty, who had applauded Faulkner so loudly for all his good work, might have helped him by dipping their approving hands rather deeper into their pockets.

One Monday morning arriving early at the School to open the post I found an envelope on my desk. In his letter Faulkner explained that he had decided to take his life and where I should find his body. Something in his mind had goaded him to a decision no human soul could have forced upon him. Something stronger and stranger than the combined force of Trumper, McDonald and Gregory.

In retrospect I wonder how he would have been accepted today and what he would have thought of cricket and cricketers. I find after 30 years that his teachings and theories are as flawless and applicable as they were when he taught them. Contrary to many sporting figures of the present day, Faulkner never tried to project any form of "image" (he even kept his flannel trousers up with string). I believe his directness and dynamism would have been accepted because of his great ability and understanding of youth.

Faulkner would have strongly disapproved of playing cricket on anything but the best available pitches. Any doctoring of wickets to suit the players on either side would have shocked him.

Himself an attacking all-rounder he would have criticised the negative wait-and-see tactics so often employed in modern cricket. He believed a challenge should always be presented. Faulkner would have applauded the magnificent fielding, both close to the wicket and otherwise, of present day Springbok sides. He loved the cricketer that give his all for the game.

Aubrey Faulkner and Eddie Barlow would have understood each other.

Tom Reddick
September 1971

and a total bag of 102 in all matches.

Most puzzling was the unaccountable eclipse of South Africa's star attacker Ernie Vogler. This caused the biggest upset to the team's aspirations and "Buck" Llewellyn and Faulkner gave Schwarz most assistance. Big Jimmy Sinclair was also a failure, with bat and ball, and the only high point of the tour came during the third test at Adelaide when South Africa held on to claim a 38 run victory in a match played over six days.

A massive innings win for Australia in the opening game at Sydney (Australia accumulated a colossal 494 for 6 wickets on the first day with Clem Hill smashing 191 and the other great Australian left-hander Warren Bardsley weighing in with 132) was followed by an exciting contest at Melbourne over the New Year in which South Africa flattered to deceive and lost by 89 runs after leading the field for most of the match.

Faulkner really excelled himself in front of a big crowd at Melbourne to record South Africa's first double-hundred in a test and the tourists replied to Australia's first innings 348 with a threatening 506. Trumper then proceeded to shred the paper-thin Springbok attack to the tune of 159 and the Australian pace attack of Cotter and Whitty hustled the nervous challengers out for an ignominious 80 second innings runs.

The following test at Adelaide was the finest of the series and, batting with greater determination, South Africa reached a first innings tally of 482 with Zulch and Snooke scoring centuries and the ever-consistent Faulkner contributing a sound 56. Australia's strong reply was due entirely to the peerless Trumper who delighted spectators and opponents alike with a breathtaking 214 not out.

Thanks to yet another Faulkner hundred and a fine 80 by Llewellyn South Africa extended their lead to 377 and Schwarz, Faulkner and Sinclair took the fight to the Aussies camp with some inspired bowling. In a match which produced the highest aggregate of runs in test cricket — 1 646 runs for 40 wickets, the tourists claimed their single test triumph of the tour.

The remaining tests at Melbourne and Sydney saw the Springboks again go down by distressing margins of 530 runs and seven wickets respectively, to bring to a sad end South Africa's first brief but glorious "Golden Age".

Next event on the international cricket calendar was the ill-starred "Triangular Tournament" between England, Australia and South Africa in the very wet England of 1912.

Conceived in his immense enthusiasm for the game by millionaire Sir Abe Bailey, the three-cornered contest ran into trouble from the start. Discord between Australia's leading players and the cricket authorities of that country resulted in the despatch of a far from representative team and, with South Africa fielding a combination which was but a poor reflection of the golden eleven of a few years before, much of the interest in the venture was lost before it even commenced.

South Africa was comprehensively thrashed in five of the six matches played and only a handful of the Springbok players came anywhere near to enhancing their reputations. Syd Pegler, who was a relative failure in Australia, suddenly came to light with 29 wickets but, apart from Aubrey Faulkner's 122 not out against England at Old Trafford, there was hardly an innings of any note.

Chief destroyers of a brittle South African batting order were Sydney Barnes of England (one of the truly all-time greats) and the little known T.J. Matthews of Australia, a leg-spinner who claimed the unique record of a hat-trick in each innings of the Australia/South Africa match at Old Trafford.

Two players, one English and the other South African, totally dominated the next international series in South Africa. The arrival of the 1913/14 M.C.C. team under J.W.H.T. Douglas (christened "Johnny-won't-hit-today" by a sharp Australian barracker') brought what was undoubtedly the strongest English combination to sail to the Cape prior to World War One.

And the grand villain of the piece (in South African eyes) was Sydney Barnes. The superlative English bowler was not a total stranger to South African matting wickets, which prevailed up to 1928, having played and coached as a professional for the Claremont Cricket Club in Cape Town in 1898/99.

The only batsman with a technical capability of sufficient quality to counter the challenge thrown down by the

JIMMY SINCLAIR 1902/03

Jimmy Sinclair's fastest test century for South Africa has been beaten by three players from other countries. The following are the five fastest hundreds on record :

MINUTES

70 J.M.Gregory — Australia vs S.Africa at Johannesburg 1921/22

75 G.L.O.Jessop — England vs Australia at The Oval 1902

78 R.Benaud — Australia vs West Indies at Kingston 1954/55

80 J.H.Sinclair — South Africa vs Australia at Cape Town 1902/03

86 B.R.Taylor — New Zealand vs West Indies at Auckland 1968/69

Since scorers have used the method of counting balls received by a batsman the fastest centuries thus recorded are:

67 balls - J.M. Gregory

71 balls - R.C.Fredericks, West Indies vs Australia at Perth 1975/76

76 balls - G.L.O. Jessop

85 balls - C.H. Lloyd, West Indies vs India at Bangalore 1974/75

86 balls - I.T.Botham, England vs Australia at Manchester 1981

87 balls - I.T.Botham, England vs Australia at Leeds, 1981

Unfortunately no record is available of the number of balls faced by Sinclair.

Lords Cricket Ground, Durban, circa 1910

gaunt and menacing Barnes was the apparently imperturbable South African hero of the hour, Herby Taylor.

If one separates the performances of the ever-resolute Taylor from that of his mostly hesitant colleagues, the contest with Sydney Barnes may perhaps be reported as having ended in some sort of honourable draw. But the Springbok batsman's companions could offer only token resistance and, as the home side boasted no comparable bowler, South Africa slid into the dismal chasm of utter defeat in four tests out of five.

Sydney Barnes actually withdrew from the final game, apparently because of a pay dispute but it has been alleged that the frustration of having to bowl continually to the unyielding Taylor had rattled the man who was always something of a law unto himself.

A tally of the judge's points in the Barnes/Taylor contest reveals the following:

Taylor - 8 innings — 379 runs (plus 42 and 87 in the game Barnes missed).

Barnes - 49 wickets for 536 runs including Taylor's in 5 out of 8 encounters.

So, perhaps, cold figures do indicate that Barnes, after all, deserves possession of the championship belt.

It is indeed unfortunate that the ensuing conflict in Europe prevented the possibility of a return bout between these two redoubtable opponents. •

Newlands, Cape Town, 1923/24

The Wanderers Cricket Ground, Johannesburg, at the turn of the century

Dave Nourse — The 'Grand Old Man' of South African cricket

CHAPTER TWO

BETWEEN THE WARS

A brief visit from the Australian Imperial Forces team in 1919 re-lit the flame of international cricket competition after the ghastly events of 1914 to 1918 had been relegated to the past and a new vision of a peaceful future had been generated by the proposal to form a League of Nations to guide the affairs of mankind.

The joyous approach of Herby Collins and his fine band of young players, sailing home after their harrowing experiences in Europe, was like manna to a cricket-starved South African public. A true sporting spirit prevailed and the experienced Australians were even observed giving serious coaching instruction to their opponents.

Although the two "test" matches played were declared unofficial, the new-look South African team approached their task with all seriousness. "Billy" Zulch played his country's innings of the series when hitting 135 in the first game (both were played at the Wanderers) and the temperamental Jimmy Blanckenberg looked to be a bowling hope for the future.

For the A.I.F. XI their captain Collins played a delightful crowd-pleasing 235 in the opening "test".

In a nostalgic prelude to the 1921/22 Australian tour of South Africa (this time a full official visit) a veteran Aubrey Faulkner, now totally involved with his famous London coaching school and no longer available for South Africa, came out of retirement to play an amazing innings of 153 at Eastbourne for a scratch XI put together by old England captain Archie Maclaren to oppose Warwick Armstrong's all-conquering Australians. Faulkner's performance has been recorded for posterity by the doyen of cricket writers, Neville Cardus, and the by now much older and burlier version of a once athletic young all-rounder was reported to have coached himself volubly throughout his long innings. The South African was also in form with the ball and, against all reasonable expectations, Maclaren's team beat the formidable Australians.

Herby Collins took over leadership for the South African sector of the tour following the withdrawal of Armstrong through injury and had to battle hard to clinch the three match series after South Africa had held out for draws in the first two games.

Aubrey Faulkner's skill and fortitude would have been a welcome addition to the Springboks' armoury and his presence may well have tilted matters in their favour in at least one of the undecided matches.

Dave Nourse wrote some years afterwards that Collins threw the first test away by delaying his second innings declaration until Charles (the "Governor General") Macartney had reached his hundred, thus giving his bowlers too little time to get the South Africans out.

Dogged defensive play by Nourse in the second match (at Johannesburg) which brought the old campaigner his single test hundred in a long and distinguished career, plus a monumental innings by new cap Charles Newton Frank, saved South Africa after the follow-on had been forced on them subsequent to a thrashing of the South African bowlers by Collins (203) and express bowler J.M.Gregory.The latter smashed the world fast scoring record with a century in just 70 minutes.

Frank, a tiny man who played with immense application and concentration for almost two days to ultimately reach 152, helped the now 43 year-old Nourse add 206 in a record breaking fourth wicket partnership.

After two stirring displays at Durban and Johannesburg the negative result in the final game at Cape Town came as an anti-climax for the Springboks, only Blanckenberg enhancing his reputation in a match dominated by Australia throughout.

The stage was now set for an absorbing series in 1922/23 when England had to wait until the final encounter to take the honours. The M.C.C. touring party was captained by Frank Mann, father of the 1948-49 skipper George Mann. Both were exceptionally popular men, with their teams and spectators alike, because of their aggressive approach to the game.

However, most of the England batsmen struggled on the unfamiliar matting pitches and, with Herby Taylor compiling a magnificent 176, South Africa claimed the first match at the Wanderers by a healthy 168 runs. Blanckenberg was chief destroyer in the first English innings with six wickets for 76 and the rising young off-spinning star E.P."Buster" Nupen, who had made his debut against Australia at the tender age of nineteen, took five good second innings wickets to clinch the match.

Lancashire born left-arm seamer, Alf Hall, bowled his heart out for his adopted country in the next game at Cape Town, but to no avail, as England won by one wicket in a tense finish. South Africa's Hall remained, however, hero of the match and was carried shoulder-high from the field having claimed 11 wickets for 112 runs in the two England innings.

High scoring drawn matches at the new Kingsmead venue (replacing the old Lord's ground) in Durban and at the Wanderers placed the series in an interesting situation for a return final test at Kingsmead.

This will always be known as "Russell's Match" — the Essex opener Alec Russell (recorded as A.C.Russell throughout his career but whose initials

Herby Taylor — Technically one of the finest batsmen South Africa has produced

HERBY TAYLOR

It is not an old book but frequent handling has made it dogeared and grubby. Along the margins there are notes scribbled in pencil and many passages are carefully underlined.

It is a book on the life of S.F. Barnes, the man whose bowling feats have withstood the passage of time so effectively that he is still regarded as one of the greatest bowlers the game of cricket has known.

This book has a place of honour in the home of Herby Taylor because in so many ways it is also a tribute to his own greatness.

It tells the story of a dour individualist who took 189 wickets at a cost of 16.42 runs a wicket and this in only 27 are now known to have actually been C.A.G.) played innings of 140 and 111 in an otherwhise low scoring fixture to swing the balance in England's favour. Only Taylor (102) and C.P.Mead (66) also exceeded fifty in the four completed innings.

An interesting re-appearance on the international scene was that of "Tip" Snooke, at the age of 42, who had last played for his country during the 1912 triangular tournament and who forced his way into reckoning with a fine innings of 76 for an East Rand XI against George Macaulay at his hostile best.

South Africa's cricketing index was dropping fast and the 1924 tour to England proved disastrous on all counts. Only eight wins could be recorded in a lengthy 38 match programme and the singular glimmer of hope came from plucky batting by the youthful Bob Catterall who tallied 471 runs in eight test innings.

It was even considered necessary to recall the now patently over-the-hill Faulkner to bolster the side for the Lord's test and, although the hero of old batted bravely he was nowhere near the bowler and fielder of before.

Injury played some part in South Africa's demise and the services of G.M.Parker, a South African fast bowler playing in the Bradford League, was called upon for the first test at Birmingham. The replacement aquitted himself admirably in what was a disastrous game for South Africa (he took 6 for 152 in an England total of 438) but strangely enough was not called upon again on the tour.

The test at Edgbaston, Birmingham is one most South Africans prefer not to be reminded of. Arthur Gilligan and big Maurice Tate actually bowled the Springboks out in just 75 balls for an appalling total of 30 runs, a score which equalled South Africa's lowest ever way back in 1895/96.

At Lord's, in the second game, England compiled an amazing 531 for two wickets declared with Hobbs (211), Herbert Sutcliffe (122), Woolley (134) and "Patsy" Hendren (50 not out) making a veritable meal of the Springboks' bowling.

Tests. He was often unplayable and was feared by the world's best batsmen of his time with the exception of one — South Africa's Herby Taylor.

The duels between Taylor and Barnes have become part of the legend of cricket. It is generally agreed that Taylor was the only batsman in the world to ever score consistently off Barnes during his heyday, yet their first encounters were certainly won by the Lancashire and Staffordshire bowler.

"The first time I ever played against Sid Barnes was during the Triangular tournament in England in 1912," Taylor told me as we sat in his spcious, cool Rondebosch home one morning last summer.

"In those days the wickets were not covered and it was a horribly wet season. Dave Nourse, Aubrey Faulkner and I were technically the best equipped to deal with such conditions, but I'm afraid Barnes and F.R. Foster formed too good a combination.

"Barnes did not worry me as much as Foster. He was a fast left-hander and he was downright unpleasant to bat against. He employed a variation of the leg theory that caused so much trouble in later years and we just could not cope.

"I still rate Foster as one of the best quickies I ever batted against and it was a tragedy that his career was cut short by an accident which cost him a leg.

"Barnes was a marvellous bowler. He bowled leg-breaks and off-spinners at about the same medium pace as Bill O'Reilly did for Australia years later. He could also roll one for a topspinner that was very difficult to detect. In fact, in 1912 we just never saw it. In addition Sid often opened the bowling and he used to swing the new ball away from the right-handed batsmen at more or less the same speed as Eddie Barlow does these days.

"On English wickets he was a real terror but I had a lot of experience batting against googly bowlers and I'd learnt to watch a bowler's finger movements as he delivered the ball. This made me quite confident that I would be able to handle Barnes under South African conditions.

"I made no secret of the fact that I was looking forward to batting against him on matting wickets, but I doubt very much if anybody took me seriously. In those days you only had to mention Barnes' name to have batsmen scurrying for cover.

"Over-emphasis on forward play and poor footwork contributed to many a batsman's downfall against Barnes, but he was nevertheless the finest bowler I ever saw."

In the 1913/14 season, J.W.H.T. Douglas brought an M.C.C. side to South Africa. After missing the first two matches because of illness, Barnes began a personal reign of terror. Against admittedly minor opposition he produced match figures like 7 for 11 in 10 overs, 9 for 57 and 13 for 48 and by the time the first Test rolled along in Durban he had the Springboks fearing the worst.

Not without reason either. He had them mesmerised from the start — except for small, slightly-built, hawkfaced Herby Taylor.

He was absolutely determined to show that Barnes was not unplayable after all and this he proved in what must rate with the great innings of all time.

"I played Barnes the way I did those magnificent googly bowlers Vogler, Schwarz, Faulkner and White when I first came into first-class cricket," he remembers. "I kept my eyes glued to the ball

Inspiring leadership by H.G."Nummy" Deane raised new hope when his bold tactics saw South Africa share the rubber with Capt R.T. Stanyforth's M.C.C. team of 1927/28. Deane had played as a batsman under Herby Taylor on the ill-fated 1924 visit to the United Kingdom and, now given the reigns, the new captain's clever field placing and general encouraging and inspiring manner assisted his attack of George Bissett, Alf Hall, "Buster" Nupen and the up-and-coming left-hander Cyril Vincent to contain the formidable England line-up of Percy Holmes, Sutciffe, Ernest Tyldesley and the mighty Walter Hammond.

The fast bowler Bissett enjoyed a particularly fine season taking 25 wickets in the tests, including a blistering 7 for 29 at Durban to give South Africa her fifth test advantage. Vincent was not far behind with 23 wickets in the rubber.

Taylor was left to concentrate on his batting to such good effect that he topped 400 runs in the series to help wipe out bad memories of the England tour. Eleven new hopefuls made their debut for South Africa during the series and, of these, much more would soon be heard of "Jock" Cameron, Denys Morkel, Cyril Vincent and Jack Siedle when Deane took his team of "schoolboys" to England in 1929.

There had been such a transformation in the composition of the Springbok eleven by the start of the 1929 series in England that yet another four new test caps were issued before the first international at bogey ground Edgbaston. Of these new boys a 20 year-old Bruce Mitchell made the most distinguished entry into the top rank by showing rock-like defence and a solid technique whilst compiling 88 and 61 not out in a drawn match.

Bob Catterall also had a good first match and in a second drawn test, this time at Lord's, Jimmy Christy, Denys Morkel and yet another 20 year-old from "Nummy" Deane's nursery, H.G."Tuppy" Owen-Smith, all reached at least fifty in good style.

The chirpy Owen-Smith's personal hour of glory arose during the the third test at Headingly. After having been

in his hand as he ran up to the wicket. And just before he delivered it I would switch my eyes to about a yard above his head to catch any finger movement as the ball left his hand. It was no use picking up the ball after it has left the hand of a bowler like Barnes because you would have no idea of what it would do off the pitch.

"Once I knew what sort of delivery it was going to be it was a case of forward to the ball you can meet and back to the ball you can't. Of course, you have to be quick with your footwork but what I have told you now is the really very simple secret of batting."

It certainly worked against Barnes on that humid December day in Durban, 58 years ago.

Springbok wickets were tumbling with nerve-shattering regularity, but Taylor never faltered. With machine-like precision, he reduced Barnes to the ranks of the mere mortals. Finally, the Springboks were all out for 182 of which 109 came from Taylor's bat. What is more, Barnes did not even have the satisfaction of taking his wicket. He was out caught Strudwick off Douglas.

An indication of how completely Taylor dominated the South African innings is the fact that Dave Nourse, with 19, was second topscorer and Baumgartner, with 16, was the only other Springbok to get double figures.

In spite of Taylor's brilliance, it was still Barnes who wrecked the South African innings. He took 5 for 57 in 19.4 overs and when England went on to score 450 runs it was obvious that they would win. In the second innings, it was Barnes' turn to win the duel against Taylor and the Springboks folded for only 111 runs. Barnes again took 5 wickets, this time for 48 runs.

Taylor and Barnes continued to dominate the series, with honours going ever so slightly to Taylor if you consider that he was a member of the weaker side and constantly under pressure. In the second Test he scored 29 and 40 with Barnes having a match analysis of 17 for 159 ! Probably even more satisfying to him was the fact that Taylor fell to him both times.

It did not happen again in the third Test. Taylor got 14 and 70 and it was Relf and Barnes who took his wicket in both innings. In this match Barnes ended up with match figures of 8 for 128 and J.W. Zulch and the tailender Jimmy Blanckenberg also showed some fight.

But the Springboks simply could not fathom the tall, poker-faced master bowler and, although the fourth Test was drawn, Barnes had the remarkable match figures of 14 for 144. Barnes took Taylor's wicket in both innings, but not cheaply — he scored 16 in the first innings and 93 in the second.

Barnes did not play in the final Test. Apparently because the South African cricket authorities had refused to contribute towards the expense of his wife and son who were on the tour with him.

Barnes always insisted that his request was turned down because he ended the matches too quickly thereby cutting the gate receipts.

Barnes' absence was a pity because Taylor, with scores of 42 and 87, was in sparkling form and another battle of wits and will between the two would have been interesting.

At the end of the series, Barnes had the figures of 226 overs, 56 maidens, 49 wickets for 536 runs at an average of 10.93 runs in 10 innings for an average of 50.80.

But the proof of Taylor's dominance over the greatest bowler of his day cannot really be found in the Test match-

"Tuppy" Owen-Smith falls as he attempts a hook. His brilliant 129 in the 1929 series against England will never be forgotten

es. It was for Natal in the 19th match of the tour — and the only one lost by the M.C.C. — that Taylor once and for all tamed Barnes.

The M.C.C. had a poor first innings and could only reach 132, but Natal, with Barnes once again taking five wickets, would have been even worse off had it not been for Taylor at his incomparable best.

He scored 91 out of a total of 153 giving his side a slender lead of 21. Taylor's must have been a remarkable knock because Chapman, with 11, was the only other Natal batsman to get double figures and the 17 extras on the board actually constituted the second highest score of the innings.

The tourists did a little better in the second innings, totalling 235 and leaving Natal 215 runs to win.

This is how Taylor remembers that golden day of long ago:

"Our first two wickets fell very quickly and then Dave Nourse joined me. From the start he was in the soup against Barnes but he somehow survived the few overs to lunch. He and I took a couple of sandwiches and went and sat apart from the others.

"Herby," he confided in me, "I can't play this blighter. That darn topspinner of his is impossible to spot." So I told him to keep his head down and I would try to keep him away from Barnes as much as possible.

"After lunch our plan worked like a charm. I was dropped with my score at 49 — off Barnes of all people. His wrath was something to behold. I decided then and there to try and hit him out of the attack and from his next three overs I took 32 runs. Johnny Douglas helped a little by keeping Barnes on too long. At the same time the tip and run tactics must have been very frustrating to a man of Barnes' explosive temperament.

"Anyway, he was given the ball again to start another over. I was just about ready to take strike when he suddenly turned to the umpire, took his cap back, threw the ball to the ground and made a few rude remarks about me to Dave at his end.

"Then, without another word, he stalked off the field while Johnny Douglas pleaded with him to carry on.

"Douglas came over to me and apologised. I pointed out to him that I could not allow him a substitute fielder but I should have known better. This fine gentleman would never have dreamed of asking. So the game carried on without Barnes, certainly to old Dave's relief.

"We were later told that Barnes had stormed into the dressingroom, whipped off his shirt and had a nice wash-up. Then he stretched himself out and drank several whiskies!

"In the meantime we were going very well, safely and at a steady pace. Imagine my surprise when Dave, who had been stealing glances at the dressingroom between overs, suddenly and quite out of character tried to hit Rhodes out of the ground only to be caught on the boundary for 59.

"For heaven's sake, Dave! Why did you do that?" I asked him.

"That . . . is coming back!" he hissed his answer as he walked past me to the pavilion. "I saw him getting ready on the verandah."

"But by that time it was a little too late for even Barnes to stop us. I got my century and we won by 4 wickets."

In later years, Barnes, who lived to the ripe old age of 94, vehemently denied that he ever left the field because Taylor so persistently stole the strike. Taylor, on the other

H.B. "Jock" Cameron — His early death at the age of thirty deprived South Africa of a brilliant wicket-keeper and a hitter who rivalled the legendary Jimmy Sinclair

told by his room companion Bruce Mitchell that the morning newspaper correspondent had stated that only rain or a century could save South Africa, the young doctor to be, in his own inimitable carefree manner, carted a formidable English attack to all corners of the famed Yorkshire ground.

Owen-Smith raced to a personal tally of 129 whilst in partnership with last man "Sandy" Bell, who was really more noted for his fairly sharp pace with the ball than for any great pretensions with the bat. The two added a record last wicket 103 in only 63 minutes and delayed England's victory bid.

England had won again but clear notice had been posted of a new fight-

hand, insists that this was indeed the case, and Barnes' well known temper and his frequent brushes with the cricket authorities during his career certainly loads the evidence in favour of Taylor's version.

His performances against Barnes established the South African as one of the best batsmen in the world, but although Taylor was born into a cricketing family (his father played for Natal against Lord Hawke's side in 1898/99), he was in many respects a self-made player. At Michaelhouse he had the benefit of keen coaching and he was the school's best batsman. He was realistic enough, however, to realise that his play off the backfoot was poor — in common with that of all his teammates and his opponents.

One day he picked up a copy of the "Boys Own Paper", a publication edited by the great England cricketer C.B. Fry. In it was an article in which Fry discussed this particular facet of batsmanship and after that, night after night, for six months he practised in his bedroom. "To my mother's great disgust," he remembers now "because I would draw chalk lines all over the floor! Had it not been for my father she would probably have put a stop to the whole project."

"I am convinced that by learning to step back sideways for backplay and forward sideways for forward strokes, I improved my batting 100%. To do this properly the front foot must point to cover point and not straight down the wicket. This is the only way to acquire a proper follow-through for maximum power. In fact, all the world's really successful batsmen down the years have been able to play back properly.

"I feel very strongly about this and for many years now I have waged a constant war against certain coaching methods and manuals. Not so long ago I had a letter from Frank Woolley, the great Kent and England lefthander, and I would like to quote from this to support my own views:

"This is what Woolley wrote: 'I do not approve of the method of coaching where the batsman is taught to have the front foot pointing up the wicket and, at the same time, is made to bring up the left elbow (in the case of a right-hander) in order to play with a straight bat. The player automatically develops the same sort of thing in his drive, thus impeding the long follow-through which is so essential to strike the ball with power to penetrate the gaps in the field.

"I regret to say that much coaching takes place in England with the accent on this left elbow business and all to the detriment of striking the ball naturally.

"When playing on a sticky wicket where the good length ball pops up, the dead straight bat is necessary, but even then it is better if the front foot is pointing to extra cover. This places the body sideways and gives the batsman, if anything, a better reach with the left arm and keeps the bat straight. On such wickets the experienced batsman usually plays his scoring shots mostly by stepping back and using the pull shot because the ball comes off the wicket slowly.

"There is another myth one hears often — get behind the ball. The ball should be struck mostly when beside the batsman.'

"That's what Woolley believes about the art of batting and I agree with him wholeheartedly. The main point is to get into the best possible position to hit the ball with all the power you've got.

"Unfortunately, there are

ing spirit having arisen amongst the young cricketers of the veld.

Twice the age of some of his colleagues, Herby Taylor stroked his way to a superb 121 in the final match at the Oval after having missed a couple of games through illness. The old master was still to play an important part in his country's cricket when A.P.F-.Chapman's England team toured in 1930/31, a season which was significant for an important innovation which changed the face of South African cricket forever.

For the first time three of the test matches were played on grass pitches instead of the customary matting and South Africa's batsmen greeted the changeover at Newlands with a massive score of 513 for 8 wickets in which Mitchell, Jack Siedle and Taylor contributed hundreds.

The introduction of grass wickets came as a lasting tribute to South Africa's fastest bowler at the turn of the century, J.J.Kotze, who personally supervised the laying of the turf wickets at Newlands.

In the *Cape Times* of 24th December 1928, Kotze was described as "the man who did more than any other to introduce the grass wicket, and so raise South Africa to her rightful place as a cricketing nation !".

South Africa claimed honours in the 1930/31 series by virtue of a thrilling 28 run win at the Wanderers in the first match, with Nupen almost unplayable on the mat still in use at that ground. The remaining games were all inconclusive, two being played on another grass pitch at Kingsmead, Durban.

A number of distasteful off-the-field controversies marred what should have been a fine season and affectd the composition of the South African team chosen to tour Australia in 1931/32. E.P.Nupen substituted for an injured Taylor as captain for the first test but was unceremoniously dumped when Deane returned for the Newlands turf wicket game. Nupen had retained his own place in the side at Cape Town but was discarded for the next clash at Durban whilst still further haggling resulted in the withdrawal of Deane for the fourth test at Wanderers, where 26

coaches who stick so rigidly to the manuals and who really have so little actual experience of topclass cricket that they leave promising youngsters hobbled and powerless by the time they are finished with them."

Herbert Strudwick, the great England wicketkeeper who was behind the stumps when Barnes had his duels with Taylor, many years afterwards said that Taylor's success was due entirely to his remarkably quick footwork. He was particularly impressed with Taylor's ability to step over to the offside to pull Barnes. "In making this pull, sometimes one leg would be behind the stumps and his bat flying around my head!" he once told an interviewer.

Throughout his life Herby Taylor has been generous with advice and help, to friend and foe alike. Although a product of Michaelhouse, he once coached Hilton to beat his old school thus ending a long and discouraging run of defeats.

It is a measure of a man's ability to move with the time that his lessons are invariably illustrated with the pictures of today's outstanding players. How often has he not phoned me in a state of high excitement on the discovery of a newly-published action photograph of Graeme Pollock executing a shot the way he likes to see it done.

Sydney Barnes. Possibly the best bowler of all time and certainly never mastered by South African batsmen other than Herby Taylor

He has in fact a very high regard for Graeme Pollock and rated him after Wally Hammond, Don Bradman, Frank Woolley and Jack Hobbs as one of the five greatest batsmen he has ever seen. Dudley Nourse, Graeme Pollock, Alan Mellville and Barry Richards are his selections as the best batsmen yet to be produced in South Africa.

Neil Adcock, Peter Pollock, Buster Nupen (on matting wickets) and Hugh Tayfield he considered to be South African's best bowlers of the past 60 years with S.F. Barnes, Clarrie Grimmett, Bill O'Reilly, Maurice Tate, Harold Larwood and F.R. Foster the greatest bowlers he ever faced on the international field. He was quick to add that he was already more than 40 years old when he played against Grimmett, O'Reilly and Larwood!

Herbert Wilfred Taylor's exact place in Springbok cricket's Hall of Fame is, of course, a matter of opinion and open to debate. To the older generation, he is still the best batsman ever to have played for South Africa. Others qualify their praise and label him as "technically" the best batsman we have had.

Chris Greyvenstein
September 1971

H.G. "Nummy" Deane's 'Nursery' OF 1929 — From the left: Cyril Vincent, Denys Morkel, 'Sandy' Bell, Herby Taylor, Bob Catterall, Deane, Neville Quinn

year-old "Jock" Cameron took over to become the third skipper in four games.

To compound South Africa's selectorial woes, Nupen and the most capable batsman after Taylor, Bob Catteral, were dropped from the final match for "reasons other than cricketing ability". The black-ball of these two fine players extended to their omission from the side which toured Australia in 1931/32 under Cameron, a move which seriously weakened the South African combination.

The typical South African cricketer of the thirties was a rather gentlemanly sort of person if compared with his Australian counterpart of the period (the Aussies haven't altered much since but the Springboks certainly have adopted a more aggressive approach to the game, and to life in general for that matter). Cameron's men were somewhat "phased" by the intimidating remarks directed towards them by all and sundry from the moment they landed "down-under".

In his little gem of a book, *Cricketers of the Veld,* Louis Duffus, possibly the best writer on the game South Africa has produced, relates an incident in the dockyard at Fremantle that occurred minutes after the Springbok's vessel had berthed.

The first words uttered by an Australian to the sixteen players, all newcomers to the land of Bradman and the kangaroo, came from a tough dockside worker who bawled up at them:

"Where's your wicket-keeper Cameron? Where's your Don Bradman?"

Not having an equivalent of the last-named in their party, several of the players pointed towards Cameron, who promptly dropped his hat. He made a grab for it but the elusive headpiece landed in the water.

"Fine bloody wicket-keeper he is!" was the onlooker's loud retort.

Duffus goes on to say that even if the cricket authorities had organised intimidating propaganda it could not have been more thorough than the spontaneous comments which, for the next few weeks, were offered to the side "to convince them that they were not likely to do much good against Australian cricketers".

Characteristic of the average Australian's disdain for the Springboks' potential to test their players was the remark made to Bruce Mitchell at the nets by a bare-footed youngster. Having commented with absolute surety that ace Australia leg-spinner Clarrie Grimmett was capable of getting all the visitors out, he quickly corrected himself on recognising Mitchell, by stating: "Oh, but you're an opening batsman. Of course, you won't see Clarrie."

Australia would probably have won the 1931/32 series without the services of the crafty Grimmett who ended with 33 wickets at 16,87 runs apiece but was not even called upon to bowl in the final test at Melbourne where South Africa, on a treacherous pitch, disintegrated for an all-time test match low of 36 and 45 all out in the two innings.

Destroyer-in-chief of the Springboks' batting in this (for South Africa) infamous test was the tall left-hander Bert Ironmonger who returned an astounding match analysis of 11 wickets for 24 runs.

And the other chief contributor to South Africa's acute discomfort that summer, the one and only Don Bradman, also took little part in the tourists' final humiliation at Melbourne when he did not bat because of injury.

Earlier, Bradman had seemingly scored at will from a fair South African attack in which fast bowler A.J. "Sandy" Bell excelled with 23 wickets at under thirty runs apiece in the tests.

Sir Donald Bradman, from the point of view of effectiveness, has had no peer as a match-winning batsman, apart possibly from that other great cricketing knight Sir Garfield Sobers, and in 1931/32 the Australian champion was at the height of his powers.

In just five innings he amassed 806 runs with two double centuries, including an explosive 299 not out at Adelaide, where he ran out his number eleven partner off the last ball of the innings when going for his triple hundred.

For South Africa only Bruce Mitchell and, to a lesser extent, the now clearly veteran Herby Taylor (he was already 42 years old), batted with much conviction, although it fell to comparative newcomer Ken Viljoen to take the honour of notching his country's lone test century of the tour with 111 at Melbourne.

Apart from Bell, the medium paced left-hander Neville Quinn most impressed the Australians, even Bradman treating hin with caution when all other bowlers were handled with total disdain.

The Springbok captain H.B. "Jock" Cameron batted and kept wicket with great determination but the firing power of the enemy was too powerful for his brave little company.

At the conclusion of the Australian tour the South African team sailed south to New Zealand for the first time (unsuccesful negotiations had taken place to bring the 1910/11 combination to that country when New Zealand was still a long way off from test match status) and Cameron's men grabbed the chance to wipe away some of the trauma induced by their recent shattering experience against Bradman and company.

Jimmy Christy, who later became a professional coach in Queensland, Australia, and Bruce Mitchell added 196 for the first wicket in the opening test at Christchurch and Xenophon Balaskas, better known for his googly bowling, slammed 122 not out at Wellington.

South Africa won both tests easily thanks to good support work from the other leg-spinner in the party, Quentin McMillan, who rounded off a useful tour by claiming 16 wickets in the two games and a first-class total of 71 in both countries.

A couple of test-free home seasons now appeared to work miracles for South African cricket. Herby Wade's team in England in 1935 travelled along a trail of triumph, starting with a grand innings victory over traditional first opponents Worcesterhire, reaching the pinnacle of ambition with a test and series win at the home of cricket Lord's, and ending with the finest tour record to date by a South African team in England.

Stan McCabe (left) and Don Bradman, Australia's most exciting batsmen of the 1930's

Wade proved to be the inspiring leader South Africa needed, and a measure of the regard with which his team was accorded by the English selectors was the fact that no fewer than 25 players were called upon by them during the series. But all their efforts at endeavouring to raise an eleven to beat the Springboks were in vain and South Africa took the rubber by virtue of the fine win at Lord's.

Twin heroes of this game were of course Bruce Mitchell, with a magnificent 164 not out in a second innings

Dudley Nourse square cuts during the 'Timeless Test' against England

total of 278 for seven wickets declared, and spinner Xenophon Constantine Balaskas, the first player of Greek extraction to represent South Africa (current Zimbabwe vice-captain John Traicos, who was actually born in Egypt, was the second) and who took nine wickets in the match.

Balaskas, because of injury,only played in that one test and missed a number of other matches that summer but was very active in the famous encounter with Yorkshire at Sheffield when his skipper Cameron so confused poor Hedley Verity.

THAT MAN NOURSE

This is a story of exceptional courage which needs a background; a prelude before the dramatic act is unfolded.

It was a cold, bleak afternoon in mid-May at Bristol where the 1951 Springboks were playing Gloucestershire and the home county were busy extricating themselves from batting difficulties. The majestic Tom Graveney was in the throes of one of those innings of charm and grace often recalling the days of his world-famous predecessor Walter Hammond.

Dudley Nourse was fielding at deep extra cover. Off his back foot Graveney unleashed one of those scorching drives for which he was so renowned. The ball shot like a bullet to the Springbok captain who went forward to field. But the ball gathered momentum off the slippery grass and caught Nourse unawares on the left thumb.

He wrung his hand in pain and, looking down, noticed that the bone was sticking up at an awkward angle. He was led off the field and immediately it was realised there was trouble afoot and that the injury was serious.

There was gloom in the Springbok camp when it became known that Nourse was seriously injured. How would they fare without their skipper and best batsman?

By fortunate chance one of Britain's leading orthopaedic surgeons was in Bristol at the time and he agreed to see Nourse after the hospital authorities had ruled that the thumb should be put into plaster for six weeks. That would virtually have ruled out any more play for the Springbok captain on the tour.

The specialist's verdict was that Nourse could choose between having the thumb in plaster and a six weeks' rest or he could have it pinned and possibly go back into action

The South African captain slammed the astonished England left-arm spinner for three sixes and three fours in one over causing Yorkshire wicket-keeper Wood to remark to his team-mate at the conclusion of the slaughter that he did at least have the South African in two minds. Twelve wickets by Balaskas, including eight for 99 in the second Yorkshire innings, gave the South Africans a morale boosting win in this match.

Other players to succeed on this tour included Eric Dalton, Ken Viljoen, and, to a lesser extent, the youthful Eric Rowan and Dudley Nourse, all as batsmen, and that fine medium-pacer in the Maurice Tate mould, A.B.C-."Chud" Langton, one of South Africa's best pre-war bowlers. The enigmatic Bob Crisp, who late in life chose to live as a semi-recluse, with boat and donkey, on the island of Corfu, after a long journalistic career, was also impressive as a new-ball bowler. He holds, of course, the unique record for a South African of twice claiming four wickets in four deliveries in Currie Cup cricket.

But just a few months later the collective failure of all these players (apart from the magnificent Nourse) against the spin and guile of Grimmett and O'Reilly when Australia made their first direct visit to South Africa in 1935/36 came as a profound shock to all those connected with South African cricket.

Bob Catterall — an aggressive stroke-player whose omission from the 1931/32 team to tour Australia for reasons other than cricket materially weakened the Springbok combination

It is probable too that the sad loss of the much loved "Jock" Cameron, who died tragically at the age of only 30 from fever contracted on the voyage home from the 1935 tour, had some demoralising effect. Only Dudley Nourse, whose technique and temperament were akin to that of the Australians themselves, took the fight into the enemy camp.

The two leg-spinners of varying styles, the gnome-like little Clarrie Grimmett and his tall and menacing partner Bill O'Reilly, invariably took over completely on Nourse's departure to tear into the Springbok batting line-up like a shiver of sharks into the carcass of an ailing whale.

Between them the arch-destroyers claimed 71 of the 98 South African wickets to fall and only a masterful innings by the South African champion at the Wanderers prevented an Australian clean sweep in the series.

Dudley Nourse was a self-made cricketer who, strangely enough received no coaching from his famous father and Old Dave Nourse first saw his son bat in a first-class match when the two opposed each other at Newlands in 1931/32.

Nourse senior then played for Western Province (he coached for years at the University of Cape Town) and the young Dudley was an up-and-coming Natal hopeful who was yet to notch his first century in big cricket.

Fittingly the auspicious occasion came when his father was on the field

continued on page 36

after ten days.

Naturally Nourse chose the pinning operation though he knew it was going to be painful. But if it meant being able to resume his active participation in the tour he was prepared for any sacrifice. And so the thumb was duly pinned.

There were ten days of discomfort and pain but at last it looked as though the thumb was on the mend.

All eyes were on the first Test at Nottingham starting on June 7 and Nourse knew that if he was to play in that match he would have to see how the thumb reacted to match play. The only chance of this was to take part in the match against Surrey at the Oval on June 2, 4 and 5 immediately preceding the Test.

His team-mates were desperately keen to have Nourse back in the side, but they knew what risks he took. It was decided that he should try the thumb out at the Oval and he had it as well protected as possible.

Fortunately nothing untoward happened and there was no setback to the injured thumb and so the die was cast. Nourse would play in the first Test and his team-mates were jubilant. Dudley was back at the helm and his fighting batting spirit would be there with the rest of them at Nottingham.

Fortune, which had been so cruel to him earlier on, relented, for Nourse won the toss and was thus able to take first choice of innings.

The early batsmen started quickly and built up a useful total, for when the second wicket fell and Nourse strode to the wicket the score was 107.

That was for him one of the most nervous moments of his career, for although he had then played in 29 Test matches, here he was leading a side in England for the first time and knowing that he was going into bat under the most appalling physical difficulties. Every stroke he played jarred that thumb.

Normally an attractive, attacking batsman, his side came first and the demands were that he stay to help build a commanding total. He accepted that responsibility and had many sympathisers around the packed Trent Bridge ground.

Herby Taylor leads the Springboks onto the field during the first test in 1924. The players from left to right are: Catterall, Ward, Nourse, Blanckenberg, Taylor, Commaille and Pegler

That night South Africa had 239 and Nourse had 73 not out.

It was a night of excruciating pain. The pin had moved and was visible through the skin. Much against his wish he decided next morning that it was wiser to have an injection in an attempt to deaden the pain. But after an hour's batting the effect had worn off and back came those jarring stabs of pain each time he put bat to ball. To play an off-side stroke which necessitated using force with the left thumb was sheer agony.

Those of us who watched this human drama from a distance saw that Nourse mopped his brow every now and again and at the end of each over would tuck his left arm behind his back. We knew he was suffering pain but did not know just how much.

On reaching his century the applause was both loud and generous.

The longer he played the more that left hand swelled. It was puffy, bruised, and that pin had moved even more.

Of necessity Nourse's scoring pace slowed down and the crowd, forgetting that the Springbok captain was playing under the most difficult circumstances, slow handclapped.

It was probably the only time in his life that the Springbok captain endured that indignity. But he took it all calmly by walking away from the pitch when the clapping started, taking off his cap and mopping his brow. As soon as the barracking stopped he took up his stance again and battled on.

Having reached his double century with the Springbok total 483, Nourse hit hard to the covers and ran in an attempt to keep the strike. But his rival captain, Freddie Brown, picked up and took a pot shot at the wicket, scoring a direct hit and Nourse was run out.

He received a standing ovation, as well he might. Surely no innings in Test history has been shaped against greater odds or played in a more courageous manner.

On reaching the dressingroom, Nourse was pale and in obvious pain, but tactics had to be discussed and it was agreed that a declaration should be made in the hope of snatching a quick England wicket before the close of play.

In point of fact that happened when McCarthy was told to stay at short fine leg because there was no time to get him to the boundary, and

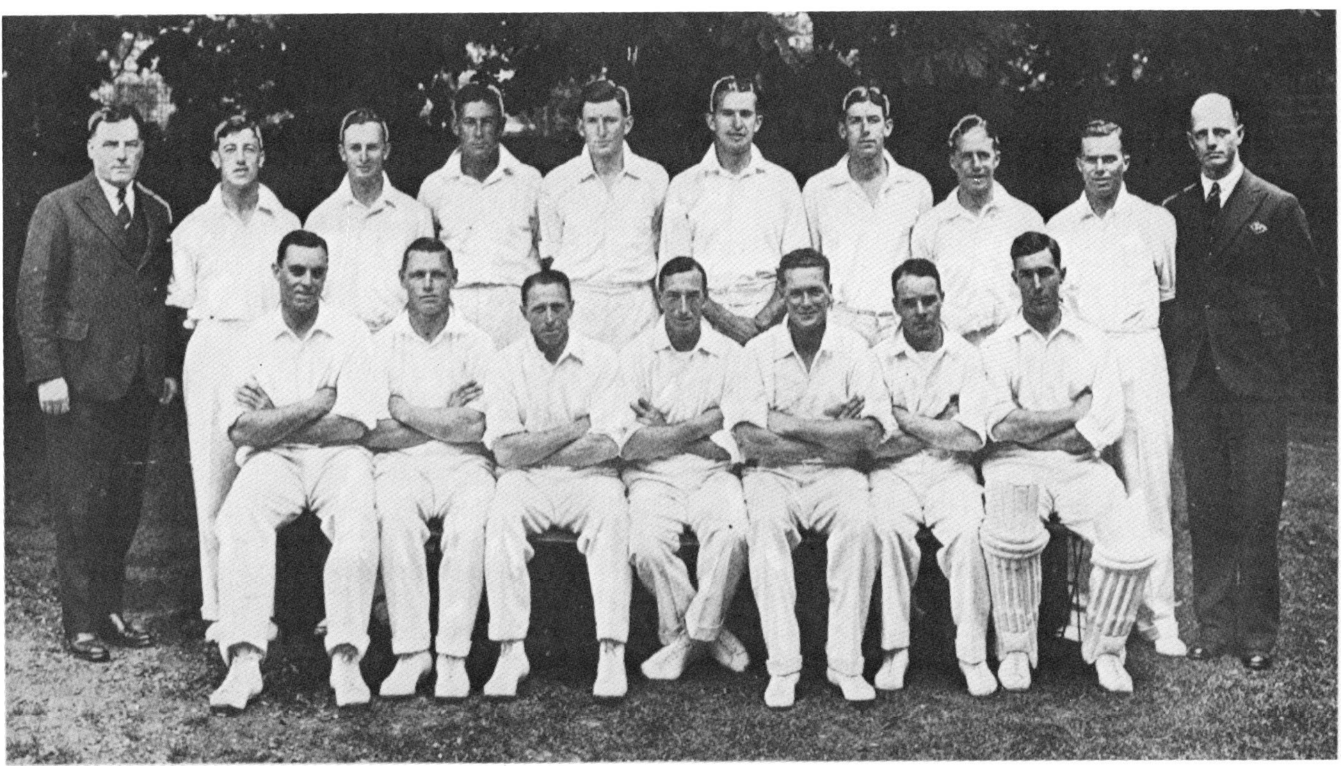

The 1929 Springbok side in England: Back row: H.O. Frielinghaus (manager), H.G. Owen-Smith, B. Mitchell, D.P.B. Morkel, A.J. Bell, J.A.J. Christy, N.A. Quinn, Q. McMillan, E.L. Dalton, A.S. Frames (Secretary); Front row: I.J. Siedle, A.L. Ochse, H.W. Taylor, H.G. Deane (capt.), R.H. Catterall, E.A. van der Merwe, H.B. Cameron

right there he caught Ikin as the clouds closed in and rain threatened. It had undoubtedly been South Africa's day; nay, Nourse's day.

When experts at the hospital that evening examined the thumb they marvelled that Nourse had been able to hold a bat let alone notch a double century. The pin had moved out further and hospital advice was that it should be removed.

But before doing that Nourse decided he would like to contact the specialist who had done the original job of pinning that thumb.

"Don't let them take that pin out. Come back to me and I will try to squeeze it back into place," the specialist advised Nourse.

And so by car back to Bristol to have that pin readjusted once again. It was more or less squeezed back into position. But somehow the pain and discomfort was eased by the knowledge that South Africa had gained her second Test victory in England and her first for the past 16 years.

"Those nine and a quarter hours' batting time had been worth it after all. When victory came at last it was my greatest moment," says Nourse. "As one gets older the game becomes harder and in achieving anything exceptional in difficult circumstances it tends to stick out in the memory. It is the ambition of every cricketer to achieve something worthwhile for his country.

"I often rate the finest innings I ever played was one at Manchester on the 1947 tour. We were 39 behind on the first innings but the pitch was taking treacherous spin with the ball coming through at varying heights, especially from Compton.

"Edrich, Wright and Hollies were all difficult and I felt I had never earned 115 runs harder than on that occasion — until, of course, the Nottingham Test four years later. The many factors surrounding it will always make that one for me a match to remember.

"It was also the reason for my withdrawal from first class cricket earlier than I had intended. But that is the way it goes and I then settled down to try to put back something into the game from which I derived so much pleasure."

C.O. Medworth
January 1963

and Dave was the first to walk over to congratulate his son when he had reached the coveted three figures.

Dudley Nourse's brave 231 off the rampant Australians in Johannesburg in 1935/36 must remain one of the greatest innings ever by a South African and, considering the odds ranged against him, one of the best test innings of all time. He finished the series streets ahead of the other South African batsmen with 518 runs at 57,55 an innings.

For Australia the dashing Stan McCabe hit 149 at Durban and a dazzling 189 not out at the Wanderers before a storm saved South Africa from certain defeat. The contrastingly dour Jack Fingleton affixed his personal seal on the series with three successive centuries.

SIR DON BRADMAN

Sir Donald Bradman's amazing aggregate of 806 runs in only five innings against South Africa in 1931/32 was not the only occasion on which this great player totalled 800 in a series. His best performance was against England in 1930 when he totalled 974, the world record (W.R. Hammond — 905 vs Australia, 1928/29 is next best), and he aggregated 810 vs England in 1936/37. The best performances by South Africans are: G.A. Faulkner 732 vs Australia 1910/11; D.T. Lindsay 606 vs Australia 1966/67; E.J. Barlow 603 vs Australia 1963/64.

Jack Siedle (left) and Bruce Mitchell who totalled a record opening partnership of 260 in the second test of the 1930/31 M.C.C. tour

The final test dual in South Africa prior to the Second World War was notable for high scoring throughout and for the exhausting "Timeless Test" which was left unfinished at Kingsmead, Durban after twelve days (nine of actual play, with two week-ends and a washout in between) and an incredible aggregate of 1 981 runs, the highest ever in a test match.

Left to score an apparently impossible 696 runs to win in the final innings England were, amazingly enough, only 42 runs short of their gargantuan target when stumps were drawn because the tourists still had to make a two-day rail journey in order to catch their ship home from Cape Town.

England had previously taken the lead in the series by virtue of an innings victory in the third test, also at Kingsmead, and when they began their final effort it looked as if South Africa could well even the odds.

But a painstaking Paul Gibb and the young and aggressive Bill Edrich, who had totalled but 21 runs in the series so far, placed their team in a position to strike for what would have been the most astounding win in history were it not for the necessity to draw stumps so that the Englishmen could meet their travel commitments.

Edrich stroked his way to 219 in what was a gruelling situation for the bowlers and fielders on a pitch which seemed to improve every day, whilst Gibb (120) and the regal Wally Hammond (140), saw the England total to a world record for the final innings of the match: 654 for five wickets.

Louis Duffus, incidentally, points out in *Cricketers of the Veld* that timeous light overnight rain twice revived "a wicket that was too good to begin with".

Hammond had always kept that other master of the willow, Australia's Bradman, close company when it came to the matter of huge scoring feats and he made no exception in South Africa

Above: The 1935 Springbok team in England: Back row: A.D. Nourse, E.L. Dalton, A.B.C. Langton, R.J. Crisp, D.S. Tomlinson, K.G. Viljoen, R.J. Williams; Middle row: A.J. Bell, C.L. Vincent, H.F. Wade (capt.), S.J. Snooke (Manager), H.B. Cameron, I.J. Siedle, B. Mitchell; In front: X.C. Balaskas, E.A.B. Rowan

in 1938/39 with three test hundreds and an average of 87.

Accustomed good form for the home team was shown by Nourse and Mitchell, whilst Pieter van der Bijl, father of the popular Vintcent and also a tall man of impressive personality, almost had his name recorded for posterity with scores of 125 and 97 during the Durban marathon.

Of the South African bowlers Norman Gordon, a lively medium pacer, most impressed the tourists but he was sadly one of the many players whose careers were to be cut short by the coming events in the northern hemisphere. •

JACK FINGLETON

Jack Fingleton's four consecutive hundreds for Australia over 1935/37 was equalled by Alan Melville, South Africa's captain in 1938/39 and 1947, who hit the first of his quartet against England during the "Timeless Test" at Durban in 1939 and followed with three hundreds on the trot against England in 1947.

The joint record held by Fingleton and Melville was beaten by West Indian Everton Weekes who recorded five consecutive three-figure innings against England and India over 1948/49.

Right: The Australian opening batsman, Jack Fingleton who hit three centuries in a row during the 1935/36 tour of South Africa

The great England fast bowler, Harold Larwood, shatters J.A.J. Christy's off stump in the first test in 1929

Bob Catterall (left) and Bruce Mitchell

FOUR IN A ROW

The physical features of the Great Karoo are many and varied and over the years some amazing phenomena have come from that vast, arid stretch. Little did the residents of Carnarvon know on that 19th day of May, 1910, when a son was born to their bank manager that he would one day become an internationally famous sportsman.

The son was christened Alan and when his father was asked why he gave his son only one name he replied: "The first name doesn't wear out so there's no need for a second."

When Mr and Mrs Melville two years later moved to Greytown, their little toddler went with them and in a few years' time he was able to attend St David's Preparatory School. At the tender age of 13 Alan was sent to Michaelhouse, Balgowan, where he was to start a great sporting career on the cricket field. His housemaster, Mr C.W. Hannah, was to play an important role in his later life.

As a colt Alan showed much promise both as a batsman and as a legspin bowler and it wasn't long before he was in the senior side as an all-rounder. His prowess had got around and in 1927 he was selected to play for a combined Natal and Transvaal Schools team against the

M.C.C. That was Alan's introduction to prominent players.

The next season, still as a schoolboy, he was included in the senior Natal team primarily then as a spin bowler though he also batted fairly high up. He had the distinction of being a schoolboy cricketing prodigy. Adventurous days lay ahead of him for upon matriculating his father sent him up to Oxford University in 1930.

Unlike many other freshmen, Alan arrived with a ready-made reputation and he went straight into the 'Varsity side which he also captained in 1931/32. But Alan gave up spin bowling, for two very good reasons as he says. "Firstly I found it so cold that my fingers were sore and stiff and as I had to do a good deal of batting I decided to give up bowling. But there was perhaps an even better reason. At the same time we had the services of one of the great spin bowlers of that time, Ian Peebles. He could do it so much better than I could."

During his vacations Alan used to stay on an estate in Sussex with his former housemaster Mr Hannah and in this way he qualified with the two years residential demands, to play for Sussex, for whom he played from 1932 to 1936 and as captain from 1933 to 1935. Those were years when he made a great impression as an outstanding cricketer; an upright batsman in the classic mould with smooth, fluid stokes, yet penetrating and productive.

He was clearly ready for the bigger issues and had a frustrating time before national honours came his way.

The year before he had gone up to Oxford he had been invited to go with Herby Wade's Springboks to England. In 1931 he was invited to accompany the Springboks to Australia. He was also asked if he could travel with Douglas Jardine's controversial M.C.C. team to Australia.

To all these invitations his father turned a deaf ear. His son was to complete his studies before he made any such excursions. Apart, thus, from playing for Oxford, Sussex and the Gentlemen of England, Alan had to bide his time for bigger cricket.

When he returned to South Africa in 1937 Alan was immediately made captain of Transvaal. At long last the national scene was to absorb him, and it was as captain of South Africa in 1938/39 against Wally Hammond's team during which series the timeless test was played.

That marathon, which produced endless runs and which did not ironically enough come to a decision because there was not the time left for the M.C.C. to polish off the match and to catch their boat back home, was to start a unique chain of runs for Alan Melville.

He scored 7 in the first innings and 103 in the second. The next time he was to play in a Test match was after the hostilities had ceased and peace restored cricket to its followers when Alan took the 1947 Springboks to England. The years lay lightly upon him for the break seemed to have made no difference to his batsmanship.

He strode to the wicket at Nottingham in the first Test of that series and cracked another century in a prolific partnership of 319 for the third wicket with Dudley Nourse. And when he hit another century in the second innings of that match he earned two new distinctions.

He became the first South African to score two separate centuries in the same Test match and he had hit three in a row.

There followed the Test match at Lord's, scene of some of his earlier triumphs, and again Alan turned on the charm to score a century and so make history with the unprecendented achievement of scoring four consecutive Test centuries. This was indeed Melville's greatest moment. It is history no South African has ever repeated.

Then, when it seemed he was at the height of his career, he decided he wanted to leave the scene of action at the age of 37 and he also decided that he would not for several years seek any election honours as an administrator.

He was reluctantly persuaded to come out of retirement in the 1948/49 season and played in one Test only before calling it a day.

For a while he went into cricket obscurity. "I have always held the view," he says, "that one should not go straight from active cricket to the selection board as was suggested to me. I doubt whether one's perspective can be quite right. One could so easily be inclined to think that one's contemporaries are better than those coming up. I felt it necessary to be away from the game for a time so that I could come back with a clear and open mind."

It was not until 1954, after seven years away from cricket, that Alan Melville came back and this time as a national selector, and he has helped to choose every Springbok team since then bringing to bear his vast experience of the game and his shrewd knowledge of players.

C.O. Medworth
November 1963

Hugh Tayfield and Trevor Goddard lead the Springboks off the field after victory in the fourth test in 1955

CHAPTER THREE

A NEW START

Most of the Springboks who toured England with Alan Melville in 1947 had seen war service of some kind or another and for many it had been a struggle to find form and fitness during the preceding South African season.

One of the main batting hopes, Dudley Nourse, had returned from "up north" in poor health and it took some time for him to regain his touch. But, on the opening day of the first post-war test for his country, he was in fine fettle and assisted his skipper to add 319 grand runs for the third wicket to take South Africa to a heartening 376 for three wickets by close of play.

Melville himself, who is described by E.W. Swanton in an obituary eulogy in *The Cricketer* as "a batsman of high talent and classic style", continued where he had left off in 1938/39. The very correct South African captain hit 189 and 104 not out in the first match at Nottingham (which ended in a draw) and followed with his fourth test hundred in a row at Lord's, where England set the standard for the series with a ten wicket victory.

The main agents of destruction for the home team were the devastating "Middlesex Twins", Denis Compton and Bill Edrich, who treated all bowlers that season as if they were merely Sunday afternoon trundlers in the local park.

If it were not for the famous England pair South Africa might have been in with a chance as, other than Nourse and Melville, Bruce Mitchell was in prolific form, especially during the final game at The Oval where he was on the field for virtually the entire match to score 120 and 189 not out.

Over four days this match drew an attendance approaching 80 000, with a crowd of nearly 27 000 on the second day, and the cricket-starved British public was not disappointed by the quality of play.

South Africa, after a disappointing start came their closest to a test win, thanks almost entirely to the herculean effort by Mitchell. Trailing by 125 runs on the first innings South Africa suffered a customary battering from the irrepressible Denis Compton and were left with the huge task of accumulating 451 for victory.

Mitchell then played an innings of great contrasts — during one period he scored only 36 in two-and-a-half hours but, after reaching his hundred in just under five hours, proceeded to move onto the attack. Nourse had earlier weighed in with a typically aggressive 97 to take his personal tally for the series to 621 runs, and Lindsay Tuckett, coming in at the fall of the seventh wicket, proceeded to almost match Mitchell stroke for stroke in a 109 run partnership. Forty-six runs flowed in the final thirty minutes but the task was, alas, just beyond South Africa's capability.

Tuckett had, incidentally, bowled with great verve and stamina throughout the rubber but it was unquestionably a batsman's year for both teams.

For England, Compton and Edrich reigned supreme and Nourse, Melville and Mitchell each scored over 500 test runs for South Africa. The only bowling feat of note on either side was a ten-wicket haul by "hop-skip-and-jump" leg-spinner Doug Wright when he bowled England to victory at Lord's.

To South Africans it was rather puzzling to see George Mann's 1948/49 M.C.C. team land without Bill Edrich, who was then still an amateur in the days of Gentlemen and Players and was unavailable for business reasons.

As events turned out the second half of the Middlesex act was not required, with the two less flamboyant northerners, Len Hutton and Cyril Washbrook, giving Denis Compton all the assistance he required to outscore the Springboks on their home arena.

Certainly the opening test performance at Kingsmead, Durban turned out to be a tragi-comedy from South Africa's point of view. After a disastrous first innings debacle against the seam attack of Alec Bedser and Cliff Gladwin, South Africa's hopes were renewed by some splendid spin wizardry from off-break bowler Athol Rowan (one of the best of his type world cricket has seen) and left-hander Norman "Tufty" Mann.

Both had bowled with immense skill and accuracy in England in 1947 and, were it not for the almost superhuman performances of Compton and Edrich, they might have sailed home as members of a winning combination.

South Africa's batsman/wicket-keeper, "Billy" Wade, who had first gained his Springbok cap ten years earlier in 1938/39, top scored in what appeared to be a totally inadequate second effort but a hostile spell of pace bowling by nineteen-year-old Cuan McCarthy, of the controversial double-jointed action, suddenly placed South Africa back on stage and with a chance of taking the winning ovation.

Intermittent heavy rainstorms and the action of the heavy roller had served to aid the bowlers in their efforts on a very difficult pitch and England needed 8 runs to win at the commencement of the final over from Lindsay Tuckett.

It was drama straight out of the top drawer. After a flurry of quickly scampered runs, Alec Bedser brought the scores level with a single off the sixth delivery in the eight-ball over.

His partner was the popular Cliff Gladwin, who had remarked to his nail-biting colleagues in the dressing room prior to his saunter to the middle : "Coometh the hour, coometh the man!". The Derbyshire bowler swung and missed at Tuckett's seventh ball and the batsmen decided that they would run whatever happened to the last.

As Tuckett ran in to bowl the fateful delivery, the fieldsman ran in to prevent the possiblity of a single. The ball missed Gladwin's furiously swinging bat but struck his ample thigh and he and Bedser galloped through for the winning leg-bye.

England's hero of the final ball was reported to have proudly offered to display his match-winning bruise to anyone wishing to view the temporary souvenir of England's close victory.

Showing complete domination of the South African attack, Hutton and Washbrook created a new first-wicket world test record in the next game at Ellis Park, Johannesburg (this new ground replaced the famous Old Wanderers for several seasons) by adding 359 in the relatively fast time of 290 minutes.

In front of a crowd of 35 000, a record for South African tests, Compton launched a merciless attack in partnership with left-hander Jack Crapp and England built up the huge total of 608. But victory eluded the Englishman when Eric Rowan, who had ironi-

THE AUSSIES SCORED 520 — AND THEN THEY WERE CHEETHAMMED!

The most important quality of a test cricket captain, "Plum" Warner, a one-time England captain himself, wrote, is enthusiasm. Enthusiasm is more important than a sound knowledge of the game, cool judgement and tact. For it is a quality which enriches life and gives it zest.

"The man who is enthusiastic about his XI and their doings will, unless his influence and authority are sapped by disloyalty and want of co-operation, soon inspire the same feelings of zeal for the common cause in his followers," declared Warner.

He might have written these words specially for tall, slim Jack Cheetham, the Springbok skipper of 10 years ago.

For what else but enthusiasm and a refusal to be depressed whatever the odds could have enabled "Happy Jack" Cheetham to coax his Springbok team to a victory over Australia in the Fifth Test in 1953 — in the face of a first innings total of 520?

Taking a team of "innocents abroad" to the home of the world champions of cricket, Jack Cheetham welded this side of young triers into a formidable side. So that by the time the fifth and decisive test was due to be played — Australia 2-1 up in the series — his players had faith in themselves.

A target of 520 runs was just another obstacle to be overcome, and it made little matter that no side in the long history of international cricket had ever managed to win a test after such a bad start. That was Jack Cheetham's biggest contribution to his country's cricket — the instilling of confidence in players who for years had taken knocks in the way of defeats by the larger cricketing powers.

Unquestionably the highlight of the skipper's career was the astonishing victory by six wickets over the Australians at Melbourne in February, 1953, when no-one, bar captain Jack Cheetham and manager Ken Viljoen, would have given any odds to the Springboks winning after Australia's mammoth 520.

They say that South African cricket is too defensive. Well, the lie was given to this adage in the pre-game talk. Cheetham said to his players that a draw would not help the side. To save the rubber cally already been dropped for the next match at Newlands, scored a painstaking 156 not out after South Africa had followed on.

Exceptionally cautious batting by the local batsmen spoilt any chance of levelling the series at Cape Town. Mitchell, in his usual phlegmatic manner, and an out of character Nourse added 190 but took far too long over their effort and the game petered out into another draw.

Dudley Nourse played one of his finest innings when he compiled 129 in the fourth test at Ellis Park but the Springboks again displayed excess caution and the result was inconclusive giving England a 1-0 lead into the final game at Port Elizabeth.

In sharp contrast to the hesitant home players, George Mann and his talented team accepted the challenge of scoring 172 to win in only 95 minutes and scraped home by three wickets just one minute from close of play. Jack Crapp was the hero of the moment, hitting ten off three successive balls to clinch the matter, but the win had been set up by Hutton and Washbrook. The former smacked the

Bill Edrich (left) and Denis Compton who devastated the Springboks in 1947

and equal the tests at two-all, "we have to win," he said.

Melbourne had been the scene of the side's great victory in the Second Test, and with the batting, bowling and also the prehensile fielding at a high pitch, the side need not have had any lack of faith in itself.

Both Ray Lindwall and Keith Miller were missing from the Australian side for the final test, but there was nothing wrong with an attack which included Bill Johnston, Geoff Noblet, Ron Archer, Richie Benaud and Doug Ring. Including speed, spin and swing, the Australian attack looked complete.

At the penultimate day's end, South Africa were 94 for one. With nine wickets standing, the Springboks needed 201 runs for victory — and "Endless Endean", as the spectators called him, was still there.

"In retrospect, that evening must have been a pleasant one", writes Jack Cheetham in his book *"Caught by the Springboks"*, but I can recall that I experienced a tension far greater than ever before. We realised that we had a chance to even the series, an achievement no other touring side had done since Jardine's 1932/33 team, which had introduced into the game the 'bodyline' era.

"What a controversy that had caused — and I can remember thinking at the time that the only 'controversy' we had caused was whether we should have been allowed to tour Australia, as we were 'too weak' to do 'justice' to South African cricket.

"It suffices to say that long after leaving Ken Viljoen's room I lay awake, wondering whether, as in the First Test, we should fall apart, flattering but to deceive and, then again, hearing a sudden squall of rain, worrying lest nature would deprive us of at least an effort to snatch a win", he said.

Both Endean and Watkins had some pre-start batting practice to get their eye in, and to become accustomed to the light. It seemed to help, for the first 30 minutes brought 30 runs.

A double bowling change by Hassett saw the stand broken, Endean being yorked by Bill Johnston for a fighting 70. Score: South Africa, 124 for two wickets.

Despite the tenseness of the game, the Australian spectators retained their normal high spirits. When a Skymaster aircraft flew overhead one fan commented: "If it lands in the middle of the pitch, we've still got a chance."

At 174 the third wicket fell, Ring bowling Watkins with a sharp spinner which took his

Left: Neil Harvey, the superb Australian left-handed batsman who amassed huge scores against the Springboks

Right: Had it not been for an injury to his left knee, Athol Rowan could well have become one of the greatest off-spinners of all time

off bail. Watkins had made a valuable 50 which, together with his 92 in the first innings, some solid bowling, and three smart catches in the Australians' second innings, gave him a proud match record indeed.

Headley Keith came in to see out the 14 minutes remaining before lunch, which he duly did.

Recalling that lunch interval, Cheetham told me: "Headley Keith sat chain-smoking with his cap on for the entire 45 minutes' break.

"Ken Funston paced up and down like a caged leopard. The room was still, and the atmosphere was terribly tense. I tried to talk to the two batsmen to take their minds off the game. That didn't help, so I told than that I had complete confidence in their ability to see the side through to victory.

"That also didn't help, so I switched on the radio and did an improvised tickey draai — and that did help. The batsmen both burst out laughing, and the ice was broken," recalled Cheetham.

After lunch, Benaud proved difficult to get away, and the spin bowler caused some consternation in the Springbok camp — everyone peering anxiously through the dressingroom window — when he bowled Funston with his wrong 'un.

Now came one of the most poignant moments of the tour, and one which is enshrined in Springbok cricket history. As Roy McLean, next man in, rose and looked round to pick up his bat and gloves, Cheetham was at his side. There had been a close bond of friendship between the older and younger man all through the tour. It was evident now.

The Natal youngster smiled and replied: "Don't worry, Pop, I'll get 'em for you." And he was briskly away down the steps.

McLean met Benaud's first ball with a powerful swing. It travelled straight to mid-wicket and into the hands of Arthur Morris — who dropped it. Another moment of truth in this match of fluctuations!

"I shall never forget my reaction to that shot," recalled Cheetham. "Next man in, I stood up with an empty feeling at the pit of my stomach, only the crowd's groan and the excited shout from Anton Murray allowed me to sink gratefully back on the bench."

When his score was 15, Keith was missed by Arthur Morris at short fine leg, and one of the Springboks in the dressingroom said with sudden confidence: "This must be our day. I'm not worried any more."

first ball he received for four to set the pace and Washbrook responded by hooking the first one he faced for six.

Overshadowed for years by the great Sir Donald Bradman, the chirpy but shrewd little Lindsay Hassett claimed his rightful place in the sun when given the opportunity to lead his country in South Africa in 1949/50.

Standing only five foot six inches, the popular Australian captain, who seemed to walk around with a permanent smile on his elfin face, was a fine batsman in his own right close behind the two brilliant left-handers, Neil Harvey and Arthur Morris, in a highly proficient squad that was virtually the same combination which had massacred England in 1948.

Only the experienced forty-year-old veterans, Dudley Nourse and Eric Rowan, possessed technique of the order required to handle the frightening array of Australian fast bowlers. Bruce Mitchell was sadly missing from the Springbok ranks after failure in two pre-test encounters with the Aussie seam attack. Strangely enough he did not even get to face a ball from the main danger man Ray Lindwall, who virtually terrorised South Africa's mostly inexperienced young batsmen into submission with a barrage of short pitched bumpers.

The glamorous Keith Miller who was initially left out of the party but was hastily recalled when big Bill Johnston was slightly injured in a car accident, was again Lindwall's chief aide-de-camp. In addition to his own battery of menacing bouncers, Miller often surprised the South African defenders with an unexpected leg or off-break of genuine quality.

Added to his vigorous but always classy batting and athletic fielding and catching, the Australian's ability to almost "psyche" the batsman out certainly proved to South Africans the verity of the claim that he was one of the finest all-rounders ever to appear in a test match.

The scintillating stroke-play of Neil Harvey was a joy and his 178 in the second game at Newlands has only been challenged subsequently by the power of Graeme Pollock and possibly the New Zealander John Reid. Harvey, however, played his best innings for Australia in a totally different key.

After Eric Rowan had exhibited outstanding strength of character in a knock of 143 in the Kingsmead test, young Hugh Tayfield, a replacement for the injured Athol Rowan, produced his own *magnum opus* with an unbelievable spell of seven wickets for 23 runs, albeit on a helpful pitch.

Australia had been dismissed for the incredibly low total of 75 and South African skipper Dudley Nourse agonised during the ensuing weekend over his pending decision about a follow-on. Apparently influenced by the possibilty of rain he decided to bat again but the Springboks, in their turn, collapsed to the combination of Bill Johnston and Ian Johnson.

Thus Australia was left with the daunting task of scoring 336 runs on a still far from easy wicket. But Harvey altered his style of play so effectively as to be unrecognisable from the gay stroke-player of previous games. He proceeded to graft his way to a match-winning 151 not out, surely one of the most commendable of his test innings.

On the credit side for South Africa in what was otherwise a totally humiliating experience, was the emergence

Eddie Fuller was the self-appointed scorekeeper — although everyone else could also see the big Melbourne Ground scoreboard. "Only 101 to go . . . only 94 . . . only 89," he intoned.

McLean had quickly appraised Benaud's possible danger on a wicket which, after five days' play, was beginning to take spin, and he singled the tall leg-spinner out for some "treatment".

Stepping out of his crease, McLean crashed anything loose to the fence. With six fours he shot to 27, and Keith with 16 was left astern.

Hassett rang the bowling changes, but McLean after his lucky early let-off, was inspired. Soon only another 50 runs were needed, and a couple of minutes later loud cheers told that McLean had reached his 50.

Off an over from Ring, 18 runs were taken, and then, with only 10 runs required, the whimsical Hassett conceded defeat. In a typical puckish gesture, he took the ball and with an 'I'll bowl you out' look, he delivered to McLean — who slammed the ball away for four.

Another delivery was square-cut viciously for four. Only two runs needed — but McLean wasn't in a mood to do things by halves. A perfect cover-drive saw the ball skim all the way to the fence — and South Africa had won, gloriously, by six wickets.

In the South African dressingroom there was pandemonium. One of the first people to offer congratulations to the Springbok captain was Sir Donald Bradman — tribute from one of the great captains of history to a plucky leader of the so-called 'poor relations'.

Cheetham recalls: "As the boys crowded around and everyone sang, shouted and wise-cracked, I felt a lump in my throat and my eyes filled with tears. It would not be wrong to say that I was overcome with joy . . . Roy and Headley came into the dressingroom, and I put my arms around their necks — what a great partnership — a great double for Roy, and a magnificent opening to Headley's test career."

By a master stroke of inspired leadership and team spirit, South African cricket prestige had been restored and the Springboks were once again rated among the top cricket nations.

Arthur Goldman
January 1964

of Hugh Tayfield as a bowler of stature who was to develop into the main cog around which Jack Cheetham built his efficient test machine of the early 1950's.

Sadly enough it was the absence through injury of one of South Africa's greatest sons, Athol Rowan, which had made clear the way for his young rival to stake a claim for a permanent place in the South African XI.

The younger of the Rowan brothers had completely baffled the Australians with his off-breaks during the Transvaal match played some two weeks prior to the first test, running out with a match analysis of 15 wickets for 68 runs, but badly twisted his already suspect knee in a fall whilst batting.

This brave player had for a time actually taken part in first division club cricket with his one leg in an iron brace and returned during the following domestic season to oust Tayfield from consideration for the 1951 tour of England. As it turned out, Rowan experienced further trouble with his leg whilst on tour and the younger man was called in as a reserve.

In the 1952 edition of *Wisden* the editor noted : "The South Africans came to England in 1951 hoping to write a new chapter in the history of cricket on the veld, but they returned home to a large extent disappointed".

An unfortunate injury to the captain and most well-equipped batsman in the team, Dudley Nourse, drastically reduced the South Africans' run-getting capability and an inordinate load was thrust onto the wiry shoulders of 42 year-old Eric Rowan.

Nourse had his left thumb broken during a pre-test match against Gloucestershire. Although he bravely took part in the first test clash with his hand strapped up, his style of play was reduced from the customary aggressive and dominating role to that of defensive sheet-anchor.

In great pain throughout, Nourse refused injections to alleviate his discomfort, fearing the possibilty that it might numb his hand and affect his grip. That he should have batted in all for nine and a quarter hours and, at the end of what must have been a harrowing experience, was able to witness a team total of 483 and an amazing personal contribution of 208 was little short of a miracle.

The South African captain took no further part in the match and leadership on the field was taken over by Eric Rowan, possibly the best captain never to have officially led his country.

Rowan, of necessity, became the mainstay of the batting for the remainder of the tour and, following a slowish start in which his first five test knocks yielded only 62 runs, he smashed Dudley Nourse's top score record with 236 in the fourth match at Leeds.

The always outspoken and oft controversial South African vice-captain was involved, with his nephew Johnny Waite, in an "incident" during the match versus Lancashire at Old Trafford. The 15 000 Manchester spectators objected to a period of cautious batting and began to slow-handclap. Rowan and Waite promptly sat down on the pitch to await a cessation of the minor hubbub.

Later, on being abused by an onlooker in the Members' enclosure as he walked onto the field after luncheon, Rowan retorted with a choice comment, unprintable but probably warranted in the circumstances.

Unfortunately the occurrence received much press publicity, especially in South Africa, and probably influ-

NEIL ADCOCK

I came to know Neil Adcock after he had made something of a name as a fast bowler. He was then around 26 and a tearaway type whether on the field in his flannels or sprucely turned out for the evening's adventures.

Somewhere along the line influences that have stabilized and mellowed Neil Adcock came into play. The once carefree and sometimes careless fast bowler of the fifties became something not far removed from an elder statesman by the sixties.

Adcock's adventures in test cricket started off much as they were to continue. His first big burst into the headlines came with his test match debut against New Zealand at Kingsmead in 1953. Adcock sent down 19 eight-ball overs taking never a single wicket but conceding 52 runs. Economical enough but not the thunder-bolt impact he had been picked to produce. His first press notices were lukewarm. The second test, Johannesburg and Ellis Park, make a different story.

That strip thirty feet wide put down as a makeshift cricket pitch while the Wanderers' Club moved on to pastures new, could on its day be a lively affair. Here around Christmas 1953 Adcock bounced one ball off Bert Sutciffe's cranium before that courageous cricketer got off the mark. He rattled Miller's ribs and thereby had two New Zealanders simultaneously under X-ray apparatus for damages to be assessed.

Head swathed in bandages Sutcliffe returned and found some modicum of revenge by carting Tayfield into every corner of Ellis Park. Sutcliffe's 80 not out with 7 sixes along the way was perhaps the most memorable moment that Ellis Park ever knew in its short story as a test match ground. In this his second test Adcock took 8 wickets for 87 runs. A newcomer and a fast bowler had arrived.

I was in Australia during the cricket season of 1954/55 with the MCC tour skippered by Sir Leonard Hutton. It was good preperation for the Springbok tour to England due to start in May 1955 and I travelled direct from Sydney to London. But if this Australian season kept me fully in touch with English cricket and the mighty bowling feats of

Russell Endean who played a major part in the Springbok revival in 1952/53

enced the decision to leave the forthright opening batsman out of the party to visit Australia in 1952/53.

After a win in the Nottingham test in which Athol Rowan and "Tufty" Mann spun England out for a low score in the final innings, the South Africans struggled and the home eleven gained a 3-1 advantage by the end of the series.

Unlike those in the previous side in 1947 the younger players of 1951 improved immeasurably as the tour progressed and Waite, Roy McLean, who looked the natural successor to Nourse, Jackie McGlew, Russell Endean, Tayfield, Percy Mansell and Michael Melle were to form the nucleus of Jack Cheetham's young battalion of giant-killers in Australia in 1952/53.

Johnny Waite, originally chosen as the reserve wicket-keeper, soon became first choice, as much for his ability as an opening bat as for his considerable genius behind the stumps. This elegant and correct player was to appear in a record 50 matches for his country and also holds the honours for most dismissals in a series by a wicket-keeper, 26 (23 ct 3 st) vs New Zealand in 1961/62.

Statham and Tyson on Australian pitches, it also landed me in England only faintly aware that a Peter Heine had emerged from the "B" Section of the Currie Cup to become Adcock's sparring partner in many a famous battle yet to be.

Looking back on this tour of 1955 it requires some effort to remember that this, the finest test series I ever watched, started off so bleakly. Agreed the Springboks won handsomely over MCC on their first visit to Lord's, but the first test at Nottingham was one long rear-guard action that failed to save the day. The second at Headquarters was a case of being always in the lead except at the winning post. England behind on the first innings by 171 runs got home in the end with a margin of 71. And for Adcock that Lord's test was a difficult match.

On a very lively wicket England batting first was put out for 133. Adcock struck the first blow by bowling Kenyon of Worcestershire for a single. Thereafter Heine making his debut in test cricket took 5 for 60 and it seemed a grand pair of Springbok fast bowlers had arrived. But Adcock's knee gave trouble in England's second innings. Later in the fourth test at Leeds trouble more serious by far came his way. At Leeds when England went into bat Adcock bowled but 4 overs (three of them maidens) when he broke down with an injury that X-ray showed to be a fractured bone in the foot. Thus for Adcock the splendid tour with Jack Cheetham was something of a disappointment.

It was fashionable among the England players and the English press in the fifties to rate Adcock's fearsome giant of a partner Peter Heine as

the more difficult and penetrating of the two Springbok fast bowlers. This was true

Tayfield, McGlew and Endean were destined to achieve great eminence in Australia and New Zealand and the others were all essential parts of Jack Cheetham's well-drilled combination.

Their departure on board the *Dominion Monarch* was a quiet affair. The author recalls being there with Alan "Porky" Dennison, scorer for Cheetham's club Alma, and probably less than two dozen other well-wishers, mostly family and officials.

When it became known that most of South Africa's experienced players were unavailable for the tour it had even been suggested that the venture be called off. Without Nourse and Athol Rowan (both retired), Eric Rowan (banned by the South African Board), Clive van Ryneveld and George Fullerton (unavailable for business reasons), Cuan McCarthy (then resident in England and ruled ineligible) and the much lamented "Tufty" Mann, who had at the age of 30 sadly passed on to other fields, the Springboks were given absolutely no chance by the critics of extending Australia, or even the major State teams.

But they had all reckoned without Jack Cheetham and his team-building formula of — as he put it in his book of the tour *Caught by the Springboks* - "application, determination and concentration".

Months before commencement of the undertaking the almost fanatically dedicated Cheetham and his main assistants, manager Ken Viljoen and vice-captain Jackie McGlew, had corresponded frequently to discuss tactics for the coming battle. The famed rugby coach Dr Danie Craven designed a course of special get-fit exercises which was used by all the team members and some of the players arranged special winter net practices, which were filmed in an effort to assist them to eradicate their weaknesses.

All this pre-tour effort soon paid unexpected dividends when the Springboks first took the field at Perth and amazed the Australians with their unprecedented speed and agility in the field. The excellence of the South Africans' out-cricket was such that it served to raise what was, apart from Hugh Tayfield, a mediocre bowling attack into a force to be reckoned with at the highest level of play.

The miraculous catches taken by Endean, Tayfield and others have become part of the legend of the game and Australian enthusiasts were soon pouring into their stadiums as much to see the Springboks field as to watch them bat and bowl.

Cheetham wrote that from the start the main emphasis was placed upon team spirit and and there could seldom have been a happier touring party. Top joker in the pack was the cheery John Watkins, a useful if unspectacular all-rounder, whose quick reply to a hotel porter when asked if he had been included in the Springbok line-up for the fifth test was: "Of course I am, I'm here to draw the crowds!."

South Africa relied to an immense extent on the pin-point accuracy of Hugh Tayfield's off-breaks, sometimes bowled to an unusually aggressive field including two silly mid-offs *and* two silly mid-ons. Cheetham himself was always at the forefront and bagged some outstanding catches of his own to set a fine example to his team.

Unexpectedly, Russell Endean developed into the mainstay of the batting, reaching his own personal peak at

when the two played together on the Cheetham tour in England in 1955 but certainly not so on South African wickets. Throughout the Peter May tour of 1956/57 Adcock was the rapier, Heine the battle-axe, Tayfield the magician and Goddard the tormentor. From these four was welded the finest attack that South Africa ever put into the field.

Peter May's team came ashore at Cape Town in mid-October and stayed with us until mid-March 1957. This was, at least I would say, the strongest team that MCC ever sent to South Africa. The outcome was a tied series devised in a manner exciting to the absolute. England won against initial expectations at Johannesburg and took a 2-0 lead at Newlands. Kingsmead was drawn — where the Springboks should have won. Again in Johannesburg England had the match and rubber for the taking when Tayfield took control.

Thus the series was still open when the Fifth test came to Port Elizabeth. There the toss and the wicket decreed the outcome; South Africa won the toss and the match thereby to share the rubber. Neil Adcock was an immediate choice for all five tests and his contributions took him to the top of the South African bowling averages with 21 wickets at 14,91 apiece.

Adcock played in all five tests against Ian Craig's Australians. With Tayfield and Goddard both well below their best it was the two fast bowlers who gave the Springbok attack its penetration. This tour of 1957/58 was an Australian triumph and one that the visitors had hardly anticipated. In fact the Springbok team never really got together.

At Port Elizabeth for the Fifth test both Adcock and Heine were throughout in somewhat "stroppy" mood and when Australia needed no more than 68 to win the St George's Park crowd was treated to the most terrifying eruption of fast bowling I have ever seen.

The light was drab and the evening chilly. Heine and Adcock between them sent down seven overs of electrifying pace and soaring trajectory. Adcock in his first over gave Colin McDonald three successive bumpers all of which missed him only by hair-breadths. Then both umpire and skipper van Ryneveld called for a stop to this style of attack. Adcock promptly sent down the daddy of all bumpers. From it McDonald was caught at slip.

Later that night, about 1 am I bumped into Neil and Piet, still very "stroppy" and quite unrepentant! As bowlers

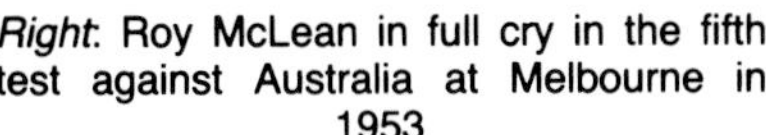

Above: Jackie McGlew. Courage and determination were his main attributes

Right: Roy McLean in full cry in the fifth test against Australia at Melbourne in 1953

maybe they had had their fill of bowling in a side that would make no runs to supplement their own prodigious labours.

So to 1960 and the tour to England captained by Jackie McGlew. For all members of the touring side save only one this was a disappointing venture. That solitary exception was Neil Adcock. Somewhere along the years between March 1958 and April 1960 Adcock's whole approach to cricket sobered and matured. In England he was without his old partner Heine and his half-section was now the ill-fated Geoff Griffin.

Adcock was the seasoned veteran and fully aware that he stood unchallenged as the fast bowler who would have to spearhead the South African's attack. He arrived in England intent on avoiding all injuries and quietly confident he could confirm his status as a great fast bowler. Throughout the tour he ordered his days and played his cricket always with something held in reserve. He set his sights on his main objective and kept them on target to be as fine a fast bowler as any in the land.

In addition he meant to enjoy England and avoid all involvements. Involvements there were aplenty — not least the Geoff Griffin saga.

In the event, Adcock lost his partner with the new ball. His counter was to attend to his own job of ensuring that there still was one big gun firing. Never has a fast bowler throughout a long tour of England bowled more consistently and effectively than did the Adcock of the '60 tour. Not often were wickets ideal for fast bowling. Always Adcock was rested when the opposition was weaker. Rarely did he get a match when wickets could be picked up cheaply. Yet when final statistics were totted up his tally was superb : in all first-class matches 108 wickets at 14,02 and in the test series 26 at 22,57.

For a fast bowler to take over 100 wickets on a tour of England is rare. Only Bill Johnston of Bradman's great side succeeded and Charlie Griffith took his hundred wickets for the West Indies in 1963.

When at Scarborough the last match ended, Adcock had come through the tour without one day lost through injury. His own words as he left the field at Scarborough were : "I went off the field only three times on the tour and each time because I'd split my pants."

Charles Fortune
September 1971

Melbourne in the second test match where his magnificent 162 not out safely guided South Africa to an 82 run win, thus enabling the tourists to draw level in the series.

Jackie McGlew, who actually stood out as an extremely brilliant cover fieldsman in a team of superb athletes, batted with dogged concentration as did his opening partner Waite. The adventurous Roy McLean blossomed in the test matches and played the innings of his life when he hit a quick-fire 76 not out to take his side to its target in the final game which South Africa won by six wickets.

Others to impress as the season progressed were Ken Funston, as an attacking batsman, Anton Murray, a fine all-rounder, Hedley Keith, a solid left-hander who forced his way into the test team with a hundred in each innings against Victoria, the two faster bowlers, Michael Melle and Eddie Fuller, and the bespectacled Rhodesian player, Percy Mansell, who was unparalleled as a slip fielder.

That the Springboks were able to avoid humiliation in this series was indicative of their total dedication to the task in hand; the fact that they eventually departed with honours even was little short of a miracle.

Sailing south after the Australian adventure, the Springboks proved their superiority over New Zealand in a two match rubber which was won by virtue of a big innings win in the first game at Wellington.

Man of the match was Jackie McGlew who shattered Eric Rowan's record with an innings of 255 not out. The little Natal player had returned to the side after a month's absence nursing a broken finger and, in an innings filled with polished strokes, he gave no chance until he had reached 175.

Jack Cheetham, one of South Africa's greatest captains

Bert Sutcliffe, the brave New Zealander who hit a brilliant undefeated 80 after being hit by an Adcock bouncer which sent him to hospital during the second test in 1953

In a return bout with the New Zealanders, this time in South Africa in 1953/54, the Springboks once more proved too powerful for their opponents gaining four wins with one game left undecided.

A new dimension in South African cricket had arrived in the form of a bowler of genuine speed whose name could be placed in the same company as the finest fast bowlers of all time.

Neil Adcock bowled with almost terrifying liveliness throughout the five match contest and was undoubtedly the main agent in the comparative failure of New Zealand's two star batsmen, Bert Sutcliffe and John Reid.

The rugged left-hander Sutcliffe played one historic innings at Johannesburg when he returned to smack seven huge sixes, three in one over from Hugh Tayfield, after having earlier been forced to retire when struck a cruel blow on the head by an Adcock thunderbolt.

Another courageous New Zealander to play in this match was fast bowler Bob Blair (now a coach in Zimbabwe), who took to the field on the second morning with a heavy heart having heard of the passing of his fiance in a rail accident back home in New Zealand.

Tayfield continued to show match-winning form in this series but most of the South African batsmen were inconsistent, Roy Mclean actually was dropped from the side for the final game after having hit a hundred in the opening test at Durban but accomplishing little else thereafter.

The 1955 South African team left their own shores for the trip to England carrying with them high hopes of success and the knowledge that they possessed one of the most well-balanced Springbok teams on record.

A second express bowler of frightening proportions, the massively built Peter Heine, had been included to complement the known firepower of Neil Adcock; McGlew had found a steady new opening partner for Natal and now for South Africa in the lanky form of Trevor Goddard, who soon also became an essential bowler of nagging accuracy; and Paul Winslow, another six-footer in a team of execeptionally tall men, soon developed into a hitter in the tradition of Jessop and the mighty Australian Bonnor.

Injury dogged the steps of the captain, Cheetham, and, after defeat at Trent Bridge and Lord's, a cracked bone in his elbow forced him to drop out of the team. McGlew took over and led the side with great concentration and dedication to proudly witness the turn of the tide at Old Trafford and Headingly.

In the first of their two great successes of the season South Africa chased a total of 145 in two and a quarter hours. McGlew and Roy McLean hit 72 in fifty minutes and Johnny Waite eventually executed a cover drive to the boundary off the third ball of what would have been the second last over, to gain a thrilling win in front of an enthusiastic crowd which had been right royally entertained to five days of cricket at its very best.

England's first innings had been held together by Denis Compton who, after a shaky start against South Africa's four-pronged attack, reached 158 in a total of 284.

The Springbok team which played in the deciding fifth test at the Oval in 1955. Back row (left to right): E.R.H. Fuller, P.N.F. Mansell, T.L. Goddard, P. Heine, H.J. Keith, J.H.B. Waite; Front row: R.A. McLean, D.J. McGlew, J.E. Cheetham, W.R. Endean, H.J. Tayfield

South Africa's three century-makers of the third test at Manchester in 1955 — Johnny Waite (113), Jackie McGlew (104 not out) and Paul Winslow (108)

The tragic picture of Geoff Griffin bowling underarm after he had been no-balled for throwing by umpire Sid Buller. This ended his cricket career

McGlew and his by now entrenched partner, Goddard, then stood fast for three and a quarter hours to add 147 before the left-hander was dismissed. McGlew retired on 77 with an injured hand and the innings appeared to be losing its momentum when Waite was joined by Winslow at 245 for 5 wickets

South Africa's wicket-keeper proceeded to play second fiddle to the impetuous Winslow's strident double-bass. Driving with exceptional power Winslow hit three enormous sixes, one of which was a hefty straight hit over the sightscreen to bring up his century. The South African big hitter raised memories of the mighty Jimmy Sinclair as he peppered the boundary with thirteen fours to add to his blows over the ropes.

McGlew returned later to become the third century maker in the innings after Waite had joined Winslow at that milestone and South Africa had gained what eventually proved to be a match-winning lead of 237.

At Leeds in the next test South Africa won by a convincing 224 runs thanks to another hundred from McGlew and a return to form and his first three-figure score of the tour by Russell Endean, followed by a marathon bowling feat from Goddard (62-37-69-5) and Tayfield (47,1-15-94-5).

The "king of The Oval", Jim Laker then humbled the Springboks on his home turf in a match marred by controversy over umpiring decisons, especially when related to the interpretation of the LBW law. Between them McLean, Endean and Keith gathered only six runs in the two South African innings and England won by 92 runs with a day to spare to take the rubber 3-2.

Although the Springboks recovered stoically to tie the series after losing the first two matches by heavy margins, the tussle with England in 1956/57 was, when it came to cricket as a spectacle, a disappointment for the majority of the onlookers. Both sides possessed bowlers of exceptional skill and accuracy and few of the batsmen at any time appeared to have the courage to go onto the attack. Thus a war of attrition developed and excruciatingly slow scoring was the order of the day.

The England pace attack of Brian Statham, Peter Loader, Trevor Bailey and Frank Tyson (the man who had wrecked Australia only played two tests in South Africa) was well complemented by the watertight spin bowling of the happy-go-lucky Johnny Wardle (a great favourite with South African crowds) and Jim Laker, who had so humiliated the Australians in 1956. The captain, Peter May, could call on such an array of talent that he was able to leave out that fine bowler Tony Lock for all but one test.

May, himself, failed as a batsman in the international encounters but scored impressively against the provincial sides.

It was left to the classical, if painfully slow, Colin Cowdrey, the ungainly looking Doug Insole and a very dour Peter Richardson to provide the bulk of the runs in the big games.

Adcock and Heine were at their fearsome best for South Africa and, with Goddard bowling in his usual run-inhibiting fashion and Tayfield in absolutely peak form there was little difference in the quality of the two attacks.

For South Africa only Goddard and, to a lesser extent, Roy McLean, showed any sort of consistent scoring form and it was basically the off-spinning genius of Hugh Tayfield which presented his country with the opportunity to recover from a poor start.

After England's two resounding wins, in the first test ever played at the New Wanderers ground in Johannesburg (South Africa all out 72 in their second innings with Bailey claiming five for 20) and at Cape Town (again a humiliating home total of 72 with, this time, Wardle grabbing 7 for 36 after taking 5 for 53 in the first innings) it was an eight for 69 spell by Tayfield that stopped England in their tracks. Thanks to his persistent form, a dreadfully slow match at Kingsmead eventually staggered to a draw after the daily average run rate had barely exceeded 200.

The fourth match at Johannesburg found Tayfield at his very best and South Africa scraped through to a 17-run win to keep the series alive. Tayfield's spell of nine wickets for 113 runs in England's second innings remains the best bowling by a South African in a test match, and with Roy McLean at last finding his rightful form with an innings of 93 the Springboks could go into the final encounter with a chance of squaring the rubber.

In another low scoring match at Port Elizabeth the South Africans achieved their goal on a dreadful pitch which had only recently been re-laid. The ball kept exceptionally low throughout on a dead-slow strip and there was much controversy over the decision to actually stage a test match on a such a wicket.

After a grand start on the opening day of the first test at the Wanderers there was little to recommend, and certainly nothing worth recalling about South Africa's batting displays against Ian Craig's 1957/58 Australian team.

HUGH TAYFIELD

His friends and foes alike would agree that Hugh Tayfield could be, and often was, a very difficult fellow. Equally would they subscribe to the opinion that never a finer competitive cricketer ever came out into the middle.

In 1949 the Australians came to South Africa captained by Lindsay Hassett and with a reputation none could dispute. Tayfield must have viewed his prospects of getting to grips with the Australian batsmen with a certain amount of negativity — there was still the hard fact to be faced that Athol Rowan would certainly be first choice for South Africa when an off-spin bowler was selected.

Athol Rowan was probably the crucial factor in making a great bowler of Hugh Tayfield. Rowan gave the ambitious and determined young Tayfield the very opposition he needed and the opportunity to show his mettle.

Rowan's reputation as an off-spin bowler, and rightly so, stood second to none. Then came that calamitous day at

Ellis Park when playing for Transvaal he skittled the Australians for 84 and 109 only himself to damage a knee that never again truly mended. Rowan's injury was Tayfield's opportunity and he played in all five Tests.

Never did a young spin-bowler face a sterner debut into Test cricket than did Tayfield at Ellis Park on Christmas Eve in 1949. Tayfield took 3 for 93 and bowled 28 overs each of eight balls.

A week later at Newlands Tayfield was called on for 37 more of those king-sized overs and for no more than two wickets while Harvey scored the first of that string of centuries he was to hit, and often, at Tayfield's expense. But if Tayfield could make little headway against Hassett's batsmen, he found sweet revenge when going to bat. When South Africa followed on, Dudley Nourse stood almost alone till Tayfield came in. Nourse with his 114 and Tayfield's 75 averted defeat by the innings.

There were those at Newlands ready to doubt Tayfield's quality as an off-spin bowler; indeed but for the runs he made at Newlands he might well have lost his Test place. Kingsmead gave Tayfield his chance and he took it to the full. Batting first, South Africa made 311: Eric Rowan 143. On a wicket now taking spin, Tayfield's bowling, 7 for

Suffice to state that McGlew and Goddard set South Africa on what should have been the victory road with a magnificent opening stand of 176 and Waite, Endean and McLean (coming in, inexplicably at number six) built to such good effect on their sound foundation that Australia were faced with the formidable task of overhauling a total of 470 for nine wickets declared.

This they could not achieve, despite a splendid hundred from Richie Benaud, coming in at number seven and seeing the total from a tottering 177 for six wickets to a respectable 368 all out.

South Africa then proceeded to succumb in disorderly array to Alan Davidson's left-arm fast-medium bowling which, angled across the right-handed batsmen, was to become, together with Benaud's alarmingly accurate leg-spin, Australia's main weapon against a Springbok team which commenced the series as favourites and ended the proceedings in a state akin to total shock.

After the South African surrender to Davidson the other "thorn-in-the-flesh" Australian, the habitually gum-chewing Ken "Slasher" MacKay played his own patented brand of unspectacular cricket for three and three quarter hours to save the day for Australia.

A complete debacle for South Africa followed at Newlands. Colin McDonald (99) and Jim Burke (189) conscientiously imitated MacKay's methods of the previous game whilst adding 190 for the first wicket in 263 laborious minutes. Facing a total of 449, South Africa obliged the Australians by scoring insufficiently well to avoid a follow-on and then throwing heart and soul away to the spin of Benaud and left-arm "chinaman" bowler Lindsay Kline for a pitiful 99 all out in their second turn at bat.

At Durban Jackie McGlew earned the dubious distinction of compiling the slowest century in history (545 minutes). The snail's pace batting of the South African opener and his partner in a 231 third -wicket stand, Johnny Waite, prevented any chance of South Africa making rightful use of the advantage gained when superb fast bowling by Neil Adcock (six for 43) and Peter Heine had seen Australia back in the pavilion for just 163 runs.

Heine (6 for 96) and Adcock (until he left the field after taking two wick-

23 from as few as 68 deliveries, put Australia out for 75.

The rest of this Kingsmead match is a poignant paragraph in South African cricket lore. Nourse could ponder through a long sabbath in deciding whether or not to enforce an Australian follow-on. On the Monday he chose to bat again and South Africa fell from grace.

When in 1951 the South African team to tour England was named, Tayfield was omitted. Athol Rowan, his knee far from fully serviceable, was the off-spin bowler. But soon it was clear that Rowan's knee would not stand up to continuous cricket. Within the first month Tayfield was called on to join the touring team.

Out in the field with Tayfield was Jack Cheetham and Cheetham in his own quiet way gave much thought to the bowler with the wonderfully smooth action and ball control who was not taking many wickets. Cheetham decided then that Tayfield was not a duplication of Athol Rowan but a bowler of markedly different style and with a high potential that was not being exploited. Soon Cheetham was to have ample opportunity of putting his thoughts to the test.

Cheetham's team of young hopefuls sailed to Australia at the end of September 1952. There was time in plenty for serious and strenuous practice in Perth before the real business began. Tayfield now was the only off-spin bowler in the party and virtually assured of a place in all the Tests.

The first Test in the steaming heat of Brisbane proved a weird affair. Melle and Watkins put the full might of Australia out for 280. Tayfield had a comparatively easy time bowling only fifteen overs. With South Africa in and out for 221 it was now a spin bowler's turn, Doug Ring's leg-breaks taking six for 72. Nor was there any flood of runs in either second innings, but now Tayfield (four for 116) and fast bowler Ray Lindwall (five for 60) did the main damage as South Africa was beaten by 96 runs. Harvey again was Australia's top scoring batsman. His batting alone tipped that match Australia's way.

Cheetham was convinced that Tayfield could be made the more effective by giving him a different field setting and persuading the off-spinner to bowl to it. With these thoughts in mind Cheetham took his Springboks to Melbourne for the second Test.

On Christmas Eve 1952 Lindwall and Miller played the major part in putting South Africa out for 227. By close of play Australia, Morris and McDonald, had wiped off 26 of those runs. There was no great cheerfulness in the Springbok camp on Christmas Day 1952.

The morrow, Boxing Day, started with rain and only 30 minutes' play before lunch: Australia 49 for no wicket. Watkins was out of action with a slipped disc. Immediately on play restarting Murray was forced to leave the field through fibrositis. All that was left was Mansell (leg-spin), Melle (fast right hand) and "Toey" Tayfield.

It was hereabouts that Cheetham's deep thinking of how best to use Tayfield began to show its wisdom. He had Tayfield bowling around the wicket to the left-handed Arthur Morris and himself close up at silly mid-off. The Australian score was 84 for 0 when Morris launched himself

Springbok opening bowler, Peter Heine, hits Alan Davidson with a bouncer during the fourth test at The Wanderers in 1957

to smite Tayfield high over the in-field. Cheetham soared up for the catch and took much of the pace off a sizzling drive that deflected away towards a point some half dozen yards, perhaps more, behind the bowler's wicket. Tayfield having delivered his ball leapt into the air a full yard in front of the popping crease as Cheetham got hands to the ball. Thereafter both his reaction and action were near instantaneous. Tayfield whipped around, took at least five accelerating paces towards mid-off and then dived low and horizontally.

Inches from the ground, arms stretched to the limit, Tayfield's hands held the catch. There have been few catches more brilliant than that dismissal of Morris. Possibly never a finer "caught and bowled". The moment showed so clearly those other attributes that made Tayfield a tremendous cricketer — rapid reaction time, physical agility, a conviction that the impossible was for him always possible and, not least, sheer guts. That catch also proved the turning point of the entire tour.

Australia was all out well before close of play on that memorable Boxing Day. Tayfield's analysis read six wickets for 84 runs taken in thirty (eight ball) overs. Those six wickets included Harvey (11) and Miller (52). Great catches that afternoon became the order of the day. As dramatic a cricket passage of arms as the famous Melbourne Cricket Ground will ever embrace.

No more than 16 runs behind on that first innings, South Africa went on to win. Endean scored 162 not out; Tayfield now completely attuned to the unorthodox fields that Cheetham had persuaded him to adopt, came again in Australia's second innings with 7 wickets for 81. The margin of victory was 82 runs.

Was that second test at Melbourne or the fourth at the Wanderers against Peter May's 1956/57 English team Tayfield's finest hour? In the latter game he again took 13 wickets, with nine for 113 in the second innings, holding too the catch that was the only one not to come from his own bowling.

In 1910 Ernest Vogler against England took 36 at an average of 21.75: Tayfield against England in 1956/57 claimed 37 at 17.18. By contrast Jim Laker had managed no more than 11 at 29.45. Just prior to visiting South Africa, Laker had had his wonderful year in England against the Australians. At Old Trafford he had taken 19 wickets in the match. All told he captured 47 in that series. In South Africa, as later in Australia, he could neither bowl extended spells of run-denying purpose nor take wickets. While Laker was a man for a camp and chilly English summer, Tayfield was indeed the Man for All Seasons.

Tayfield's bowling achievements will in all probability never be surpassed in Test cricket by a future Springbok.

Hugh Tayfield was unique among cricketers. On the field ambition and sheer courage — even vanity and near foolhardiness — were so blended in him that anything less than notable success appeared to him as abject failure.

Charles Fortune
September 1971

ets) again bowled with fire in the next game at Johannesburg but Benaud tied the Springbok batsmen in knots and the Australians went into the final round with the series already firmly packed in their tucker bag.

Davidson took another nine wickets at Port Elizabeth and Benaud and MacKay also rounded off the tour with good performances in an eight wicket win.

South Africa's 1960 team to England, under Jackie McGlew's captaincy, came under fire from two separate directions soon after their arrival. Anti-apartheid demonstrators were waiting for them at the airport, and there were minor demonstrations throughout the season and, to add to the Springboks' discomfort their new young fast bowler Geoff Griffin was called for throwing before the series proper had begun.

After being "called" in two seperate matches the unfortunate Griffin saught advice from former opening bowler Alf Gover, one of England's top coaches, and took part in a three-day coaching course under the guidance of the old test player.

It was all to no avail. Griffin passed muster during the first test at Edgbaston (England won by 100 runs), but the keen young South African was again called during a dramatic second test at Lord's. Griffin actually claimed a hat-trick in this game, the very first by a South African in a test match, but was no-balled eleven times for throwing.

Farcical events followed during an exhibition match which was played because England had claimed an innings win soon after lunch on the fourth day. Umpire Syd Buller no-balled the hapless South African four times out of five and, when he switched to bowl an under-arm lob, he was no-balled again, this time by Umpire Lee for not notifying the change.

Poor Griffin did not bowl again on the tour and, with wet weather adding its own peculiar problems, the South Africans were more than a little demoralised.

Only two South Africans could look back with any satisfaction on this tour : Roy McLean started with a rousing double-hundred against Worcestershire and was the Springboks' only century maker in the tests and the apparently inexhaustable Neil Adcock, for once not plagued by any injuries, took 26 wickets in the test matches and a grand total of 108 for only 14 runs apiece on the tour. Both players were honoured by inclusion amongst *Wisden's Five Cricketers of the Year.*

The unhappy venture to England in 1960 completed a downward cycle in South Africa's cricket — a welcome upturn was soon to become apparent, short-lived but leading to heights never before attained. •

TEST DOUBLE CENTURIES

Eric Rowan's record test score at Leeds in 1951 was eventually beaten by Jackie McGlew, against New Zealand in 1952/53, and by the player who has come to be regarded as probably the greatest batsman ever produced by South Africa, Graeme Pollock. The following is a list of test double centuries scored for South Africa :

- 274 **R.G. POLLOCK** vs Australia, Durban 1969 /70
- 255* **D.J. McGLEW** vs New Zealand, Wellington 1952/53

- 236 **E.A.B. ROWAN** vs England, Leeds 1951
- 231 **A.D. NOURSE** vs Australia, Johannesburg 1935/36
- 209 **R.G. POLLOCK** vs Australia, Cape Town 1966/67
- 208 **A.D. NOURSE** vs England, Nottingham 1951
- 204 **G.A. FAULKNER** vs Australia, Melbourne 1910/11
- 201 **E.J. BARLOW** vs Australia, Adelaide 1963/64

The 1960 Springbok team: Back row: J.E. Pothecary, H.J. Tayfield, A.H. McKinnon, P.R. Carlstein, M. McLennan (baggage master), J.P. Fellows-Smith, N.A.T. Adcock, C.A.R. Duckworth, A.J. Pithey, S. O'Linn; Front row: G.M. Griffin, R.A. McLean, D.J. McGlew (capt.), A.D. Nourse (Manager), T.L. Goddard, J.H.B. Waite, C. Wesley

TREVOR GODDARD

Once they have established themselves most present-day South Africans have been quick to play an innings of three figures. Barry Richards accomplished the feat in his third test innings, Graeme Pollock in his 4th, Eddie Barlow in his 10th and Jackie McGlew in his 13th.

One reason given why Goddard took so long to attain the cherished landmark was the sinus trouble which plagued him for many years and particularly in Australia.

When he had an operation in Melbourne which relieved the complaint the surgeon maintained that enduring pain in the region of his eyes sapped his mental energy and concentration and affected his stroke-play. Yet there were some occasions when his innings was broken and he was given a fresh start the following day and still without overcoming the bugbear of premature dismissal. On the other hand it was often overlooked that he had already undertaken long spells of masterly bowling before going out to open an innings.

There came a time when his bowling was so important to the side that it was felt that he could not do justice to himself if he were asked to bat immediately after doing gruelling work in the field. So he was dropped down the order. In the end the theory was abandoned because of the exceptional physical condition which Goddard maintained and which continued when he had given up the game.

By choice a non-drinker and non-smoker he has never found it a hardship to keep up exercising and training for sport. It began when he was a lad preparing for soccer and when he was captaining the team in Australia where, goodness knows, he seemed to have enough exercise through long days of cricket, he made a point of following the schedules for keeping fit offered in the book compiled on Canadian Air Force methods.

South Africa's greatest batsman-wicket-keeper, Johnny Waite

Australian left arm spinner, Lindsay Kline, is congratulated by his team-mates after his hat-trick at Newlands in the second test of the 1957/58 tour

His accuracy as a bowler throughout his 15 years of test cricket in which he took 123 wickets — a total exceeded only by Tayfield — was a priceless asset to South African cricket. No cricketer of this country in my experience, and surely not in earlier days, contributed so much as Goddard in physical effort to the game. Nor did any Springbok of my time mature so quickly or with so much versatility as Goddard. After just one series he was already established as a highly competent all-round test cricketer.

Whatever the cause of his continual frustrations it seemed part of the destiny of his cricket that throughout his long career he had to struggle by ceaseless hard work to reach the goals that won him so much distinction.

When South Africa played England in the dreary series of 1964/65 Goddard made 60 in the first innings of the fourth test at the Wanderers. At this point he announced his retirement from test cricket. That meant that if he were ever to attain his century he had a maximum of three more innings in which to do it.

Two years later, after missing the 1965 tour to England, he rescinded his decision, to everyone's approval, but when he went out to bat a second time against Mike Smith's team it was seemingly to be his last summer as a South African cricketer.

As though his decision to retire had lifted a weight off his shoulders he played a confident, carefree innings that proved to be the most colourful of his career. Batting with complete assurance he hit fours through the covers and to long-on with perfect timing and gave the stamp of class to his display by lofting the ball over the bowler's head to the inviting vacant area. When he had scored 22 he reached his 2 000 runs in test cricket.

In a rare feat for him he hit three sixes and with the first brought his total to 50. It was Goddard at his best using sparingly his sweep to leg which was sometimes fraught with uncertainty, yet he was left with one more nagging period of suspense.

By the evening of the second last day he had carried his score to 89 and both he and his many admirers faced a night on which to speculate whether now at last he would achieve the one major honour in cricket which had eluded him for so long.

Next morning the drama moved slowly to its climax. He scored two twos and six singles to bring him to 99, the total which had proved so fateful at the Oval in 1960.

The 4 000 spectators shared the tenseness with Goddard and when he tapped a ball off Tom Cartwright to mid-off and scrambled home for his hundred they rose and gave him a tumultuous ovation.

Goddard was not a demonstrative player but this was such an exceptional event for him that he threw his bat in the air. It was, he maintained later, the most satisfying innings of his life. It had taken him 62 innings in 32 tests to reach his moment of glory — by now almost magnified into a matter of national interest after its long delay.

Louis Duffus
September 1971

The irrepressible Eddie Barlow. He looked explosive at all times

CHAPTER FOUR

AT THE CROSS-ROADS

by Peter Pollock

While Richie Benaud's Australians and Peter May's Englishmen were doing battle during the English summer of 1961, a team of young South African cricketers, headed by veteran gladiator, Roy McLean, arrived at Heathrow Airport.

They were called the "Fezelas" — meaning the sting in the tail of the scorpion — and they were to make something of an impact during their short tour. The visit had been sponsored by the late Stanley Murphy, a generous benefactor of cricket and manager of the team was the late C.O. Medworth, then sports editor of the Natal Mercury.

The 1960 Springbok tour of England had been a disaster and South African cricket, according to the pundits, was at the cross-roads. Stan Murphy wanted to make his contribution and he gathered his team.

I do believe that this team had a lot to do with a decade of South African cricket which will probably go down in the annals as the greatest ever. It extends over a period of thirty tests. In the early stages you see the teething pains and the transition; then follows the puberty, but also a certain lack of conficence and killer instinct and finally you have the maturing into a force which was generally acknowledged as the finest cricket team in the world.

The Fezelas trip produced eight Springboks, namely Peter van der Merwe, Eddie Barlow, Colin Bland, Peter Pollock, Denis Lindsay, David Pithey, Jackie Botten and Kim Elgie. Graeme Pollock was so nearly invited but he was just a bit young at that stage. But out of this nucleus came the motivating power behind an almost incredible rise to fame. When it is considered that in 1961-62, the Springboks shared a series with the lowly New Zealanders but by 1970 had murdered just about any side that had cared to cross their path, then you appreciate the tremendous impact and significance of it all.

The Fezelas came, saw and conquered. They went to England to learn but ended up giving lessons all the way round, even to three first-class opponents in Combined Services, Gloucester and Essex.

Back home the critics were a little cynical. They doubted the standard of the opposition and while appreciating that there was much potential in the Fezelas line-up, they felt that a sterner test was needed. There is only one way to the top — the hard way. Certainly in sport there is no easy way to success and I do believe that the Fezelas, arrogant as they might have seemed during the early stages, did always appreciate that the game does not come easy.

In my early days as a Springbok I was once asked by a certain veteran while we were arguing a point:

"How many tests have you played in?"

My immediate reply was "How many more are you going to play in?"

That to us was a major criterion. You were as good as your position on the day. It is performance in the middle that brings the results. You don't get rewards for the number of years you have served.

JOHNNY WAITE

1955

Johnny Waite is without doubt South Africa's most successful wicket-keeper. Apart from having played in more tests than any other (and in fact he holds the record for most tests by any Springbok), he also claims the record for most dismissals in a series and is second to Denis Lindsay for most dismissals in a match and innings. South Africa's wicket-keeping statistics run as follows:

Most dismissals in a career
141 J.H.B. Waite (124 ct 17 st)-50 tests
59 D.T. Lindsay (57 ct 2 st)-19 tests
51 H.B. Cameron (39 ct 12 st)-26 tests

Most dismissals in a series
26 J.H.B. Waite vs N.Zealand 1961/62
24 D.T. Lindsay vs Australia 1966/67
23 J.H.B. Waite vs N.Zealand 1953/54
17 P.W. Sherwell vs Australia 1910/11

Most dismissals in a match
8 D.T. Lindsay vs Australia 1966/67

Most dismissals in an innings
6 D.T. Lindsay vs Australia 1966/67

Thanks to the likes of Jackie McGlew, Roy McLean, Neil Adcock and Peter Heine, the era got off to a fair start, not in results, but in teaching us quickly the methods and the realities of Test cricket. Maybe some of the others won't agree but I do single out Jackie McGlew as an outstanding tutor in those more formative days. Maybe he had a chip on his shoulder over certain aspects of that New Zealand tour but if you were prepared to listen and learn, there was much to be gleaned from McGlew. He was the dedicated never-say-die, lead-by-example skipper and I say it again, he taught us plenty.

Two veterans, Trevor Goddard and Johnny Waite, stayed, and they proved to be the guiding lights on our first overseas tour, the one to Australia and New Zealand. I have heard certain criticisms of Trevor Goddard's captaincy and probably some of these are justified but I do firmly suggest that not enough praise is given to Trevor for what he did in fact achieve with a bunch of "Cinderellas", as Dick Whitington labelled us. The same can be said of Ken Viljoen, that martinet, who managed the Springbok team. At the time he might have appeared a bit harsh and strict on such issues as the curfew but perhaps it was needed? A bunch of youngsters like we were could so easily have gone off the rails.

The Australian trip saw the emergence of Eddie Barlow, Colin Bland, the Pollock brothers, Graeme and Peter, Joe Partridge and a few others. Then came Mike Smith's English tour of South Africa when a "cabbage patch" pitch at Kingsmead for the first Test virtually ruined the entire series. It gave the English "underdogs" one-up in the series and they were quite happy to hold on to this lead by employing the most negative of tactics.

But revenge was to come in England, this time under Peter van der Merwe and with new names like Ali Bacher, Tiger Lance, Jackie Botten, Richard Dumbrill and Athol McKinnon added to the list. Who will ever forget Trent Bridge?

Back to South Africa, a 3-1 triumph over Bobby Simpson's Australians, in the summer that saw Denis Lindsay play immortal cricket, and later a 4-0 white-washing of Bill Lawry's side with such exciting new Springboks as Barry Richards, Mike Procter and Lee Irvine in the line-up. It is a beautiful story, one that does not lack incident, controversy, heartache and humour. And during the era under review the Springboks conquered a peculiar South African sporting affliction — lack of confidence in their own ability.

Modesty is a most commendable trait in any sportsman's make-up and in this respect South Africa has always had reason to be proud of its ambassadors abroad. Unfortunately, in many instances the modesty stemmed from an inherent inferiority complex. The Springboks of the years between 1964 and 1970 managed to overcome this handicap. I am prepared to stick my neck out and suggest that the players of this particular era were not necessarily all that much better than some of their Springbok cricketing predecessors. But when it came to a question of the right frame of mind, the teams led by Peter van der Merwe, Ali Bacher and to a lesser extent, Trevor Goddard, certainly had "their minds right".

South Africans are basically sensitive. We love winning but we are not so gracious in accepting defeat. We are positive in enjoying victory but perhaps a little negative and tentative in anticipation of it. The weakness in our mental attitude was first brought home in Australia at the conclusion of the 1963-64 drawn series. We were quite happy about sharing a series with the might of Richie Benaud's Australia, indeed illustrious foes. But our complacent bubble was soon burst by certain Australian critics who suggested that we should in fact have won. "You fellows were too scared to win". This hurt as only the truth can hurt.

Yes, we reflected, perhaps we had been too timid to take the intiative, too possessed by the fear that we might come unstuck. Slowly, the pieces of this psychological puzzle began falling into place. South Africans had become generally accepted as late starters in a cricket series. Possibly the underlying cause was that we only started playing our best cricket once we had sized up the opposition and convinced ourselves that perhaps they were not invincible.

I will always give Eddie Barlow the credit as the instigator of a new mental approach. No single person deserves greater recognition than Eddie for his contribution to our development into a world cricket power. Technically, he was inferior to many who played with him during those fantastic nine years

Ken MacKay caught behind by John Waite off the bowling of Michael 'Kelly' Seymour but mentally he was probably always better prepared and, quite frankly, that is what really counts.

It was nine years of team spirit, of great individual feats, of some brilliant cricket, some spine-tingling excitement and bitter frustration but, above all,it was nine years of dedication from talented cricketers who had decided that they were good and that they were going to prove to the rest of the world that they were indeed the best.

By 1970 they had achieved their ambition but unfortunately their triumph turned a little hollow because they were never given the opportunity of really conquering the world. Certainly, Ali Bacher and company had the equipment and the motivation for such a task.

Butterflies and wide-eyed expectancy. That is how it all started and no doubt many other sporting decades have begun in similar circumstances. Personally I felt a little like a naughty schoolboy who had cheated on his homework and who was not quite sure whether he was going to be caught out.

Indeed, I had no right to be playing in this test. Statistically and on current form, the faith shown by Jack Cheetham and his panel in me was probably justified but they didn't know, nor was I going to let on, that my left ankle was swollen and sore.

The injury had been sustained the previous Saturday when Eastern Province took on John Reid's New Zealanders but even though I say it myself, I should have earned an Oscar acting award for managing to keep my disability a secret. Yet, deep in my heart of hearts, I knew this could be one of the most foolish things I had ever done in my life. But when you are young you are sometimes prepared to fight the odds.

Standing trial, as it were, that Friday morning of December 8, 1961, were seven new Springboks. It was as hot and sultry as a mid-summer's day can get in Durban and the beads of perspiration caused by nervousness and heat in equal proportions poured down our brows as Jackie McGlew, striped Springbok blazer and all, went to the middle to toss the coin with John Reid, that burly batting cavalier of New Zealand cricket.

To Eddie Barlow, Colin Bland, Kim Elgie, "Goofy" Lawrence, Kenny Walters, Harry Bromfield and myself it was our entry into test cricket. The 1960 Springbok tour of England had been a fiasco. What with the Geoff Griffin throwing controversy and the rather poor showing of the South Africans. The pundits spoke of South African cricket being at the cross-roads and the selectors had answered the challenge by injecting new blood.

One of us three fast bowlers was in the team only because Neil Adcock had been side-lined through injury. Anyway, there we were, thrown into the hurly-burly of test cricket with only four veterans to guide us.

There was skipper Jackie McGlew, a man whose tactical genius, grit and determination and utter dedication could never be questioned. Then there was Roy McLean, who stroked the ball with a grace and ease that suggested that he was a cut above the other mere mortals playing with him. Also in the team was Johnny Waite, who as a wicket-keeper had no peer while Sid O'Linn, though not in the same class as the other three, had been one of the few to emerge with some credit from the 1960 tour of England.

It was such a mixed bag that one couldn't have blamed McGlew for feeling perhaps like a martyr on his way to the lions but such was Jackie's tenacity and enthusiasm that we fledglings did manage to feel just that little bit wanted.

Jackie had no option. He was going to make the best of what was available and he got the ball rolling by doing the right thing — winning the toss.

At one stage the Sringboks were sitting rather handily placed at 185 for two but the next eight wickets fell for the addition of only just over 100 runs. With about 40 minutes to spare on the opening day, we were all out for 292.

The "babes" had made little contribution. They had all failed but none as miserably as my own "duck". South Africa managed to get a first innings advantage of some 47 runs, although Paul Barton and the plucky Zin Harris did at one stage threaten to take the Kiwis past our total.

My one lasting memory of that New Zealand innings however, revolved around the dismissal of the New Zealand captain, John Reid. Reid, on that tour, was like the little Dutch boy who kept his finger in the dyke. He was regarded as the single saviour of New Zealand and naturally his wicket was the ultimate prize as far as his opponents were concerned.

I was fielding at mid-on and "Goofy" Lawrence was the bowler. With the New Zealander on that unlucky 13, "Goofy" varied his pace to entice Reid into an on-drive but unfortunately for him he played a fraction too early. The ball skied in my direction. I didn't pick it up until rather late and then, in adjusting myself, I happened to utter "God, it's mine!"

"He won't help you" came a retort from the direction of mid-off and after what seemed like an eternity the ball eventually nestled into my hands.

Our second innings was a disaster, to say the least. Only Johnny Waite (63), Colin Bland (30) and myself (15) scored more than ten runs and we were all out for a meagre total of 149.

RICHIE BENAUD
1957/58

Richie Benaud's 106 wickets in first class matches during Australia's tour of South Africa in 1957/58 created a new record for a visiting bowler and a comparison of his figures with those of the two great Aussie leg-spinners of 1935/36 makes interesting reading:

R.Benaud 743,6-185-2057-106 : 19,40
W.J.O'Reilly 662,5-250-1289-95 : 13.56
C.V.Grimmett 663,1-229-1362- 92 : 14,80

New Zealand batsman, Zin Harris, hit by a bouncer from the youthful Peter Pollock

Dick Motz, Frank Cameron and Jack Alabaster shared the spoils and the Kiwis were set for a well-earned triumph. At this stage, the critics still believed that the New Zealanders, as the obvious underdogs, deserved moral support and that it would be good for the game if they notched up a victory.

But losing, in fact, would have been the death-knell to us youngsters. Nothing motivated me more than a comment that was made by Roy McLean, after play on the third day with the New Zealanders appearing to be in complete charge. I don't believe that Roy made this remark in the sincere hope that the New Zealanders would win but he was probably preparing himself for a let-down. I know he hated losing as much as anyone of us, but he did suggest that "perhaps a victory for the Kiwis will give cricket in their country a much-needed boost".

I am forgiving Roy for what I'll regard in retrospect as benign diplomacy. But what Roy said really upset a few of the younger players. Maybe that was what he had in mind all along. If so, I can only apologise belatedly for not recognising his method to motivate us. The survival of us younger Springboks suddenly depended on New Zealand's demise and we were not going to allow it to be otherwise.

The Springboks won the match with 30 runs to spare and afterwards I was accorded the honour of planting a tree. This was supposed to have been the last test at Old Kingsmead but they are still playing there today. I took nine wickets for 99 runs in a dream debut but whatever the personal glory, it would all have been in vain had the Springboks not won that particular match.

Those four sultry days at Kingsmead way back in December 1962, set in motion a mighty wheel that may have lost or added a spoke or two on the way, but which did eventually crush all available opposition. In the final reckoning that test was the starting point of a cricketing era that could stand for all time to come as the most glorious in South Africa's cricket history. I suggest that it was because of the simple fact that we came to realise that "We had to win".

The second test was a pawky affair. It never quite got off the ground and this often happens when rain reduces the first day of a four-day encounter to a mere 80 minutes. It really shouldn't be possible to get a result in a test match in just over three days and this is exactly what happened. To be honest, the game dragged itself from one day to the next and only the brilliance of individual contributions left the spectators with some memories.

Three days later we were back in action, this time at Newlands with the New Year spirit very much in the air. The Coon Carnival was doing its "thing" down Sea Point way while New Zealand and South Africa were fighting it out at Newlands. But will I ever forget that first morning of the match.

I was nominated among the twelve but with just on 45 miutes to starting time Jack Cheetham, convenor of the selectors, came up to me. I thought at first that he was going to wish me luck. But no.

"Peter" he said "it's a case of horses for courses. We don't think that Newlands will suit your bowling, so you will stand down and be twelfth-man while Syd Burke will be playing".

Well, the Kiwis certainly made hay while the sun shone relentlessly and the Springboks had to reach 408 for victory. John Waite (113), Jackie McGlew (63) and Colin Bland (42) all

Peter Pollock lauded by Leyden after his first test match

tried their best but it was a target beyond their capabilities.

What annoyed Jackie McGlew most of all was the "bumper" warfare his batsmen were subjected to in this innings. Gary Bartlett only took two wickets for 40 runs in 22 overs but he bowled enough bumpers to get tempers between the two sides to a boiling point. I have never seen McGlew so furious as he was when he got back to the pavilion. He was not concerned about the game in progress.

"I am going to insist on the recall of Neil Adcock and Peter Heine" he fumed. "We'll show these New Zealanders what intimidation is all about".

Gary Bartlett was quick. That he was a "chucker" was undeniable but no umpire had the "guts" to call him. This also annoyed Jackie McGlew, especially after his experiences in England the previous year when Geoff Griffin was hounded out of the game.

And so it was back to the Wanderers and an innings victory for the Springboks. Revenge came, and it was sweet but with it came further controversy.

Neil Adcock and Peter Heine were recalled, as Jackie McGlew had vowed. Bouncers flew, verbal barrages were common-place but in the final reckoning the powers-that-be in South African cricket decided, in their wisdom or folly, that cricket was a game that needed no side-issues or controversy. I have often argued that legislators tend to be moved rather by circumstances than principle for I doubt if what happened in that Wanderers test would have happened had it involved a stronger cricketing country than New Zealand.

All is fair in love and war and I regard test cricket in the latter category. Heine, an old campaigner, was not prepared to take John Reid's verbal hand-outs and he answered with interest. The cauldron was stirred, animosities came to the fore but this is all part and parcel of the test scene. If you can't take it, you shouldn't be there.

The Kiwis needed 300 to avoid an innings defeat and missed the target by 51 runs. All but 105 of their reply came from John Reid's bat and while he was at the crease he suffered everything imaginable in the way of bumpers; both physically and verbally he was attacked.

I was not on the field but from what I have heard he was subjected to a "third degree" that would have turned a non-believer into a believer. I had no sympathy for John Reid then and I have none now because as I have said before, if I had had the experience I would probably have done exactly what Peter Heine did to him. Reid got what he deserved but the irony was that the critics took up the cudgels on his behalf! I have got news for those critics who regarded Reid and his team as poor under-dogs. John Reid, thanks to those very critics, perpetrated perhaps one of the biggest "cons" in South African cricket history.

Reid's confidence trick carried him through the tour and was only eventually revealed over some drinks three years or so later with Jack Alabaster, the Kiwi leg-spinner.

John Reid was, without question the touring team's number one trump card but his achilles heel was his intense dislike of spin bowling. Speedsters he didn't mind, and medium-pacers he murdered but spinners were a severe test of his pugnacious rather impetuous temperament. And when the Kiwis arrived in South Africa, Hugh Joseph Tayfield, one of the world's finest spinners, was still doing the rounds, albeit less effectively than in his prime.

So the plan was put into motion. Tayfield had to be blown right out of test recognition and the story had to get around that he was "over the hill". Well, when Transvaal came up against the tourists early in November 1961, the massacre of Tayfield was number one item on the Kiwi menu. They took every possible risk and their boldness paid off. Tayfield was hit out of the Transvaal attack and almost automatically out of test consideration as the critics built up John Reid as the supreme plunderer of spin bowlers.

And it figures that each time a spinner was brought on against Reid in the series, he took his life in his hands and lofted them to all corners of the field. He could so easily have got himself out but he was enjoying one of those golden seasons and everything went right. But, had we only known that behind the bravado was a weakness that, had it been exploited, could have turned the whole series! It is easy to talk from the advantage of hindsight but the fact that the New Zealanders actually planned the destruction of Tayfield deserves the highest compliment for tactical one-up-manship. Certainly it still brought a smile to Jack Alabaster's face while he was relating the story years later.

It would be remiss for me not to mention one of the real highlights of the fourth test, a highlight that heralded the emergence of a new facet to the

GRAEME COULDN'T GET A KNOCK

Four years ago, the man whom Sir Donald Bradman, among others, has described as "the most exciting young batsman in the world", couldn't get an innings for a club side in England.

That, indeed, is what happened to Robert Graeme Pollock, when he was invited to play in a club game for Sutton.

Big brother Peter was on tour in England at the time with the late Mr Stanley Murphy's first and last Fezelas touring side overseas, and the Pollock family, Dad, Mom, Graeme and kid sister, Helen, decided to give him moral support while on a holiday trip to Britain.

Graeme had already established himself as a player for the future. Stepping out of the examination room at the Grey High School, as it were, straight into the Eastern Province Currie Cup side, at the age of 16, he rattled up a quick half-century against Border in his first innings, took 41 off Griquas, clipped Rhodesia for 60, got a half-century at Newlands, and then went to the Wanderers to hit his first century and become the youngest century-scorer in first-class cricket in South African history.

Many there were who believed that had the invitations to the Fezelas gone out some few months later, Graeme Pollock would have accompanied his big brother as a playing member of the side.

Anyway, while pottering around in England he found himself in this Sutton XI.

The story-teller would go on from there to say that he was asked if he could bat, came in low down and won the game for his side with a dramatic century.

But the fact is stranger than fiction. Graeme Pollock did nothing of the sort.

When he said he did a bit of batting, he was invited to go in at No. 8, and the innings was declared before he had had a chance to get a knock.

Little did the members of the Sutton club realise that in their batting line-up was a young man who, on his next trip to England, was to score one of the greatest Test hundreds of all time, and to hit a double century in fantastic time off the Kent bowlers at Canterbury, having in the meantime hit five centuries on a tour of Australia and another against England in his own country.

Jimmy Hattle
May 1966

game. Fielding, in most circles, had been regarded as a necessary drudgery but Colin Bland was bringing a new meaning to this department of the game. A superb athlete and fitness fanatic, Bland's dedication to the art of fielding was to prove one of the most important developments of the emerging era. In fielding alone, Bland was worth 20-30 runs an innings and that is really a valuable asset to any team.

In the New Zealand first innings John Reid, or "Bogo" as he was nicknamed, was dismissed by perhaps one of the greatest catches of all time. "Goofy" Lawrence was the bowler and he let one go which to Reid appeared to be a half-volley. He launched into his drive but was not quite there. He hit it beautifully and with all the power and timing at his disposal but the ball carried inches off the ground into the covers. The ball appeared destined for the boundary boards anyway but Bland, diving forward, scooped the ball literally fractions off the ground for a sensational catch.

So brilliant was the effort that even Reid stood his ground for a few seconds to applaud South Africa's "Golden Eagle", as Bland later became known. Lawrence shook his head in disbelief and he was not the only one to be stunned before the crowd erupted in their excitement. Superlatives can never do justice to Bland's magnificent catch that day at the Wanderers but suddenly fielding took on new proportions as far as South African cricketers were concerned.

And so to the final test, a game studded with records, injuries and prematch controversies. Bowlers opened the innings and Jackie McGlew came in at number eight with his thumb in splints and his shoulder encased in what was virtually a straight-jacket of plaster.

Artie Dick, the Kiwi wicket-keeper crowned a maiden series by equalling the previous world record for wicket-keeping dismissals — 23 victims — but Johnny Waite, besides passing 2 000 runs in test cricket, topped that by establishing a new wicket-keeping record of 26 dismissals in the series.

Then there was Neil Adcock and I setting our own batting record and "Goofy" Lawrence, with 28 wickets in a five-match series, set up a new record for a fast bowler.

It was all very exciting and yet, in the final analysis all so diappointing, as we had lost the fifth test by 40 runs. To us youngsters, sharing a series with the lowly Kiwis was a failure, but perhaps we shouldn't take all the blame. There were extenuating circumstances and in the process of learning about test cricket we were perhaps most fortunate to have had to battle the hard way and not to have had it laid on the proverbial plate.

Clearly, the McGlew-McLean-Adcock-Tayfield-Heine era was over and the game was waiting for their replacements. But were they in the wings? Only time would answer this poser.

History was to repeat itself when Trevor Goddard and his "Cinderellas" boarded a Quantas flight bound for Perth, Australia, in October 1963. Almost a decade earlier, Jack Cheetham and a team of "no-hopers" had set off

South African and New South Wales' players stand in silence as they pay tribute to President Kennedy who had died from an assassin's bullet

One of the few times the Springboks dismissed Brian Booth cheaply during the 1963/64 tour of Australia. The bowler was Joe Partridge

on a similar mission — to tackle the might of Australian cricket. And as was the case with Goddard's side, they had returned, having shattered all the pre-tour predictions, to share the rubber.

Perhaps there had been a little less pessimism with Goddard's side for with Cheetham's team it was seriously suggested in many quarters that the tour should be cancelled as they feared it would be a sheer waste of time. For us a jolly good thrashing was predicted but most thought that it would be a worthwhile experience for the future. The McGlews, Adcocks, Tayfields and McLeans had retired and the only real experience in Trevor Goddard's line-up was the skipper himself and Johnny Waite.

The odds were stacked against us though I must admit that within the tour party we didn't feel any sense of hopelessness. Waiting for us were the like of Richie Benaud, Bobby Simpson, Peter Burge, Wally Grout, Bill Lawry, Brian Booth and the "golden boy" Norman O'Neill.

"I'll be feeling for you when you take that third new ball and the Australian total is in the 600's", was a quip that I won't easily forget for it was one of the last uttered as we boarded the plane. But with us was a quietly-confident manager, Mr Ken Viljoen. He had heard all this before because he had in fact also managed Jack Cheetham's side.

It would be fair to say that the Australian public was also a little sceptical about our side but by the time we reached the first test, this scepticism no longer existed.

Suddenly names like Pollock, Barlow, Bland and Partridge started to mean something. I do believe that the Australian selectors, convened by the one and only Sir Donald Bradman, also allowed themselves to panic a little. The loss of that famous left-arm speedster, Alan Davidson, through retirement (much to our relief) rattled them into including Ian Meckiff for the first encounter. We were stunned by his selection and the only person who seemed to be at all pleased was Ken Viljoen.

He just smiled that knowing smile and said: "It's a great compliment to us".Some said that Bradman was outvoted for he was acknowledged as being a firm member of the camp which believed that Meckiff was a thrower. Others suggested that Bradman, sick and tired of being continually pestered by Meckiff's claims, wanted him put out of the game for once and for all. Maybe the real truth lies between these two theories. But the Ian Meckiff saga we will never forget.

The eve of the test was tense. The teams assembled for an official mayoral function and there was an air of uneasiness. "Will he or won't he?", was the headline that blazoned across the back page of the local newspaper in its preview of the match. Yes, will Meckiff or won't he be called for throwing?

The cocktail party provided the calm before the storm. I watched Ian Meckiff, a delightful personality, as he joked and laughed with the aplomb of an academy award actor, when deep down in his thoughts his fears must have been considerable. He was being thrown to the lions of cricket justice — umpires Colin Egar and Lou Rowan. And to make it worse, Egar was a personal friend of Meckiff.

The Springboks fielded first and thus the judgement of Meckiff was postponed for a day-and-a-half. In that time the Aussies piled up 435 runs, thanks largely to a magnificent 169 by Brian Booth and a typically cavalier 82 from Norman O'Neill.

I thought I had done an outstanding job in finishing with six wickets for 95 but despite my weariness following a longish spell to clean up the tail, it did not take me long to swallow a few glasses of orange drink, remove my boots and get out onto the balcony to watch what was going to happen to Meckiff.

The crowd tensed as Richie Benaud handed Meckiff the ball and Egar took up his stand at square-leg. The first ball was passed but the second was as if an atomic bomb had hit the place.

"No-ball", screamed Egar. The over produced five more calls and Benaud was forced to whip the Victorian from the attack. Benaud was criticised for not trying him again at the other end to guage Lou Rowan's reaction but somehow I think that it would have been pointless. As Meckiff walked around the field getting sympathetic cheers from the crowd each time he touched the ball, one could not help but feel sorry for him. He was a completely dejected figure and what a tragedy that the final chapter of his career, an illustrious one at that, had to be one so inglorious.

Colin Egar became the villain and there were personal threats from some quarters. He was accorded police protection but, as usual there were also the amusing aspects to this unfortunate affair.

Arriving at the ground the one morning, we were told that some bullets had been found on the pitch. It turned out that the night-watchman had, in fact, dropped them during his rounds. But this did not stop a classic quip from Wally Grout, who was always full of fun. Egar was standing at square-leg when Grout put up his hand to stop play. He then shouted at the Aussie umpire: "Col, there is a chap in the crowd pointing a gun at you. Will you move a little to your right because I am a bit scared that if he misses you he will hit me. I am in direct line at the moment!"

Later that same day, Bill Lawry continued in the same theme. He walked into the Australian dressing-room with his rain coat draped over his shoulders and a hat neatly cocked on his head, looking rather like James Bond. He had a newspaper over his right arm. He walked over to Richie and demanded to know why Meckiff hadn't been bowled at the other end. He produced a toy pistol, a very realistic one, and Richie fell out of his seat in fright.

These little incidents helped to ease the tension but there is no doubt that the calling of Meckiff had spoiled the test. All else paled into insignificance, even the brilliant century scored by Eddie Barlow. What with all the rumpus at the start of the innings, it wasn't that easy to concentrate but Eddie really kept his wits about him to keep a rampant Richie Benaud at bay. The

Bobby Simpson clean bowled by Peter Pollock for a duck

Trevor Goddard and Australian skipper, Richie Benaud in conversation during the 1963/64 tour

wicket was turning quite sharply, suggesting that there could be trouble for us on the fourth and fifth days. But our problem was eased by the third day being completely washed out. The scoreline says a draw but it had certainly been a match to remember — thanks to the unfortunate Ian Meckiff.

The finest cricket stadium in the world belongs to Melbourne. The "MCG" has a seating capacity in the region of 90 000 and had been packed just once — the previous season for the final test between Frank Worrell's West Indians and the Aussies. The total aggregate for our second test there was just over 100 000 but for us it was a game we wanted to forget in a hurry.

We started as favourites, not because we had shown any real form but simply because the Australians were going to be without their three stars of the first test — Richie Benaud, Norman O'Neill and Brian Booth. Benaud and O'Neill were injured and Booth was sick. Bobby Simpson was nominated the new skipper but all the critics favoured us. But from start to finish it was a nightmare.

"Bunter" was not nearly as confident as at Brisbane, but he was resolute and took four hours over one of the pluckiest innings I have seen him play. It is all very well making runs when you are in form, but if you still manage to get runs when you are scratching, then you deserve the highest praise. This was sheer guts and tenacity at its best.

Eddie survived a few "lives" and I like to claim that perhaps I had something to do with this. At the start of the tour Eddie failed three times in a row. I decided to change his luck and before he went out to bat the fourth time, I plucked a hair from his rather hairy chest. It worked: he notched a double ton! For the rest of the tour I kept plucking and Eddie finished the Australian trip with an alltime South African record aggregate of 1 532 runs.

Anyway, back to the Melbourne test. Our first innings was worth a rather poor 274 — not a good score by Australian standards — and Bill Lawry and Ian Redpath, the new opening

DENIS LINDSAY — THE JET AGE BATSMAN

There was hardly a word or even a comma that I did not consume avidly each week in those wonderful weekly papers, the *Magnet* and the *Gem,* back in the late 1930's. I followed the cricketing careers of Harry Wharton, Tom Merry and their colleagues faithfully — for these were my schoolday heroes.

But faithful though I was to author Frank Richards, never would I have accepted a story in which one player scored 69 runs (top score) in the first innings, hit 182 runs (again top score) in the second innings, took six catches behind the wicket to equal the world wicketkeeping record, and then clinched another two wickets with the big gloves in the opponents' second knock.

For that would have been stretching the imagination too far. No, not even Harry Wharton, the hero of Greyfriars, could have done that.

Well, there in front of my eyes Denis Lindsay of Benoni did just this when playing for South Africa in the first test against the Australians at the Wanderers over Christmas week. And, what is more, in his 13th test match.

The "truth is stranger than fiction" platitude was never more clearly shown.

Slim, modest Denis Lindsay was rated just a useful Springbok wicketkeeper-batsman when the match began. He had played 12 times for South Africa in series in England, Australia, New Zealand and at home, but his batting and wicketkeeping had set no rivers on fire.

"A useful player, Denis", they said, "and our best replacement for the great Johnny Waite who retired too early".

Suddenly, after five days of dramatic cricket at the Wanderers, with South Africa winning a memorable test by 233 runs, Denis Lindsay had become a modern "great".

Famous former Australian players dubbed him "the greatest wicketkeeper-batsman in the world". Denis Compton murmured: "A beautiful player . . . he has improved out of all recognition". Denis Lindsay was finally accepted in the ranks of the internationals.

Denis Lindsay was a star of the Springbok side, a player who — as Waite before him, Jock Cameron before him, and Percy Sherwell long before him — was indispensible in the South African team. For both in front of the wicket and behind it, he was a great international.

In an era or allrounders, Lindsay was now worth two places in the Springbok team. For whoever heard of a player who, after equalling the world record for catches behind in one innings of a test, could come out at No. 7 and hit a magnificent 182 runs with 25 fours and five sixes?

And so, Denis Lindsay had come to stay.

That's an expression that many opponents use about him when describing his batting. An ultra cautious opener he takes a long time to get his first 15 or 20 runs. But suddenly there is a *moment critique,* some instant when Lindsay decides that he is seeing the ball so clearly that he can go on the attack.

And when he attacks — Graeme Pollock and Gary Sobers included — there is probably no more thrilling sight in cricket.

Always a graceful batsman,

pair, answered by setting a 219-run partnership.

Barlow, once again, Tony Pithey (76) and Johnny Waite (77) did their best to fight back for the South Africans in our second turn at the crease, facing a deficit of 183 runs, but defeat was inevitable. It came mercifully early on the fifth morning when Bobby Simpson hit Peter van der Merwe's first and only test delivery for four runs.

Incidentally this test did present the first occasion in the history of test cricket that two sets of brothers — the Pitheys and the Pollocks — appeared in the same side.

One week separated the second and third tests and this was the week of the Peter Pollock miracle. It was more like ten days, if you consider that I was injured on the second day of the Melbourne game, but the doctor's diagnosis in Melbourne that I would be out for at least three weeks turned out to be quite inaccurate. It was a routine of ultra-sound treatment morning, noon and night that saw me successfully negotiate a fitness test at Sydney on the first morning of the third Test. I hadn't been given a chance of playing. The fitness test was quite a trial.

"How do you feel", asked Ken Viljoen.

"It seems okay boss", I replied "but how it will stand up to five days, I don't know".

Ken consulted Trevor and then said: "We'll take that chance. Go and get showered and get ready to play".

The pitch was well-grassed and Bobby Simpson looked long and hard before he decided that he would bat. He had been right in sending us in at Melbourne; this time he was wrong in deciding to bat. Joe Partridge and I had a ball. I enjoyed the pace and the bounce and Joe thrived on the gentle breeze that came in from the main score board. Between us we took nine of the wickets in dismissing the Aussies for 260.

The stage was now set for one, Robert Graeme Pollock. A drunken wag in Melbourne had tempted fate by shouting: "Pollock you won't make a half century in this series, let alone a

---

Lindsay times the ball like a Rubinstein delivering an arpeggio on a concert grand. It is all timing and fluency — and the ball scuds across the turf, and often over the boundary, as if rocket-propelled.

In his great innings of 182 for South Africa, incidentally the highest ever made by a Springbok wicketkeeper, Lindsay struck five towering sixes. They soared effortlessly over the fence. Such was his certainty of timing that, as Jackie McGlew wrote in a graphic description in the *Rand Daily Mail,* he "mauled the Australian attack".

Over the past seven or eight years, I must have seen Lindsay bat a score of times or more, and almost without exception I have seen him adopt this approach of cautious start, followed by a devastating attack.

Let's take his record partnership of 221 runs for the sixth wicket with Peter van der Merwe in the Springbok second innings at the Wanderers as an example. When Van der Merwe came in at 349 for five, Lindsay now in the 20's, had already been in for some time and along with Tiger Lance had added 71 for the fifth wicket.

Lance had been the senior partner but with his dismissal, Lindsay took over the driver's seat.

The scoring timetable went: 50 partnership in 47 minutes; 100 in 81 minutes; 150 in 111 minutes; 200 in 148 minutes; and 221 runs in 166 minutes. Test match rate? No, jet-age rate. For, how often has a test side battled its way through a full six hours' play to reach the 220-odd. Here, in their death-or-glory partnership, the Springboks added this much in less than three hours.

Of the 221 runs, Van der Merwe scored 76, so Lindsay got 145 runs in 166 minutes.

That's really going some, in any level of cricket.

Not that Lindsay is a newcomer to fast scoring. He is the holder of the world record for the number of sixes struck in succession in a first-class match. Playing for Roy McLean's Fezelas against Essex at Chelmsford in 1961, he blocked the first ball from W.T. Greensmith and then blasted the next five deliveries for sixes. In so doing, Lindsay equalled Arthur Wellard's twice-performed world record of 30 runs in a six-ball over. (the incomparable Sir Garfield Sobers of course smashed this record when he hit six sixes in a row off M.A.Nash of Glamorgan in 1968)

What influence did Johnny Lindsay, wicketkeeper in the 1947 Springbok team to England, have on his son? Not all that much. The decision to become a wicketkeeper was Denis's alone. And when he decided to don the bulky gloves — he did not model himself on his father or on any other famous player.

Said Denis: "I did consult my Dad when I had a particular problem to iron out, but that was about all. He helped me with advice, and then I went my own way."

Like many top-class cricketers, Denis Lindsay is superstitious. One of his pet beliefs is that to score well he must wear a favourite pair of trousers when going out to bat. Did he wear them for his epic 69 and 182 against Australia? That's probably why he made the runs — he did, of course!

Arthur Goldman
February 1967

Above: The Springboks before departure to Australia in 1963

Left: Brian Booth who was a prolific scorer for Australia against the Springboks in 1963/64 snicks one from David Pithey between Graeme Pollock and Johnny Waite

Below: The second pair of brothers on the Australian tour, Tony (left) and David Pithey

century!" Norman O'Neill had also once shown indignation when he was touring South Africa with a Cavaliers side and had been told "there was a Bradman in the making in Port Elizabeth".

"We have promising youngsters like him by the score" he replied, "but they don't always make the grade in the big time".

It is dangerous to scorn a genius, as Norman O'Neill and that unknown spectator were to find out.

Unfolding some of the grandest cover drives and hooks the Sydney cricket ground had ever seen, he annihilated all who came to challenge his authority. He notched his maiden test century — 122 — and in the process caused Lindsay Hassett to write: "I never have heard a sweeter note than the one young Graeme Pollock brought to Australia in his bat".

But alas, there was not all that much support from Graeme's team-mates.

Lawry O'Neill and Benaud then all just failed to get centuries and even Garth McKenzie weighed in with a highly competent 76 to enable Simpson to declare at 450 for nine, leaving us 409 to get in 433 minutes.

This was going to be our "make or break" innings for we couldn't afford to lose and go down 2-0 in the series.

Skipper Goddard didn't have to say a word to us. We all know what the next seven hours were going to mean. We didn't really contemplate winning, for it was a long, long way to go but an honourable draw we simply had to get. I doubt if I have ever sat through seven longer hours as we hit back with a magnificent team effort. Nobody made a century but nobody failed. The main accolades went to Colin Bland, especially because he curtailed his natural inclination to hit the ball and played an innings of unbelievable circumspection.

What happened in the fourth test at Adelaide should be recorded in letters of gold — rather green and gold. This was the triumph of all triumphs.

Yes, who could possibly forget the realisation of a dream? At some stages it might have appeared to be an "impossible dream" but as Eddie Barlow always said: "Nothing is impossible if you believe you can do it". And Eddie who had played such a role in convincing his team-mates that the positive approach was the only way to success, was quite fittingly the major figure in this triumph.

It started with a hassle. Johnny Waite wasn't fit and only minutes before the toss he decided to stand down. In came Denis Lindsay vowing that Johnny would never get his wicket-keeping berth back. We lost the toss for the fourth time in a row, but round one went to me. I had had an altercation with Norman O'Neill at Sydney. Once the wicket had flattened out in the Sydney match Norman was full of back-chat describing my bouncers as "cream-puffs".

Well, I struck early that morning at Adelaide getting Bill Lawry. In came Norman O'Neill and six balls later he was back in the "hut" with a duck. In attempting to fend off a bouncer he nudged the ball into Trevor Goddard's hands in the gully.

"You can't handle cream-puffs", I shouted as I marched triumphantly down the wicket. Yes, the action was on. Bobby Simpson, Peter Burge, Brian Booth and Barry Sehperd all played extremely well but as seemed to be the case with the Australian batsmen in the series, they inexplicably got out when centuries were in sight. Thank heavens, anyway. The Aussies totalled 345 with Trevor Goddard being awarded for his nagging accuracy with a bag of five wickets.

Out went Goddard and Barlow and as they did so regularly in this series, they got us off to a comfortable start. Trevor nudging them here and there, Barlow whacking the odd boundary. The score mounted and reached 70. Then came the crisis and the turning point.

The bowler was Neil Hawke, whose action is anything but textbook but who moved the ball around quite disconcertingly. He started the over by clean bowling Goddard and then back went Tony Pithey, second ball. Seventy for two wasn't looking so good. In strode Graeme Pollock.

The next ball Graeme met with the full face of the bat and sent it scurrying into the covers. It was an effortless shot but the ball seemed to gain momentum as it sped into the pickets. And this was to be the pattern for the next four hours and forty minutes of play. Barlow and Pollock took complete control. They massacred the Australian bowling in a display of ruthless authority that would have made even Hitler look like a weak-kneed diplomat. The song that Barlow and Pollock sang was so sweet that even the most ardent Australian supporter couldn't begrudge the sheer magnificence of it all.

Eddie finished with a brilliant double century and Graeme eventually succumbed to the wiles of bowler Hawke for 175. But they had compiled a mammoth 337 runs in their glorious batting duet.

Bill O'Reilly, Australia's greatest bowler of any era and at that time doyen of cricket writers Down Under, stood hatless in the pressbox to applaud as Graeme — the first to go — left the arena. It is not customary for cricket writers to clap their hands in applause but O'Reilly couldn't let an occasion like this go by without showing emotion and appreciation. Without wishing to detract from Eddie's innings, there is little doubt that the role of "Prince Charming" belonged to Graeme. His innings was compiled with a laconic mastery almost incongruous and quite unbelievable from one so young and innocent of countenance.

An incredible chapter had been written into cricket history by these two fair-haired Springboks. Records tumbled and so too did the reputations of the Australian bowlers. The Springboks finished with 595.

A first innings lead of 250 was all the inspiration the Springbok bowlers needed. The Aussies didn't give up easily — they never do- but the leeway was too much. However, by late afternoon on the fourth day a spirited sixth wicket partnership between Richie Benaud and Barry Shepherd was starting to cause a little consternation. Everything had been thrown at them but they were going along a little too nicely. Came five o'clock, an hour to close and Eddie Barlow went up to the skipper.

"Give me a go. I have a feeling I'll do them", demanded Eddie.

In his very first over, Eddie sent down a long-hop and Shepherd, going for the hook, mistimed his shot and sent the ball skywards in the general direction of fine leg. Denis Lindsay, pads and all, realising that the ball wasn' going to carry to me at fine-leg, set off and a full length dive climaxed a miraculous catch.

But this was not to be the end of

continued on page 77

Tony Pithey caught by Australian wicket-keeper, Wally Grout in the third test at Sydney

COLIN BLAND — THE GOLDEN EAGLE

I well remember the first time I saw Colin Bland. It was at the new Wanderers ground, Johannesburg, in 1959 when Rhodesia were playing Transvaal. A tall, splendidly-built young man was fielding at fine leg underneath the great cantilevered stand as the opening overs of the match were bowled. His name meant nothing to me, just another cricketer representing a country not renowned for its prowess at the game.

One of the Transvaal batsmen pushed the ball hard off his legs towards deep square leg, a stroke off the middle of the bat and four runs all the way . . . or so I thought.

The Rhodesian fine leg erupted into action. With sprinting speed that would have done Olympic sprinter Bob Hayes credit, and the ballet grace of Nijinski, Bland set off after the ball.

The scene is still crystal clear in my memory. He reached the ball just before it was about to cross the boundary line, picked it up in his left hand at full speed, transferred it quicker than the eye could follow into his right, and threw, all in one motion, with a rocket-like flat trajectory right over the top of the wickets into the keeper's waiting gloves. The batsmen managed a scampered two!

The details of the game itself I cannot remember, but this electrifying solo performance by Kenneth Colin Bland made an indelible impression on me as I sat in the stand.

Since then Bland has matured from being merely a wonderful fielder who can bat a bit, into a Test class number three or five with an enviable international record.

He arrived in England at the start of the present short tour by the Springboks with a reputation which had long preceded him. The M.C.C.

Bobby Simpson edges the ball through the slips during the test at Sydney. The fielders from left to right are Goddard, Barlow and Graeme Pollock

players, who recently toured the Republic, talked only of two men — Graeme Pollock and Bland.

Ian Thomson, that valuable stock bowler in South Africa, is no great enthusiast about opposition batsmen, but when he said to me, "Colin is not only the greatest outfielder I've ever seen, but also one of the best half-dozen batsmen I've bowled against," then I for one am impressed.

The success story of K.C. Bland is not without its ups and downs.

He achieved only moderate results when he first played for Rhodesia. He made his first class debut while still at college in 1956, against the M.C.C., but was a somewhat surprise selection for the 1963/64 tour to Australia.

His first six matches on the trip saw him average a mere 24.5 and he failed to gain a place for the first Test. Brittle batting, however, plus loss of form by Carlstein gave him his chance in the second Test in Sydney, where he scored a brilliant half-century before being tragically run-out.

This was the innings that transformed the young potential into a world-class batsman, and he finished the series third in the averages behind Barlow and Goddard with a figure of 61.61, including 126 at Sydney in the fifth and decisive Test. On the tour of New Zealand which followed, he emerged top, again aggregating over 60 runs per innings.

He had arrived as a player of no mean consistency, but it was really not until the M.C.C. tour to South Africa in 1964/65 that he became an indispensable cog in the re-emergence of the South African cricketing machine.

English players who were on that tour have told me that in their opinion the taking of Bland's wicket was by far and away the most important task of the England bowlers. His mere presence in the covers eschewed any thoughts of a run in that direction while if the ball entered his hands on the boundary, a frantic cry of, "get back" flew from one batsman to the other!

A more cheerless atmosphere to play cricket in could hardly be imagined when the

The incredible Colin Bland. Possibly the finest outfielder in cricket history

1965 Springbok touring team flew into a grey, wet and depressing London Airport late in the so-called "flaming" month of June.

Outdoor practice was severely restricted and when the tour proper got under way, persistent showers of rain heavily curtailed play. In spite of this, Bland immediately established himself with several good innings, including a masterly 60 in the first Test at Lord's. But it is his fielding that has created a stir, the like of which has not been known since the pre-war days of Sir Learie Constantine.

The late Wally Hammond remarked to noted cricket writer Ron Roberts, "Bland is in the same category as Learie — no, on reflection he has the edge over even the great West Indian allrounder.".

When Bland ran out Ken Barrington for 91 just when the English batsman was in the process of placing England in an impregnable position at Lord's, the English Press went quite lyrical in their praise.

The *Daily Express* even carried a diagram of how the tall Springbok had raced from his fielding position next to the square leg umpire, picked up the ball level with the bowler's wicket, and with one stump to aim at, hit the wickets direct! Pat Marshall in the same newspaper headed the whole of the back page with 'THE EAGLE STRIKES' in two-inch black type.

The following day — will the English never learn — Parks was run out, again from a direct Bland throw onto the stumps. The *Daily Mirror's* cricket correspondent, Brian Chapman, wrote:

"This man Bland is superhuman. It seems indecent that one player without bat or ball in his hand can dictate the course of the game just by whichever side of the wicket he happens to be fielding."

E.W. Swanton, doyen of English cricket writers, described Bland's fielding and throwing as "breathtaking".

Certainly the Springbok had made a deep impression on the most critical journalists in the world!

So much publicity accrued from his Test performances

Eddie's contribution. A couple of balls later Richie dragged one from outside the off-stump onto his wickets. In came McKenzie. Eddie accidentally — though he insists otherwise — let go a full toss which Garth hit in the meat but straight back at Eddie.

"Bunter" relished the offering and in the space of a few minutes had changed the whole complexion of the Australian fight-back. It just goes to show what can be achieved when you are a "believer" like Eddie Barlow.

The rest of the match was a mere formality, with the Springboks the victors by ten wickets. What a grand celebration we had. And no curfews either!

The final test at Sydney could be best described as the "one that got away". We were accused in many quarters of "not knowing how to win" or how to clinch victory with an aggressive attitude. Maybe these critics were right for at certain stages of the final test the Springboks were perhaps timid when they should have taken the bull by the horns.

It had indeed been a most memorable summer, a summer which taught us much and saw many reuptations being enhanced. Eddie Barlow became a household name and his pugnacity was admired by friend and foe. At times he might have appeared a bit brazen but his message of confidence got through.

Graeme Pollock had arrived, so had Colin Bland and except for a lack of spinners, South African cricket was starting to earn a place alongside the likes of Australia, England and the West Indies.

New Zealand, after four-and-a-half months in Australia, is an anti-climax. Such magnificent grounds as Sydney, the Melbourne Cricket ground and even Adelaide are replaced by little better than a showground "shed" at Dunedin, rugby changing-rooms at Wellington and Christchurch followed by a little sanity at Eden Park, Auckland.

From the country that was vitally aware of the latest test score or the form of Norman O'Neill, we moved to a nation who were more interested in just how strong our Springbok rugby team was going to be for the 1965 tour than whether the Kiwis would be able to hold us in the forthcoming three-match series.

We should have won that series three-nil but it was drawn and Goddard's Springboks could only console themselves with moral victories as compensation for six weeks of absolute cricketing agony. Ill luck, bad weather, tragedy and injuries followed us from

Richie Benaud

that in the following match against Kent, their captain, Colin Cowdrey, arranged a fielding exhibition to be given by Bland before the start of the first day's play. A 15-minute solo performance ended with the last two throws from 30 yards knocking out of the ground, first two, and then the remaining stump!

As well as great accuracy, Bland can hurl the five-and-a-half ounce leather ball prodigious distances. The official record (for some unknown reason no one, not even Bland, has tried to break it) stands at 140 yards 2 feet.

This was set up by R. Percival, at Durham Sand Racecourse, way back in 1884. When the South Africans played at Swansea recently I talked to Bland and Herbert "Tiger" Lance. I was surprised to learn that "Tiger" claims to be able to throw around the 140 marks but with a huge shrug he nodded towards his Rhodesian teammate and said, "My friend here can beat me easily — and what's more he could do it with his jacket and suede shoes on!"

I looked over to Colin for an affirming grin, but he remained modestly impassive. This is typical of the man - for he, least of all, draws attention to his redoubtable gifts.

Colin Bland has done, and is doing, what Bradman, Hammond and Larwood did in the past. He is drawing people into the playing fields of England just to see this one-man performance. His performances so far have already assured him of a place in English cricket memory.

Way back in 1790, a cricketer by the name of T. Ray was picked for England. Not because of any outstanding ability with either bat or ball, but simply because he was the finest fielder in the land.

One hundred and seventy-five years later the same phenomenon has burst upon the scene, for if ever a man saves 50 or so runs every time he strides out onto a cricket field, Colin Bland of Rhodesia is that man.

Peter Walker
September 1965

Above: At last . . . Players gather around to congratulate Neil Hawke after bowling Graeme Pollock for 175 during that memorable fourth test at Adelaide in 1964

Below: Norman O'Neill, idol of the Australian cricketing public during the sixties, takes a nasty blow from Peter Pollock

the moment we arrived in New Zealand. It had been a travesty of cricketing justice but we had to learn to accept that victories only count when they are in the record books.

It is interesting to note that during those six weeks not a single Springbok notched a first-class "ton", but messrs, Barlow, Bland and Goddard came deperately close. And with Graeme Pollock, the team's number one, out of action for all but three innings, the team's four-pronged batting might was depleted. The bowling honours, just as in Australia, were shared by Joe Partridge, myself and Trevor Goddard, with David Pithey coming into the reckoning thanks largely to the clay-pit at Dunedin.

I do believe that those six weeks have been shelved away in the recesses of the memories of most of us. What I do remember of New Zealand are the beautiful pastures, the sheep-covered hills, the snowy mountains, big fat trout (the largest you can find) and the amazing Rotorua where hot air bubbles out of the drains and the smell of sulphur kills even the most potent deodorants. Maybe it is just as well that rugby rules supreme in New Zealand!

If ever a series turned out to be one long yawn it was the 1964-65 visit to South Africa of Mike Smith's English side.

"You chaps play the attacking cricket and we'll win the matches" — this was the comment they made early on in the trip, at Port Elizabeth to be specific. Certainly this typified the general strategy of Mike Smith's side throughout that series.

Their basic tactics were to start a test with the intention of first securing a draw and then only considering a tilt at victory if the odds were heavily in their favour. This dour approach has tended to make English sides most unpopular with the crowds the world over. The 1964-65 English side had natural stroke-makers of the calibre of Ted Dexter, Bob Barber and Jim Parks and the potential to produce memorable cricket. But no, all we are left with are memories of hours of dogged survival from the likes of Geoff Boycott and Ken Barrington.

The Springboks, led by Trevor Goddard and rampant after their tour of Australia, started as firm favourites.

Graeme Pollock started the series badly against the M.C.C. in 1964. Here he is bowled by Titmus in the first test in Durban

Perhaps the under-dog tag helped drive Mike Smith's side into their defensive shells. But what really killed the series was the fact that the tourists won the first Test at Durban on a pitch which by the third day could only be described as a "cabbage patch".

Spinners Fred Titmus and Dave Allen had a ball on it and once the 1-0 lead had been established, one could perhaps not blame Mike Smith for being happy to sit tight. Smith obviously came in for a lot of stick from the press for being content to play negative cricket but you couldn't blame this most likeable man for his methods. Except for the rare occasions when South African pitches helped his spinners, his attack was only moderate.

Towards the end it was further depleted by injuries and his hands were further tied. Mike's job was to win the series against a side with greater potential than his own. He had a lucky start, accepted this good fortune gratefully and left it to us to make the running. The task proved beyond us although they had a narrow shave at the Wanderers.

It is a pity that it wasn't a better series from the public's point of view and maybe the pitches were to blame.

The one at Durban was a "freak" and the others were just too good and too full of runs to give the bowlers any assistance. When we first saw the Kingsmead strip, we were shattered. The ground-staff had been asked to prepare a hard, fast and bouncy pitch. they obviously felt that to meet these demands a pitch should be rolled hard as a rock and then shaved!

You didn't have to be an expert on pitches to know at first glance that this pitch would be slow and could crumble in a day or two. Batting first was the number one prerequisite and as luck would have it, Mike Smith called correctly.

In my very first over I tried a bouncer at Geoff Boycott. I put everything I had into the delivery but it was so slow that it looked rather ludicrous.

The new ball was worthless within six or seven overs, having been torn to shreds by the pitch and the Englishmen made hay in Durban's intense humidity. Ken Barrington and Jim Parks scored centuries and nobody looked in any trouble. It was more a case of getting yourself out rather than falling before the skills or wiles of the Springbok bowlers.

An interesting side-issue to this test was the sudden suggestion that Graeme Pollock was vulnerable against spinners, particularly off-spinners. Whether the British pressmen took this up as a means of psychological warfare we'll never know, but repeatedly it was written that Graeme had at last been

Eddie Barlow is clean bowled by Ian Thomson in the first test at Durban in 1964 and below he is caught by Barrington in the same test sorted out. Graeme wasn't at all worried. After all, at Kingsmead all the Springboks looked hopeless against spinners. The Kingsmead pitch was a travesty and only the wicket that we played on at Dunedin in New Zealand deserves a lower rating.

The Wanderers test followed much the same pattern as the Durban encounter, with Mike Smith winning the toss and the Englishmen piling up a massive first innings 531. Barrington scored his second successive century, reaching the three-figure mark with a mighty six, which was most out of character. But we did see a magnificent contribution from Ted Dexter.

"Lord Ted" was surely one of the aristocrats among batsmen. He had an almost nonchalant disposition at the crease, an arrogance which was charming, and an effectiveness which could be quite brutal. He is said to have played the finest innings ever to have been seen at Lord's batting against Charlie Griffith and Wesley Hall when those two West Indian hurricanes were at their best and on a green wicket. Ted decided on aggression as the only answer and his innings of 70-odd is still rated today as the most devastatingly defiant ever to have been produced on the sacred turf of "Headquarters".

At the Wanderers against us he was irresistable, though he played in moods. There were times when he seemed to lose interest and merely tapped the ball back. And then there were times when he felt that he should show just who is master. His 172 was a magnificent contribution.

But salvation and hope for the future came in the form of Colin Bland. We were invited to follow-on after a poor first innings effort and just when the second innings looked as if it might be a repeat of the first, in stepped the "Golden Eagle". He showed us all how to really use the feet to the spinners and suddenly messrs. Titmus and Allen didn't look like ogres. He wasn't scared to loft the ball. In fact, he clouted a few soaring sixes and for the first time in the series Mike Smith had to pull his two trumpcards out of the firing line.

And so we were off to Newlands where a change in fortune, albeit on the first innings only, in a painful struggle, and a good deal of controversy helped to rekindle interest in the series.

One of England's mainstays during the sixties, Ken Barrington

Thanks to Trevor Goddard, Eddie Barlow and Tony Pithey the Springboks after winning the toss, compiled 501 for seven declared. England then occupied the crease for just on two days and finished with a first innings deficit of 59 runs. Thereafter, with only seven and a half hours remaining a draw was inevitable.

The controversy started with ebullient Eddie Barlow. It was followed up by Ken Barrington and it resulted in the game being tagged the "Tarnished Test". Wisden, cricket's most authoritative publication summed up the proceedings in these words: "Long after the unenterprising cricket of this test is forgotten, people will talk of two incidents which brought to a head the question of whether a batsman should 'walk'. With close-in fieldsman convinced both times that umpire Warner was wrong to turn down appeals for catches, the first at short leg and the second by the wicket-keeper, Barlow of South Africa stood firm his ground and Barrington of England, made his way to the pavilion."

Whether it was by design or not, the Wisden's report does tend to make Barrington out to be a hero and Barlow the villain. In the first instance, let me correct an inaccuracy concerning the South African's dismissal. It was in the gully, not at short-leg, that Parfitt took the "catch". Barlow had played forward to Titmus, got his legs in a tangle and the ball had popped up amiably into the eager hands of gully. Barlow stook his ground, the umpire signalled not out and the circus was on. Titmus accused Barlow of being a "cheat"; Barlow retaliated with a few choice words of his own plus a threat of putting his bat across the bowler's head.

Eddie then proceeded to concentrate even harder and he went on to make 138. This incident had occurred when he had 40 on the board and it was clear that the Englishmen were displeased for they failed to applaud any of the milestones he reached in the process. Their attitude was made clear when they applauded Tony Pithey, who batted with Barlow in a second wicket stand which yielded 172 runs, with exaggerated enthusiasm. One must learn to accept the rough with the smooth. Eddie was convinced that he was not out and he had a sore toe to prove his contention that the ball had come off his boot, not his bat. He was within his rights to leave the decision to the umpire. It was by no means an open and shut case.

Titmus, on the other hand, did not have any right to make harsh accusations even in the heat of the moment. Later in the match, Titmus ventured into our change-room to tender an apology.

"My captain has ordered me to apologise though it is against my true feelings on this incident" he said. His poor grace did nothing to repair the ill-feeling that had been stirred up between the two sides although Eddie joked: "They asked me why I didn't walk. I couldn't. My toe was too sore".

This was, however, not the end of the drama. Barrington's personal tally was nearing 50 when I was brought on for a spell just before tea. One delivery rose sharply outside the off-stump and Barrington tickled it neatly into the hands of wicketkeeper Lindsay. The whole team joined in the appeal and triumphantly I marched down the pitch, arms held aloft. But then I stopped. Barrington had not moved. I swung round and looked at the motionless umpire. Horrors of horrors — he was not going to give him out!

Seconds ticked by like an eternity and it was clear that in umpire Warner's mind Barrington had not touched the ball. He was not going to put his finger up. Finally, after waiting long enough to make a mockery of the umpire, Barrington put his bat under his arm and "walked". I was most relieved and at the time applauded the gesture.

Was Barrington's "walk" an act of sportsmanship, an action designed to make a fool of the umpire or merely designed to take a "stab" at Eddie Barlow? I still firmly believe that Ken's gesture was sincere and in the best interest of cricket but it certainly helped to stir the hornet's nest in the press box. With the professional critics having very little to enthuse over on the actual playing side, they made merry with the controversy. As much as I admire Barrington for "walking", I think that this test did convince me that we should allow the umpire to make the final decision and accept his decision, whether it be right or wrong.

The hours preceding the fourth test at the Wanderers were full of high drama for the Springboks. I was sharing a room with my comrade-in-arms, Joe Partridge, and following our team talk on the eve of the test, we had a team dinner. At this dinner, Joe and I, rather unwisely, decided on prawn cocktails as the "starter". These turned out to be anything but "amorous prawns" and in the middle of the night both of us became sick. I was not quite so bad but poor old Joe couldn't stop vomiting.

The selectors were informed early the next morning and they tried to make alternative arrangements. They even thought of getting an air force jet to fly in Mike Macauley, who had done extremely well for Free State against the tourists, as a last-minute replacement for Joe. But it could not be arranged. Joe was a very sick man when we set off for the Wanderers that morning and I didn't feel all that much better.

It was a hot day and all we needed was to have the field but Dame Fortune smiled on us.

On what appeared to be a perfectly good batting wicket, Mike Smith won the toss and then must have suffered some kind of mental lapse. He sent us in to bat. What a tremendous relief. Joe went back to the hotel to spend the rest of the day in bed and our batsmen, thanks to an opening partnership of 118 between Barlow and Goddard managed a reasonable total of 390 for six declared.

It was in this match that Trevor managed to notch his maiden Test century, a feat which had eluded him for nearly a decade. He reached the target by taking a quick single which nearly saw him run out.

Rain intervened to the extent of about three hours on the first two days but we managed a six-run first innings advantage on the tourists. The Springboks then set them a final target of 314 runs to make at a rate of 78 to the hour. It should have been a comfortable draw but I managed to effect an early break-through, including Dexter's wicket. At one stage we appeared to be on the victory path but snap went my ham-string. Deeply frustrated, I had to watch the final tw hours' play while Geoff Boycott, with a typically stubborn 76 not out, spearheaded an England recovery which saw then 153 for seven wickets at close. Most definitely this was a moral triumph for the Springboks but moral triumphs don't count. You have to bowl the other side out twice in five days to win and we

A great moment: Trevor Goddard is congratulated by the M.C.C. players on reaching his first test century during the 1964/65 tour

had failed to do that. But in our hearts we had now firmly established ourselves as the aggressors in the series.

The series ended in Port Elizabeth where the most notable achievement was Graeme Pollock's century in a Springbok first innings total of 502. As can be guaged from the scores, the pitch once again was a beauty which did not really give the bowlers much chance. As usual in this series, England made a fighting response but they also took their time about it. In such a situation batsmen like Geoff Boycott, who scored 117, Ken Barrington (72) are in there element. It was only after tea on the fourth day that the two first innings were completed and the Springboks had a lead of a mere 67 runs. There was no possibility of forcing a result and the Englishmen were already starting to celebrate their series triumph.

Unbeknown to many, the series did have an unpleasant under-current in that the selectors, messrs. Coy and company, found themselves in the embarrassing position of wanting to make a painful change. They had nominated Trevor Goddard as skipper for the whole series but in Cape town during the third test, they felt that perhaps they should reverse their decision. Apparently they felt that Trevor was not providing the positive and dynamic leadership that was required to salvage the series.

I don't believe that it was Trevor's fault for the type of wickets that we played on only made it easier for the Englishmen to keep us at bay. The balance in favour of the batsman, as the scores suggest, was quite unfair and however resourceful Goddard had been, I doubt whether it would have changed the final outcome.

The English batsmen played the percentages. They were not prepared to make mistakes in seeking runs. They knew that as long as they stayed at the crease the runs would follow. Anyway, the selectors hoped that Trevor would give them an easy way out. They prepared a statement for him in which he was going to relinquish the captaincy because it was interfering with his play. Well, and I admire him for it, Trevor refused to play ball. If they wanted to drop him they had to have the courage of their convictions.

He was then retained as captain but this, as much as anything else, probably persuaded Trevor not to be available for the forthcoming tour to England.

Trevor Goddard was certainly not a leader in the same mould as Jackie McGlew, Peter van der Merwe or Ali Bacher but he should be given his due. He was present during the birth-pains as well as the teething troubles of a team of emerging world-beaters. You can't take that away from him and while the records will show that he was not as successful as those who followed him. Trevor Leslie Goddard deserves recognition as the man who helped the flowers to blossom. Someone else might have done a better job but at the time, he was the best man around and he did what he had to do with utter dedication.

Trevor Goddard gave South African cricket everything he had and all he received in return were two slaps in the face.

The first was at Newlands when he was asked to sign his own death warrant and later against Bill Lawry's Australians when he was left out of the team for the final test. Sometimes it really astounds me just how short memories are and just how thoughtless some people can be. •

Graeme Pollock in typical mood

CHAPTER FIVE

THE STING IN THE TAIL

If ever a team had the odds stacked against them it was Peter van der Merwe's 1965 Springboks in England. There was no Trevor Goddard and to make matters worse Tony Pithey withdrew from the original side leaving Eddie Barlow without an opening partner.

I felt that the selectors had also erred in not choosing Joe Partridge, despite the fact that he was moving into the veteran class and was anything but a brilliant fielder. Joe's control of swing and seam, to my mind, would have been perfectly suited to the English conditions.

With the tour starting in mid-June it meant that we lacked match practice. The England players had already had the opportunity of gaining confidence and running into top form against the New Zealanders in the first half of that summer. To make matters worse we were plagued by incessant rain almost from the moment we arrived. It not only reduced several of our opening matches to a shambles but continually interrupted net practices. We even went so far as to consider indoor nets, so short of practice were we.

Tiger Lance and Denis Lindsay did their best as "make-shift" openers, Jackie Botten took over Joe Partidge's mantle, Richard Dumbrill reached great heights as an all-rounder and Peter van der Merwe, Manager, Jack "Tackies" Plimsoll and Eddie Barlow proved to be an excellent motivational trio at the helm.

Typical of Peter van der Merwe was his comment after we had lost our very first match against Derbyshire. "I am pleased about that", 'Murphy' said. "Now we won't have an unbeaten record to worry about".

Three weeks later when the Springboks arrived at Lords for the first test they had only one victory to show in seven matches — and that, a triumph against the lowly minor countries. Victory in the other matches had, in point of fact, gone to the rain. My, how it poured down and the clouds seem to follow us around England, even to the extent of washing out our nets on the eve of the first test.

Not many pressmen gave us a chance, but deep down, though we had no right to feel this way, there was a certain quiet confidence in the Springbok camp.

The Springboks got first use of the Lord's pitch, a wicket which had a bit of grass but nevertheless didn't look dangerous. It was a Jekyll and Hyde innings. the start was shaky, followed by a gem of a partnership between Colin Bland and Graeme Pollock which added a glorious 80 runs in ninety minutes. Then came another collapse. At 178 for seven, the Springboks were not looking good but Jackie Botten and I at the tailend eventually managed to take the final total to 280, which wasn't all that bad.

The England total exceeded our by 58 runs and would no doubt have been much higher but for the "Golden Eagle" — Colin Bland. A fielder has never been given such publicity before and the National British Sunday papers blazoned Bland's name in banner headlines across their sports pages, the next morning. He deserved the credit. His two run-outs (Ken Barrington and Jim Parks were the victims, of direct hits of the stumps) were probably more vital to the Springbok cause than we cared to acknowledge at that stage. Colin had made the vital breakthrough at a stage when none of our bowlers seemed capable of doing so.

Colin Bland became a national hero and he firmly established a new respect for the art of fielding. His mere presence on the field, patrolling the covers

The Springboks arriving for their 1965 tour

like a hungry lion saved us runs, for the batsmen refused to take the slightest risk.

Finally England were left 191 to score in just four hours. This was by no means an impossible task. In fact, they should have cake-walked it.

"We could have done it in singles" said Mike Smith ruefully after the match, but they paid the penalty for being too cautious at the start. Perhaps they felt that if they kept their early wickets intact the Springboks would crack and the last 100 runs would be a mere formality. Well, as it turned out, England were lucky to survive. They finished with 145 for seven wickets but in real terms they were eight down because John Edrich was in hospital with concussion, the result of ducking into one of my deliveries.

The Trent Bridge test was the turning point of our England tour. Personally I believe it was one of the greatest tests of this era and I am not biased by

PETER VAN DER MERWE

Keith Miller is a great admirer of Springbok captain Peter van der Merwe and his leadership. "Peter is more audacious as a captain than I would ever have dared to be, yet everything he tries seems to come off," Miller told me at the Wanderers.

"His improvement as a captain since he went to England in 1965 has been extraordinary," Keith said. "When I first saw him lead a team in Australia in 1963 he seemed to be just a boy as a captain. I felt much the same about him early during the 1965 short tour of England.

"Today he is a splendid captain, fit to rank with some of the best test captains of history. He also sets a fine fighting example to his men."

Keith Miller was one of the most audacious cricket captains New South Wales, Australia's most formidable Sheffield Shield State, ever owned.

When Keith followed Arthur Morris as new skipper he was told that those who chose him expected him to do his utmost to produce entertaining and highly competitive cricket at the Sydney Cricket Ground to bring back the crowds who had been driven away by negative tactics and declarations and by selfish and slow batting from Jack Moroney and Jim Burke.

Keith fulfilled his brief to the satisfaction of most people, was criticised for being too adventurous at times, yet he believes Peter van der Merwe is more adventurous than he ever was.

"What a pity he has announced his intention to retire," Keith said. "Cricket needs captains like him today at the international level. There have been far too many drawn test matches, especially when England and India and Pakistan have played one another."

I agree with Miller. The improvement in Van der Merwe's leadership since I first watched him lead the 1963/64 Springboks at Adelaide Oval against South Australia, has been almost unbelievable.

Peter always has had a first-class brain. He had to learn how best to apply it to leadership at cricket. It is the speed with which he has learnt to do so that is most remarkable. He must have made a profound study of the game when selector Arthur Coy singled him out as the Springbok leader of the future early in 1963, maybe before then.

He must have determined that if ever the national leadership fell to him he would become a captain in fact as well as in name. He would make his own decisions and take the responsibility for them. He would be the "boss", as Trevor Goddard rarely was in Australia in the fact that it proved to be a personal triumph for the Pollock family. It was just one of those games that had everything the game of cricket can produce — drama, tension, uncertainty and the beauty that only a genius like Graeme Pollock can produce with his flashing bat.

When Eddie Barlow and Tiger Lance strode to the wicket that first morning to take advantage of their skipper's correct call of the toss, there were not expecting many problems from the pitch. It looked a bit grey and grassless and with the sun having shone the whole day prior to the test, there shouldn't have been any problems. But, as Eric Rowan once said to me, "Anyone who thinks that he knows how a pitch is going to play is only fooling himself."

There were devils that we didn't anticipate and while Barlow and Lance struggled against John Snow and David Larter it was Tom Cartwright who caught us with our pants down. He wobbled the ball about the place most disconcertingly, both through the air and off the seam. By the time the Springbok total had reached 40, messrs. Barlow, Lance, Lindsay and Bland were back in the pavilion. When it got to 80, Ali Bacher joined them in the showers.

I couldn't bear the tension. I locked myself up in a backroom as Peter van der Merwe joined Graeme at the crease. Graeme was looking good and he was taking the fight to the Englishmen. Whatever the cost he was going to be the aggressor, working on the theory that attack is the best form of defence.

With the help of Van der Merwe, who merely kept his end up, Graeme took the England attack, particularly Cartwright, in his teeth and shook it like a dog does a rag doll. Before his innings ended, Graeme was being compared with legend-like Stan McCabe and Frank Woolley. Personally, and I am sure all the other Springboks agreed, our Graeme Pollock on that day was beyond comparison with anyone.

His 125 was brutally brilliant and yet, you could never use the word brutal to describe such charm and elegance. Even the doyen of English cricket writers, Jim Swanton, was lost for words, such was the magnificence of Graeme Pollock. In the 70 minutes after lunch, Graeme and 'Murphy' put on 102 runs.

Graeme was not happy when he was finally given out, caught in the slips by Colin Cowdrey. Graeme was thus not in the happiest of moods when he arrived back in the changing-room. He was pretty abrupt with Sir Leonard Hutton, who came in to add his congratulations. Graeme was still flushed and sweating, not to mention annoyed over his dismissal, and he didn't recognise Sir Len. Fortunately, Graeme is rarely downright rude and once he rea-

1963/64.

But when you are the "boss" you have to make the right decisions most of the time or you will lose the respect of the men you lead and, eventually, your appointment.

Peter had many advantages. He is a man his fellow men like when they get to know him. His modesty, his quiet and receptive manner, his deep understanding stood him in fine stead. So did his willingness to take the rough role on or off the field when he felt it would help his team.

Peter does not "bounce" people. Quiet, but firm persuasion is his tool of trade. He thinks deeply and acts from well reasoned judgements.

But he had disadvantages which lesser people would have found impossible to overcome. By nature he is not a great cricketer.

He began, I understand, as a batsman, changed to bowling as his main forte then switched to batting again. All the time he kept improving his fielding in interception and dispatch and today he is one of the most accurate returners of a ball to the stumps from a middle distance in test cricket. He is meticulous in this respect, almost machine-like.

That a player of his limited cricketing talent should rise so high in the game is greatly to his credit. People were apt to scoff at Peter's cricket. They do so no longer.

Those unwritten laws of the game, which at times are being honoured rather in the breach than the observance, are sacrosanct to Van der Merwe.

I spent a lot of time studying him at the helm during the recent series against Australia. He is no ostentatious figure at mid-off or wherever he chooses to station himself.

As you watch the play you are apt to forget he is there. There are so many more colourful cricketers on view — Colin Bland, for example, alongside him at cover; Eddie Barlow, bounding about with such effervescence in the close cordons.

But you can almost see Peter thinking and planning, weighing one idea against another, on one side or other of the bowler. And when he acts he does so in that quiet, yet decisive manner of his that brings conviction and usually the desired results.

Peter reminds me of a spider spinning his web. You can see the web but rarely notice the spider. He reminds me also of Professor Moriarty, that creation of Conan Doyle's — that master mind of the underworld who, despite his aims, earned one's respect and sneaking admiration.

Van der Merwe as a captain has become a master at applying pressure on opposing batsmen and at maintaining it. He detects weaknesses and has the attack to probe at them hour after hour. Bowlers respect his opinions and give him their ultimate in loyalty and application.

Dick Whitington
April 1967

Denis Lindsay whips off the bails in the split second that Colin Cowdrey lifts his foot. This brilliant dismissal put the Springboks on their way to the Trent Bridge triumph

After Trent Bridge: from left to right: Peter Pollock, Athol McKinnon, Graeme Pollock and Eddie Barlow

lised to whom he was speaking, he turned on the charm. But perhaps officials and enthusiasts should appreciate that a changing-room is best left to the players.

The Springboks finally totalled 269, which by English standards is not all that bad. Considering our predicament at one stage, it was a brilliant recovery.

The first evening saw England having to bat out half-an-hour and those thirty minutes were to belong entirely to the Springboks. Off the second ball I bowled, Boycott got an edge and the ball flew to Tiger Lance in the slips. I had palpitations as he juggled with the ball but he finally got it under control.

Before the total reached double figures, Geoff Boycott had been joined by Ken Barrington and we all had much reason to enjoy our beers in the dressing-room that evening.

Highlight of the second day was a faultless century by Colin Cowdrey. Though he is rather portly in build, Cowdrey is extremely quick on his feet and his reflexes are such that he appears to have a lot of time to play his shots. When he is on form, he makes you feel like you are only bowling at half-pace, so quickly does he move into line and so effortlessly does he time his shots.

Five wickets was my contribution as England failed by 29 runs to reach our first innings total and we began our second knock with Lindsay and Lance going out to face the new ball. Eddie Barlow had hurt his toe and Lindsay and Lance agreed to pair up as "cannon fodder". Denis survived but Tiger didn't quite manage it to close of play. And so to the dramatic third day and six hours of play that were to prove the most thrilling of the tour.

The Springboks owed thanks to three batsmen — Ali Bacher, Eddie Barlow and Graeme Pollock. Bacher's was the innings that set the solid foundation, Pollock's was the masterpiece and Barlow's was the one which ensured that England would have a target in excess of 300. But it was still anybody's game even though up till then England had never made 300 or more in a final innings to win a test. We were not prepared to put too much reliance in history. The wicket was still true and England had the batsmen to accomplish any task.

Forty-five minutes' play remained

Graeme Pollock addresses the enthusiastic crowd of 3 000 who gathered to welcome home the three Eastern Province Springboks at the end of the 1965 tour. In the picture are Peter Pollock, Eddie Barlow and his wife Helen, Inez, Peter's then fiancee and Mr and Mrs Pollock on the extreme right.

that Saturday evening. We needed a quick break-through. It was absolutely vital. In my second over our prayers were answered, this time in the form of Bob Barber who got a neat edge to Denis Lindsay. Then, in the final over of the day, burly Athol McKinnon had night-watchman, Fred Titmus caught.

What an exciting and momentous final day it proved to be. Fortunes fluctuated remarkably, almost as if the script had been written by the mistress of intrigue, Agatha Christie.

With the total at 41, Denis Lindsay brought off one of the finest stumpings I have ever seen. Athol McKinnon was the bowler and Colin Cowdrey, in attempting to leg-glance, missed the ball but lifted his foot for just a fraction of a second. It was enough time, however, for Denis to whip off the bails and to have his feat acknowledged by the square-leg umpire. I have often said and I do so again, that this particular dismissal was the turning point in this enthralling contest. As things transpired later in the day, a bigger contribution from Colin Cowdrey could so easily have led to a dramatic English triumph. It is worth appreciating the significance of this stumping in the light of Colin Bland's run-outs in the first test — yes, fielding was a vital factor in that series.

Boycott held on grimly, sometimes methinks too grimly, for had he shown a little more willingness to put bat to ball I am sure England would have benefitted later in the day. Though he was keeping his wicket intact, he was still allowing the Springbok bowlers to dictate terms and Peter van der Merwe could retain his close-in fielders. Finally Boycott fell and then the real fun started as first Peter Parfitt and Mike Smith and then Parfitt and Jim Parks launched spectacular rearguard actions. The highlight was the Parks-Parfitt episode, a partnership which had us very worried.

Both are exciting stroke-makers and they took full advantage of the rainy conditions. The ball was very slippery and poor Athol McKinnon couldn't grip it. However, the wet ball and outfield should not detract from the performance of Parks and Parfitt for I daresay that had the ball been dry, these two would have carried on in much the same adventurous mood. their buccaneering approach showed up the folly of the earlier batsmen, who between them had occupied the crease for 270 minutes in scoring a paltry 127 while in just an hour Parks and Parfitt, by pinching quick, cheeky singles and smashing out against anything loose, added 80 priceless runs.

I said we were worried. That would be an understatement. The damp conditions had taken the edge off our fielding and bowling. I was beginning to visualise the match slipping away and for the first time in my cricketing life I secretly asked God to help our cause.

Next over, I was summoned by Peter van der Merwe. Success didn't come straight away, but when it did, a few overs later, it was most spectacular. First Parfitt played across the line and was clean bowled. I don't think I have ever been more relieved to see someone head back to the pavilion. In the same over Tom Cartwright went lbw and only Larter stood between South Africa and victory. There were a few close shaves but Larter had decided on a policy of attack. He got away with a few streaky shots and then attempted just one too many. Trying to drive he lofted the ball towards mid-off. There, waiting under it was skipper, Peter van der Merwe, his big hands looking the size of the Grand Canyon, ready to swallow the small, red ball. It was like an eternity waiting for it to drop out of the sky but finally

The Pollocks. An artist depicts their triumph at Trent Bridge

EDDIE BARLOW

"For years we have been the gentlemen of cricket. We were so nice we even let other teams win so that there could be no problems."

An exaggeration perhaps. But these words written by Eddie Barlow in an article in *The Argus* in January, 1970, were a reference to the new tough approach adopted by South Africa's cricketers before the third test of the 1963/64 series in Australia and they typified the man.

The Springboks, captained by Trevor Goddard, had drawn the first test of that series and lost the second. It was then, according to Barlow, that the team got together in a spirit of "we're going to beat those so-and-so's" and, as everyone knows, South Africa won the fourth test in Adelaide and shared the series after coming desperately close to winning the fifth test in Sydney.

It was appropriate that Barlow himself should be associated with Graeme Pollock in that devastating partnership of 341 in 283 minutes at the Adelaide Oval, with the 23 year-old Barlow making 201 (27 fours) and the 19 year-old Pollock 175 (three sixes, 18 fours).

The Australian attack, comprising McKenzie, Gaunt, Hawke (who dismissed both Pollock and Barlow in taking six for 139), Benaud and Simpson were the victims of a calculated, merciless assault that had Bill O'Reilly rising in the Press Box to applaud the Springboks.

Barlow went on record later as asserting that "this partnership definitely established an attacking approach in South African cricket", though adding with a personal modesty that forms a strange contrast to his cocky, uncompromising approach to the game : "I happened to be part of it, but I believe this was circumstantial only."

Louis Duffus, over the years the most authoritative scribe on South African cricket once wrote :

"I am inclined to contend that he had more influence over South African cricket than any single player I know. Perhaps it would be more accurate to say that he had more influence on the country's spirit, tempo of batting and approach to the game. He did more than anyone else to break down the timid, defensive tactics which for so many years kept South Africa a second-rate cricket country — and that, to me, is a tremendous achievement."

His fellow-cricketers long ago dubbed him "Bunter", because of his spectacles, owlish look and undeniable facial resemblance to the Greyfriars schoolboy character created it did and as Peter tossed the ball heavenwards, the whole team erupted in sheer joy and elation. Our frustrations were over. We had finally beaten England. I don't think that I have personally had a prouder moment in my life then when I was allowed to lead the team off the field, having taken a further five wickets in the second innings for a match tally of ten. In our changing-room it was sheer chaos with all the well-wishers around with the bubbly flowing.

What happened in the first three hours after victory was great fun. Some of the Springboks even ventured onto the pitch in their underpants and performed the famous "jukskei" march, with Field Marshall Athol McKinnon in charge. Even some of the local constabulary joined in — one to the extent that he was severely reprimanded the next morning. It was a night to remember and the celebrations continued into the small hours of the morning.

Trent Bridge — just the mention of this ground will still stir the emotions of any of the Springboks involved in the 1965 Springbok tour. It was an unbelievable experience. Even the imperturbable Gerhard Viviers, the cricket commentator who has brought a new meaning to the game to our Afrikaans countrymen, got carried away by the excitement of it all just after the game. He introduced Dr Carel de Wet, who was then ambassador of South Africa in Britain, as Dr van der Merwe. Dr de Wet had watched the full four days and he too joined us in the changing-room as we celebrated with real relish that wonderful sense of achievement.

And so to the final Test at the Oval and the recall of Brian Statham. A great guy is Brian. We did consider it as a great compliment to us that the England selectors had to resort to resurrecting the old campaigner in an attempt to gain revenge. We wondered how come they had left out Freddie Trueman? Though then 35 years old, Brian was still regarded as the most accurate fast bowler in the country and we knew that we couldn't take any liberties.

We left England the mammoth target of 399. I must admit that I didn't believe England would even consider the challenge but they did and in the process played their best attacking cricket of the whole series. In fact, it was the best batting I saw from England in eight tests, and that is saying something.

The "Pommies" had a real go. And what an outstanding finish. A splendid partnership of 135 between Ken Barrington and Colin Cowdrey virtually set up the target and with seventy minutes to go and only 91 runs required — with six wickets in hand — it looked like England were going to snatch a fairy tale victory.

That final day, as England set out boldly for the challenge, the clouds had dominated the ceiling above us. In fact, several times we would see a huge black cloud pass over, wish that it

by Frank Richards. It is, however, a singularly inappropriate nick-name, for those who read the Magnet in their school-days know Bunter as an indolent, perpetually impecunious good-for-nothing.

Burly, broad-shouldered, ruddy-faced, Barlow is an unmistakeable figure on the field. He exudes a pugnacious belligerency as he peers at the bowler when batting or glares at the batsman when bowling.

Bowlers, whenever Eddie plays a long innings, become sick and tired of the sight of him wiping his glasses but it is as a bowler that he positively bristles with combative energy.

Barlow gives the impression of expecting to take a wicket with just about every ball and when the batsman has kept out a good one or just missed getting a touch he reacts by staring fixidly down the wicket for a few seconds as if unable to comprehend his opponent's good fortune.

And the man who generally takes more catches in a test series than anyone save the

wicket-keeper is always concentrating at slip, though he likes to exchange pleasantries between balls.

In a sense Barlow has always been the "Angry Young Man" of South African cricket and has always seemed to have nurtured the ambition to do something one day to change South Africa's image as "good losers".

A.C.Parker
September 1971

would pour out its wares, only to see it move on. It was becoming most frustrating.

"You'll have to bowl for the rest of the afternoon", Peter van der Merwe told me after tea. "It's the only way we'll save the match". I wasted a bit of time and was consequently booed on the odd occasion. But I didn't feel all that bad about it for in the previous seven tests, it was England who had played the negative role, not us.

With 91 to get in 70 minutes, Fate took over. It appeared to me that the rain-bearing clouds had left us but, no, along came a lone little, black cloud. It was all on its own but it decided to sit right above the Kennington Oval and to pour onto the ground every bit of the moisture it was carrying. What a relief!

The series was won and Peter van der Merwe, Eddie Barlow and Jack Plimsoll had achieved all they had set out to do. It was a great tour, one that saw team spirit and cameraderie rule supreme. If anything, it proved to the Springboks that they were in fact an invincible bunch and that the world was theirs provided they had the courage and the confidence to take it.

Several individuals made themselves household names during those three months. Five of us became regular members of the annual World XI series sponsored by Rothmans International but to me the real strength of South African cricket, emerging clearly for the first time, was the depth, the tremendous all-round talent and the fact that no game was over against South Africa until the final ball had been bowled.

Everybody played their role for, as I have mentioned, it was a stumping by Denis Lindsay and two run-outs by Colin Bland which virtually turned the tide. In cricket it is often these little things that count and South African cricket was becoming a giant because there were eleven men around to back up and give support to the one or two who might just be enjoying the limelight at that particular stage. Cricket is a team game and our success in England in 1965 was due to team effort.

When a critic of the calibre of Richie Benaud, suggests that only the 1960-61 clash between the West Indies and Australia produced more thrills and entertainment than the series between Peter van der Merwe's Springboks and the Aussies led by Bobby Simpson during the southern hemisphere summer of 1966-67, then I find myself inspired to relate my thoughts on a five-match contest that virtually had everything that is best in cricket.

It was an historic series, culminating as it did in South Africa's first ever triumph over Australia but just how often the Springboks, like true champions, had to pick themselves off the canvas to fight back against seemingly impossible odds, makes it a series that often reads like fiction.

It was a hard fight, with no holds barred and with plenty of gripes about the South African umpires. In essence some of these complaints were justified, certainly in my opinion, but they should not be allowed to cloud the issue or to tarnish the Springbok achievement. Maybe it could be argued that in a series as tight as this one a vital decision, made the wrong way, could make the difference between winning and losing. Cricket, intriguing game that it is, has produced so many thrillers born out of apparently hopeless situations that I wouldn't dare to contest the validity of such arguments. But — and I know that this is almost a truly unanimous opinion — the Springboks under Peter van der Merwe fully earned their 3-1 success.

It was a summer that saw Denis Lindsay emerge as South Africa's golden boy. Time and again he came to the rescue but it was the aggressive manner in which he turned the tide, as much as the statistical significance of his efforts, which really captured the imagination of the South African cricketing public. It wasn't a one-man effort, for in cricket it just can't be this way, but when all was said and done, Denis did present the one major difference between the two sides. It was his ability to inspire the bottom half of the batting to match-winning accomplishments. On several occasions he did this hand in hand with his skipper, Peter van der Merwe, a cricketer who is by no means over-blessed with technical attributes but who more than made up for any deficiencies with sheer guts and determination.

The daggers were out long before the tour got under way. First thrust came from Bobby Simpson in the form of a comparison. Dave Renneberg, his new fast bowling mate for Garth McKenzie was, in his estimation, "much quicker than Peter Pollock". This was psychological warfare and, needless to say, I swallowed the bait hook, line and sinker.

"What utter rubbish", was the quote I gave one of the Sunday newspapers and I followed it with the obvious "I'll show them". As things turned out, I didn't really prove my point for it was to prove a most agonising and frustrating series for me.

But it was great to get the adrenalin pumping even before the Aussies arrived. Interest was at fever pitch, so much so that the sports-writers dedicated daily columns to the Aussies at the nets. If you took their writings seriously you couldn't have been blamed for thinking that we were up against a team of world beaters. In South Africa we do have a tendency to boost opposition teams in our media whereas overseas, visitors get absolutely nothing.

What really fired enthusiasm for the series was the tremendous triumph of the Transvaal team in beating the tourists at the Wanderers early on in the tour. Australian teams enjoyed something of an invincible tag but thanks to Ali Bacher and his side's exciting 76-run victory, the Springboks did not have to overcome any psychological hurdle they might have had. As we agreed at our team meeting before the crucial first test, "if Transvaal could beat them, why can't the Springboks". The Transvaal triumph was thanks largely to a magnificent 235 from Ali Bacher and a century by Tiger Lance, two men who were going to play big parts in the series.

And so to the Wanderers, to a packed stadium, for the first Test. "Have you heard the latest Van der Merwe joke?" asked Dougie Laws on Springbok Radio during the breakfast session on the second morning of that Test. "No", replied his co-announcer. "We'll bat, Bobby", came the punchline from Duggie as he burst into laughter. The test had taken on such a wide interest that it even made the Springbok Radio "funnies" and poor Peter van der Merwe was in the hot seat. The morning papers were full of criticism. What had tempted him into batting first on a pitch which was obviously full of life. It had been raining quite consistently on the Rand and we in the Springbok camp felt that perhaps it was a good toss to lose. Rather let Simpson make a decision. But it fell to Van der Merwe and he took the brave line. It wan't his fault that we batted so ineptly, so badly in fact that at one stage the scoreboard read 41 for five wickets.

Garth McKenzie, who was to emerge as the bowler of the series, had a lovely time, working for some of his wickets but being virtually presented with others. Forty-one for five is dire trouble but just as Garth McKenzie that morning gave warning of what lay ahead in the series so too did Denis "Sporty" Lindsay.

Helped by Tiger Lance, these two set about putting some sanity in the proceedings and their partnership of 110 couldn't have come at a more valuable stage. Lindsay was not scared to hit the loose balls and bouncers were always regarded by him as potential sixes. Lance was more circumspect but once this partnership was broken, the innings finished as it has started, in a flurry of dismissals. All our for 199 and with the Aussies 99 without loss and Simpson and Lawry well in command, the first day had proven an absolute nightmare. That evening as we sat in our changing-room, sipping coke and beer, we were about as sombre as a graveyard at midnight. We had nobody to blame but ourselves.

But if the first day had belonged entirely to the Australians there was some consolation for the Springboks on the second, though it didn't seem that way for the first two hours.

By lunch the Aussies were three runs behind our meagre first innings total and still had nine wickets in hand. Thanks to the irrepressible Eddie Barlow, who on his deathbed would probably be confidently considering reincarnation, and the systematic Trevor Goddard, what looked like becoming a mammoth Australian first innings lead was eventually trimmed off at a mere 126 runs. And joining in the action was Lindsay, who with those "sticky" gloves of his latched on to a magnificent six catches. Denis had a hand in all of Eddie Barlow's dismissals as "Bunter" rocketed in with three wickets in a mere 21 balls. Barlow's ability to turn a match with an inspired spell, first experienced at Adelaide way back in 1964, had now become part of his armoury as an all-rounder. Eddie seemed to be able to turn on the screws whenever the situation was desperate. In fact, it was suggested that the more confident the batsmen, the more likely Barlow was to strike. So often was Eddie carted through the covers a couple of times only to have the last laugh a few balls later.

The Springboks gather round to congratulate Peter Pollock on his 100th test wicket during the fifth test against the Australians in 1967

"He lulls you into a false sense of security because he is not really regarded as a front-line bowler" was the way one of the Aussies described Eddie. Whatever the secret, there was no doubting Eddie's ability to be quite lethal. And so, with twelve minutes remaining on that second day and the Springboks back with an even chance, Barlow and Goddard saw us through to fight another day. It was almost symbolic that these two should have been at the crease, parrying off the venom of McKenzie and Renneberg that evening. The beers and cokes tasted just that little bit sweeter in the changing-room, and what was a morgue had turned into a haven for tired sportsmen!

The next ten hours were as nailbitingly tense as any I have ever known. The tension at times was unbearable. In the changing-room cigarettes were being smoked by the dozen; silly little superstitions like retaining your seat for fear of causing a wicket to fall were being observed and each time the capacity crowd of some 30 000 roared, our hearts dropped into our boots.

The Springbok gladiators were fighting like men possessed. Barlow, though battling with his form, scratched around with the determination of a fowl trying to locate a mealie. He contributed a half-century. Ali Bacher was working the leg-side with such application that it was a sheer tragedy when he was run-out for 63 — a decision which sparked the wrath of the crowd. Certainly, we and 30 000 others, felt that he had made his ground. Umpire Baxter disagreed and he had the final say. Graeme Pollock then played what I still regard as one of his finest innings. His first scoring stroke was a soaring six off a Tom Viviers long-hop and the elegant left-hander smashed his way to 90 in a mere 114 minutes.

His attitude was hardly that of the underdog battling to save a match. His was the role of aggressor from the word go and gradually the contest was moving into the Springbok's favour. But at 349 for six and Peter van der Merwe joining Denis Lindsay were were still by no means in the driver's seat. We all felt that to be in with a chance on a pitch which was becoming easier and easier, a target in excess of 350 runs had to be set for Simpson's lads.

Lindsay and Van der Merwe were to put together a seventh wicket partnership of 221 runs, made in only 166 minutes. However, controversy was to

It's pure reflex action as Ali Bacher brilliantly catches Bob Cowper during the 1967 tour

raise its ugly head. The Springbok skipper is not a good starter and he seemed ill at ease. He sparred at a ball from Renneberg outside the off-stump and the Aussies let rip with a most confident and vociferous appeal.

The crowd waited in silence for the umpire's decision. He didn't move nor did his finger. What a relief! But Simpson was furious, so were some of the others. They strutted around in anger, shaking their heads in an exhibition that did the game no good whatsoever. Maybe they had reason for their disappointment, but what about Ali Bacher's run-out?

There was no doubt that Van der Merwe edged the very next ball from Renneberg. It went straight to Simpson in the slips but he grassed it. And in the next over, Van der Merwe was dropped again. The Aussies had thus been presented with two chances of correcting any umpiring mistake but they had fluffed them both.

Denis Lindsay's innings of 182 was positively brilliant. It deserved the accolades usually reserved for Graeme Pollock. He drove and hooked with power and interposed his display of aggression with a few delicate late cuts. He wasn't afraid to attack, even to the extent of moving down the pitch to the new ball and hitting Renneberg back over his head for a six. And keeping a cool head, while pushing for singles at the other end, was Van der Merwe. His role was as important to the overall Springbok cause as Lindsay's and though not as memorable in style and power, it was nevertheless as commendable for its sheer concentration. By the time these two had finished, the game had turned the Springboks' way, leaving a target of 495 for an Australian victory. Conversely, the Springboks had eight hours in which to bowl the opposition out. When the final day dawned, Australia had already knocked off 97 of the runs with Bill Lawry back in the pavilion.

Trevor Leslie Goddard was the colossus on that historic last day, so much so that the game finished some hour and a half before the scheduled close and the crowds ran onto the field to carry him shoulder-high back to the pavilion. Trevor's control of line, swing and length was immaculate as his figures 32,5-14-53-6 suggest and so did he bog down the Aussies that they only managed a further 164 runs to their overnight total, making the Springboks the victors by 233 runs.

The Aussies played and missed with such regularity that Trevor might have been excused for thinking that it wasn't his lucky day. Ian Chappell and Tom Veivers and then Garth McKenzie, with a last gasp effort, showed some resolution but nobody was at ease against Goddard. Fielding in my position I couldn't quite appreciate why there was so little contact with the ball.

I asked Denis Lindsay. He just smiled "Trevor's swinging them in circles. I would rather keep to than bat against bowling like this".

It had been an outstanding fightback but despite all the celebrating and fun that goes with victory there was sorrow in my heart, for Colin Bland who in chasing a ball, had crashed into the fence and had injured his suspect knee. He wasn't going to be available for the next test but the chances were that this injury could put him out of test cricket for ever. Sadly, this was to be the truth.

Newlands had never been particularly kind to me or to Springbok teams and from the moment Bobby Simpson called right and chose first use of the rather grassless batting strip, the Aussies assumed the initiative.

"Simmo" compiled 153 in as good a fashion as you could wish to see; Redpath (54), Cowper (36) and Chappell (49) helped along and then finally Keith Stackpole, with 134 well-smote runs carried the final tally to an impressive 542.

In the Springbok dressing room the scene was very much like that of a Red Cross station during the war. The walking wounded were Richard Dumbrill, Graeme Pollock and I, and out in the middle there were three substitutes. Well, if we were invalids in real terms, the Springbok batsmen soon became invalids in the figurative sense thanks to an inspired spell by big, burly Garth McKenzie.

He was extracting life from the pitch that none of the Springbok bowlers could manage and obviously one-and-a-half days in the field had not helped to prepare Barlow, Goddard and company for the fight ahead. But Graeme Pollock was all right. In fact for six hours prior to batting he had been off the field and as such was fresh and eager to get amongst the runs. This caused some controversy. The Aussies felt, and probably with some justification, that this was "not cricket", but there was nothing they could do to prevent him batting.

Graeme really turned on the charm on that third day. There was the usual superb timing and magnificent strokeplay in an innings which was to be worth 209 runs.

Simpson decided to enforce the follow-on which suited us down to the ground. Dumbrill and I were injured; Denis Lindsay had stitches in his head after being hit by a bouncer, Graeme Pollock now had a septic toe on top of his injured muscle and the Newlands wicket could only deteriorate. And the Aussies must have been just that little bit weary. But all is well that ends well and when, with six wickets and 25 minutes to spare they clinched the test two days later, Simpson's decision was justified.

The third test saw a few changes in the Springbok line-up, notably the inclusion of two new bowlers, Mike Procter, the blond speedster who was going to make such a devastating difference to the series, and Pat Trimborn, his fellow Natalian whose seam bowling proved to be an excellent foil. The Kingsmead pitch looked a little

Bobby Simpson, the 1967 Australian captain plays quietly while facing the young Mike Procter

Australian Ian Chappell who toured South Africa in 1967 and 1970

green when Peter van der Merwe lost the toss and the Springboks couldn't have been surprised when "Simmo" asked them to bat first.

Simpson's gamble so nearly paid off. The very first ball of the day saw Eddie Barlow hit a simple return catch to McKenzie, which the big Australian grabbed with utter glee. A very dejected Barlow made his way to the pavilion for, although he was having a good trot with his bowling, his batting had been desperately poor.

"Don't worry Ed", I said "even Bradman made ducks".

"Who the hell wants to emulate Bradman", came his short, sharp retort.

Despite a gritty 47 by Bacher, we were battling the odds against inspired bowling on a helpful pitch and with six wickets down for 94, Bobby Simpson was smiling. Then — yes you've guessed it — Peter van der Merwe joined Denis Lindsay. It was more or less a carbon copy of their previous rescue acts — Lindsay the plunderer, Van der Merwe the custodian. It was becoming downright uncanny and just as amazing was how each time at the start of the partnership the Aussies would help with a fielding lapse or two.

Lindsay and his skipper added 103 but the real fireworks came when he was joined by David Pithey. Pithey was happy to play the prop-up role and of the 89 runs they added he made only a paltry 15. But I doubt whether David has ever made 15 more important runs. Lindsay's confidence by now was bordering on the outrageous. He didn't give a damn for anyone, not even Garth McKenzie as he swished his mighty willow. It was just a continuous mixture of fours and sixes — quite delightful for us but most frustrating for Simpson.

Mike Procter had a lovely debut with the ball, his first scalp being that of the prized Simpson. He added two more and Barlow did his usual trick of a couple of "scorchers" in the middle of the innings, this time claiming Stackpole and Lawry in quick succession. No Aussie reached the half-century mark and they were all out for 147. My meagre contribution was hitting Bill Lawry on the head with a bumper and forcing him off to hospital. He returned later with a heavily bandaged head and made a valuable 44, the top score.

The follow-on was enforced and this time the Australians really looked like making an issue of the outcome. Lawry and Simpson put on 94 for the first wicket and Redpath, Cowper and

MIKE PROCTER

"That can't be me" exclaimed the somewhat shocked hero. "Surely I don't look as different as all that?" An inquisitive patron in the next row turned his head, satisfied his curiosity and then whispered in his chum's ear. Yes, indeed, there was Mike Procter, flanked by other Springbok team-mates, sitting in the stalls of a Johannesburg cinema on the eve of the fourth test between South Africa and Bobby Simpson's Australians in 1967.

Procter's surprise was perhaps understandable, as he gazed almost hypnotically at the flimlet of the prvious test at Kingsmead, where he had made such a notable international debut. This was the first time he had seen himself in bowling action on celluloid and obviously he did not realise that his delivery was that non-conformist.

"I thought I looked pretty much the same as everyone else" — a comment which drew some amusement. "You're a freak, mate," he was informed, "but a pretty effective one at that" came the re-assurance.

But, unorthodox or not, it is a sight of some athletic grandeur as Michael John Procter, unruly thatch of blond hair bobbing at each stride, pursues his fiery errand as a spearhead fast bowler. A thrilling spectacle is that long run, starting at the sight-screen on some of the smaller grounds; that initial canter which breaks into a full-blooded gallop and that catapulting, arm-flurrying crescendo as every erg of thrust and timing is wrenched from his sturdy young frame. It is a sequence of unrestrained energy and power which cannot but delight all, save the poor, padded, flannelled fool some 22 yards away.

Perhaps the connoisseurs, the compilers of coaching manuals and the technical purists might find him guilty of misrepresenting basic bowling principles, but few can deny that fast bowling the Procter way is both ruggedly attractive and brutally efficient, the latter always being the major criterion.

Incidentally, the "wrong-foot" label is not quite accurate, though admittedly at first sight it does appear so. A slow motion film will prove that it is an optical illusion. Procter lets the ball go just before his left foot hits the ground, unlike the orthodox fast bowlers who pivot on the left foot in the delivery, thereby bowling against a straight left leg and with a braced left side. This is the reason why most fast bowlers dig a great big pit at the bowling crease. However, with Procter there is practically no impression left on the ground by his front foot. But, despite this, Procter does get a lot of body into his action, though admittedly it requires a higher degree of fitness for that long run.

It would be fair to say that he does subject himself to hard labour and for this reason the pundits don't feel that he will last as long as fast bowlers with orthodox actions. When, in 1968, he broke

Stackpole all weighed in with notable efforts to have the total standing at 266 for three at one stage. But two quick wickets to me, for a change, and a Procter tailend clean-up altered the whole complexion of the fight-back.

I found it most refreshing to have an opening partner like Mike Procter. He was young and fiery and it helped motivate me at the other end. Despite my bruised heel I managed to regain some of my lost fire in this particular test and I can give most of the credit to Procter's influence at the other end. Perhaps I was just not prepared to be over-shadowed by this promising young colt and the team as a whole obviously benefited.

What a remarkable series it had been to date. Three matches and three decisions and South Africa 2-1 up after countless cliff-hanging situations which could hardly have been rivalled in a novel.

The fourth Test at the Wanderers was a disappointment, not because of the standard of play, but because of the intervention of rain and the fact that it was inconclusive. Australia needed 189 to avoid an innings defeat when rain washed out the match.

The series should have been all over by the fourth test but it was perhaps a blessing that it wasn't for it gave the final encounter some meaning. I am also led to believe that it helped to prevent complete chaos in the Australian camp. I heard a lot of rumbles but unfortunately mostly from the players who had not done particularly well and whose moans one tends to take with the proverbial pinch of salt.

I had come to regard Bobby Simpson as a thorough gentleman. While he might have been a little aloof with his team-mates we Springboks couldn't find fault with him and we respected him highly as a cricketer. Even his dissatisfaction with the umpiring standard was handled with a certain degree of decorum.

The Port Elizabeth test, though interesting throughout, was probably as inevitable in its final result as the previous contest at the Wanderers. Clearly the Australian batting was not up to the demands required to deal with our non-stop attack. The Springboks knocked off the required 179 runs with seven wickets to spare. Tiger Lance finished the series with a mighty six and by so doing typified the ascendancy the Springboks held in the final three outings.

The final match was a tremendous occasion for the brothers Pollock, who celebrated their "hometown" finale with a century and a milestone.

down with a knee injury, the "I told you so's" were heard from every quarter. Others reckoned his back would give.

But Mike is still going strong, improving with every season and it is clear that whatever idiosyncrasies his bowling action might have, he can compensate with sheer physical strength and durability. Furthermore, as Mike argues: "This action just came naturally". Surely, the natural action is the easiest action and as such is the action which places the least strain on the individual. Mike feels it would be hard work bowling the orthodox way, and that's as good an answer as any!

The South African all-rounder took his own giant strides into the realms of batting greatness in the South African summer of 1970/71 when he wrote his name alongside that of C.B.Fry and Sir Donald Bradman by scoring six successive first-class centuries.

Almost as if to prove to his schoolboy rival and close friend, Barry Richards that Bradman's legendary feats were also within his grasp, Procter's sixth record-equalling century — a double at that — came shortly after Richards, playing for South australia in the Sheffield Shield, had surpassed Sir Don's record aggregate for a season with the Adelaide-based State.

It is no secret that Mike has always regarded himself as a better batsman than fast bowler, but such has been his success with the new ball at all levels that it required something extra special to validify this personal preference in the eyes of his multitude of admirers.

With his pace bowling still brimful of fire and venom, there is little doubt that Procter will eventually be recognised as perhaps the greatest all-rounder this country has produced. He is already being tagged as the "white Gary Sobers", praise sufficient.

Certainly his effort in reeling off six consecutive centuries was an achievement of the highest merit even though some pundits pointed out that five of his knocks were against lowly B section opposition. But he silenced these critics and convinced all that his batting has now blossomed to full potential when he pounded his majestic way to a brilliant 254 against Currie Cup runners-up, Western Province, in that historic sixth innings.

Spellbound, the Western Province bowlers could do nothing, save acknowledge that more than a hint of genius lay behind those broad shoulders and even broader willow.

Every year an award is made in England to a county player who is voted by all the other teams as the "players' player". This is a popularity award. And despite the fact that in 1969, Mike Procter bounced, bruised and bowled out over 100 victims, he was the unanimous choice. To be succesful and popular is an achievement worth more than all the runs, wickets and catches in the world. South Africa can be justly proud of this sportsman, who typifies every meaning of the word.

Peter Pollock
September 1971

Bill Lawry bowled by Mike Procter without playing a shot.

Another wicket for Peter Pollock in 1970

Graeme whose birthday fell during the test, took his aggregate for the series to an impressive 537 with innings of 105 and 33 not out while I became the fourth Springbok bowler in history to reach 100 test wickets.

If one looks at the bare results it would suggest that the Australian team was below par. Yet everything suffers by comparison. Maybe it was just that the Springboks were a great side.

Anyway, from every aspect it was a tour to remember and it gave tremendous pleasure to both spectators and players. In fact it must rate as one of the finest cricket tours to South Africa.

There was the peerless batting of Graeme Pollock, Denis Lindsay's fantastic wicketkeeping and batting, the fine bowling of Goddard, McKenzie and Procter, the tactical skill of Peter van der Merwe and the teamwork of his side. The type of cricket played gave enjoyment all round and this reflects on the general approach and attitude of both sides.

After the 1960-61 tour of Australia by the West Indies, it was the losers, Frank Worrell and company, who got all the bouquets. This time, maybe, the bouquets should have stayed in South Africa as they did but it must not be forgotten that it always takes two teams to tango in the quest of bright, attacking cricket.

Yes, I will always agree with Richie Benaud; it was a series to remember.

Those South Africans, who had perhaps been a little over-enthusiastic in celebrating New Year's Day 1970, were probably still recovering from their hang-overs when Bill Lawry's Australians, having finished three months of campaigning in India, arrived at Johannesburg's Jan Smuts Airport.

The angular-featured Lawry was full of confidence, claiming a better balanced attack than Simpson's side and certainly a better set of fielders. And, the gem of all gems was his observation: "In my opinion Ian Chappell is equal to any batsman in the world on all types of wickets".

How could he have suggested that anyone other than Barry Richards and Graeme Pollock ruled the batting world? Anyway, two-and-a-half months later it was the Australians who were suffering from king-size hang-overs after having been thrashed so conclusively that even their few valid excuses sounded hollow.

For Ali Bacher's Springboks each victory was easier than the previous one and by the end the Australians were so demoralised and dispirited that they had less fight in them than a wet chamois. It had been three years since the Springboks had seen test action while the Aussies had twelve months earlier put the skids under the West Indies, not to mention their notable triumph of 3-1 against the Indians on their way to South Africa. It is never easy to beat the Indians on their home grounds yet Lawry's side had come through pretty convincingly, and they had reason for the confidence they showed on arrival at Jan Smuts airport.

Personally, I had never visualised Bill Lawry as a skipper, perhaps because his cricket seemed to me so dour and negative. And as a personality he always appeared rather withdrawn. Yet, until the 1970 shambles against us, his captaincy record was pretty impressive, having won nine out of 16 encounters with only three defeats.

We were also told that his batting had blossomed, in that he was prepared to put bat to ball, rather than merely allowing the ball to hit the bat or to glide off it. Well, no changes were forthcoming and as a leader he revealed his own emotions too often to the detriment of his team's image. In fact, the series finished off on a sour note when he refused to appear alongside Ali Bacher to make the traditional after-test address to the public. He also refused a sincere gesture made by one of the umpires, Mr Charl Coetzee. He preferred to sulk.

Quite frankly, his team had taken

Ali Bacher, Springbok captain in 1970

There's a strong unity among fast bowlers. Here Mike Procter is hugged by speed-twin, Peter Pollock.

Lee Irvine in action during his test century against the 1970 Australians

such a trouncing it should have been easy for him to merely shrug his shoulders and to laugh it off with a "better-team-won" type of remark. I have always found it that much harder to accept a defeat in a tight, close encounter than when I had been obviously outclassed. But be that as it may, let's put the horse before the cart and get back to the start of a series which was memorable only if you were a South African!

Newlands had always been something of a "hoodoo" ground to Springbok teams. Its scenic beauty belies its hate of the green and gold and its total disregard for the feelings of fast bowlers, or so it has always seemed. Six times the Australians had been to Newlands for tests and six times they had triumphed. The Springboks had not won at Newlands for some 60 years and personally, what with Currie Cup experiences thrown in, I was quite used to the idea of leaving the ground at the conclusion of any with my tail firmly between my legs.

Vital to any cause at Newlands is the winning of the toss, hence Ali's tremendous grin as he strutted back to the pavilion. Lawry tried hard to hide his disappointment but that is not easy for at the best of times his is a face that does not convey happiness.

The first day was a grind but at Newlands this grind always pays its dividends and the Aussies helped with a few missed catches. There was quite a lot of pad play, especially to Johnny Gleeson whom we all found rather difficult to read. Gleeson's "flick-finger" action shot out leg-breaks and off-spinners with what looked pretty much like the same action. Australian wicket-keeper Brian Taber reckoned he could "read" Gleeson but if he could, he certainly fooled us. He missed several stumping chances in the series by going the wrong way to Johnny.

Barry Richards also claimed he could detect the difference but even he couldn't claim a 100 per cent record. We mere mortals decided that the best solution was for right-handers to play him as a leg-break bowler and the left-handers vice versa. This meant that the "wrong-un" merely beat the bat into the pads and hence the over-abundance of pad play and the many appeals.

One could detect, almost from the start, that Lawry's men were looking to harrass the umpires and the head-shaking started from the very first day, followed by screeds of moaning from some of the touring pressmen.

I'll be the first to admit that the umpiring standard in South Africa, both in this series and the one against Simpson's side, was not of the best and that there were quite a few dubious decisions. Furthermore, in the final balance, the Springboks probably had a better share of the luck when it came to bad decisions. But that these mistakes could have altered the course of the series is rather ridiculous wishful thinking. To allow yourselves to become frustrated over bad umpiring only affects your own concentration and application and it was sad to see that Lawry, instead of setting an example in how to accept bad decisions gracefully, was a major instigator in displaying disgust. To put it quite bluntly, the Aussies were busy demoralising themselves from the start.

At the end of the first day, the Springboks were 254 for four off 109 overs and thanks to a six-hour century by Eddie Barlow (127, including a six and eleven fours) by ten to three on the second afternoon the home side was all out for 382. This was by no means a mammoth total by Newlands standards but it was nevertheless useful and most had contributed in one way or another.

But at three o' clock that Friday, January 22, a most momentous two hours of cricket began that was virtually to set the seal on the remainder of the series. Bill Lawry, until then undefeated in three weeks of batting on the tour, and Keith Stackpole strode to the

Barry Richards scored 508 in the four-match test series in 1970, including two centuries

crease to a capacity crowd and Mike Procter started the attack downhill and down-wind. Ali Bacher had said to me "you take a few overs up-hill, then I'll whip you off and you can follow Mike down-wind when he has finished his spell".

Yes, Ali had everything planned. But it worked out just a little differently.

The second ball of my second over pitched just outside the leg-stump to the left-hander. It obviously hit the seam and "tracked" back but the Aussie captain had shuffled into his wicket, almost preparing for a leg-glance, and he left his leg-stump unguarded. The ball just clipped the top of the leg-stump sending the bail flying over wicket-keeper Dennis Gamsy's head. I couldn't believe my luck as the crowd roared its approval and all the Springboks came rushing around to congratulate me.

But that was not all. Four balls later, Ian Chappell, Bill Lawry's "best batsman in the world", was also back in the hut. He had attempted to pull a bouncer, did not quite latch on to it and the ball flew at a height of about seven feet in the direction of Lee Irvine at leg-gully. Lee responded in cat-like fashion hurling himself into the sky and managing to push the ball into the air with his palm for Grahame Chevalier to move in from leg-slip to make the catch with arms fully extended. Sheer chaos broke loose. We must have looked like a bunch of soccer players hugging and congratulating each other as I took my jersey and moved to mid-on for the beginning of Mike Procter's next over, the crowd rose as one in applause which must have lasted a full minute.

BARRY RICHARDS

On January 20, 1963, a very bold headline in the Johannesburg *Sunday Times* stated: Compton: "Send Richards to Australia." — a reference to a 17-year-old Durban High School boy cricketer.

Few people had even heard of this cricketing prodigy; even fewer agreed with Denis Compton's views — certainly not the South African selection committee. So the fair-haired Richards did not go to Australia later that year with Trevor Goddard's Springboks. Nor, in the intervening years, has he made his debut in Test cricket.

Yet Richards, now 23 — a connoisseur's delight at the wicket — has in five vintage cricket years, risen to become one of the truly outstanding batsmen in world cricket.

He could, if he so desired, also become a formidable all-rounder as a batsman-offspinner.

The first-mentioned assessment will not really surprise the many, many famous cricketers of yesteryear and others with long experience in the game, for they recognised the skill and taste in his batting when he was still a fledgeling. Compton, as I recall, was the first overseas man to really enthuse about Richards.

He said at the time: "I've seen Richards play. I've also bowled to him for a full hour in the nets. Therefore, I think I can judge his potential. I wouldn't hesitate to include him for the trip to Australia.

"I like his batting technique. He always seems perfectly balanced when playing a stroke and at the moment of impact with the ball.

"Now I always pay particular attention to balance at that instance of the stroke. I was supposed to have been a somewhat unorthodox batsman, but I still maintain that I must have been perfectly balanced at the moment of contact on so many occasions, otherwise I could never have scored half the runs I did in first class cricket.

(The Ex-England man scored more than 38 500 runs in all first class cricket).

"I feel confident that Richards' technique is so good at this early stage of his career that he would do extremely well in any grade of cricket in England where the ball moves about quite a lot. And any batsman who can make runs in England should do well on more favourable run-getting wickets.

"Yes, I honestly think Richards has the talent to become a really great player and there seems no point in delaying his entry into the top grade of cricket."

Within six months many other former famous players were agreeing with Compton's assessment of Richards' ability and potential.

This, then, is the young man who, at the age of eight, used to take cricket books by such immortals as Sir Donald Bradman and Sir Leonard Hutton and practise the strokes illustrated in the family garage.

Nobody watching him play a long innings in modern com-

Two hours later, at five o'clock the Aussies were in a sorry state. Mike Procter, a blond-haired fury operating at full thrust, had joined in the party and the Australians were five wickets down for 58 runs. By close they had improved to 108 for six, thanks to a plucky Doug Walters — but what a tumultuous day it had been for the Springboks!

Next day their innings folded up at 164 and Bacher, very wisely, decided not to enforce the follow-on. There were those who criticised him for not driving home the nail there and then but there was so much time available and I am sure that in the back of his mind, Ali had this dreadful fear about Newlands.

Having won the toss he was not going to give away the advantage of having his opponents bat last on a wearing pitch. That third day and the fourth, while the Springbok batsmen piled on the pressure, was not all that spectacular to watch but it certainly contained much incident, mainly on the umpiring issue. Time and again the Aussies showed their disgust at decisions made by umpire Wade and a sour note was introduced into the proceedings.

Australia were finally set the enormous task of scoring 451 runs in ten-and-a-half hours for victory. Lawry and Stackpole were clearly not overawed by the task and they had obviously written their first innings off as just one of the inexplicable nightmares. They set about the bowling almost in Sunday-afternoon-picnic fashion and were particularly harsh on Mike Procter.

But, just as in the first innings, the match was to change in a mere quarter of an hour, this time just after tea when Mike Procter came back into the attack. This time he concentrated on line and length rather than speed and the consequences were too beautiful to behold. Suddenly it was 136 for four and the rest of the match proved to be a mere formality, finishing just after lunch on the fifth day.

Ten of the twenty Australian wickets that fell went to the Procter-Pollock combination and as such a Newlands "hoodoo" had been broken in two respects — victory for South Africa and with fast bowlers rampant.

So it was off to Kingsmead and a test that will ever linger in the memories of those fortunate enought to have witnessed perhaps the finest day of batting, test cricket has ever produced. All else in this test, including a Springbok triumph by an innings and 129 runs, Eddie Barlow's three wickets in nine balls and records galore, paled into in-

---

pany would imagine that as a very young sport enthusiast he had a weak ankle structure, which eventually he overcame through swimming. This, however, has left a mark because he is somewhat flat-footed, though it doesn't appear to affect his footwork at the crease. He is extremely quick.

Already he has many achievements of batsmanship to his credit and he is probably the first player to score 2 000 runs in his first season of English County play.

What makes him such a very great player? I think I would put it down mainly to his being an instinctive batsman — a brilliant stroke-player with a wide variety of shots which he is not afraid of playing at any stage of his innings, be it at the start or when in the nineties.

In fact, it is quite thrilling to watch him hook or go on the drive — if the length and direction of the ball invites such response — almost as soon as he reaches the wicket to start an innings. He seems to see the ball earlier than the majority of batsmen and he is so technically sound.

Like Graeme Pollock, he is a "natural" batsman. By that I mean he does not really have to work at the game and though, also like Pollock, he is a trifle lazy over training matters, he is tremendously good for team spirit.

Richards is also a keen student of the game and is a most enlightening person to talk with at the end of a day's play. A match which brings him into opposition with more experience, and famous players, doesn't worry him. Rather does he take a delight in studying his opponents.

I mentioned at the start of this article that he could become a most formidable all-rounder, for he has the potential to be a very successful offspinner. Possessing long fingers, with which he can impart considerable spin, and with a high action, he can get bounce into his deliveries, a type of delivery which worries the majority of batsmen. The trouble is that he doesn't really seem to enjoy bowling.

In addition, he is a good fielder in any position. He gets to the ball very quickly and not only is he a safe catcher, but also has a strong throwing arm.

Perhaps there is just one flaw in his cricket make-up. This concerns his running between the wickets. He gives the appearance of allowing his mind to wander and get out of the game when he is the non-striker, whereas he ought to be alert.

Just what the future holds for this accomplished cricketer is difficult to forecast in the context of recent decisions. But with two years of his present contract with Hampshire still to run, it is certain that the county in which cricket has so much tradition will enjoy the benefits of a batsman in full bloom. The Irishman "youthfully mature" appears to describe the present Richards which, of course, is no more or no less than was expected by those, like Denis Compton, who recognised his potential when he was still a schoolboy. For he is the type of player whom one could go on watching for hour after hour without ever getting bored.

Jackie McGlew
December 1968

Runs for Bill Lawry in the first test at Newlands in 1970. Denis Gamsy is the wicket-keeper

Doug Walters was the only Australian to score runs in the first innings of the first test at Newlands in 1970

significance when compared with the batting feats of South Africa's two blond batting giants, Robert Graeme Pollock and Barry Anderson Richards.

They ravaged the Australian attack with such precision and timing that even the Australians should have considered it a privilege to have been the victims. It wasn't that Bill Lawry and company bowled badly, fielded badly or lost heart. Gamely they stuck to their guns but when two geniuses like Pollock and Richards take control, there is absolutely nothing mere mortals like Garth McKenzie, Allan Connolly and Johnny Gleeson can do to stem the tide. The Australian attack received the biggest thrashing in the history of tests between the two countries and it was Barry Richards who started the ball rolling, or should I rather say, crashing into the Kingsmead pickets.

Bacher won the toss and out went Trevor Goddard and Richards to face Garth McKenzie. Usually there is a bit of life in a test wicket on the first morning so one would have expected a little careful play for at least the first 45 minutes. But, no, Richards was not interested. He was going to prove a point and at lunch he was a disappointed man, disappointed because he had failed by a mere six runs to notch his century in the two hours before lunch!

Eddie Barlow, a study in dejection after his first ball dismissal in the 1967 Durban test

By doing so he would have joined a very elite band of batsmen who have achieved this notable feat. The Springboks tried to make it possible and in fact, Ali Bacher got himself out trying to give Barry the strike in the over before lunch.

To give an indication of Richards' dominance, he and Goddard put on 88 for the opening partnership of which Trevor managed only 17 runs. At 126 for two, the final over before lunch, Graeme Pollock strode to the crease for a couple of balls. He survived. And so the stage was set.

An hour after lunch, twelfthman Ashley Mallett was ready at the player's entrance with the drinks and while he waited he watched Richards being clean bowled by Eric Freeman's slower ball. But what had happened in that 60 minutes, the Oxford Dictionary and all its superlatives could not do justice to. In that hour, Graeme Pollock and Barry Richards added an unbelievable 103 runs.

Never had South African test cricket enjoyed such utter domination. In simple terms, the formula was pretty basic. Pollock took the one crease, Richards the other and between them they peppered the pickets with an array of shots that were majestic in execution and brutal in effectiveness. I just couldn't believe my eyes and when Barry was eventually out, the poor shell-shocked Aussies stood at the wicket applauding him all the whole way back to the pavilion. Lawry waited until the Springbok had left the field before summoning the drinks, which was a fine gesture.

Next man in, Eddie Barlow, lasted a very short while but when he got back to the pavilion he remarked "It was like after the Lord Mayor's show. There is no room for me out there. Those two have made a mockery of batting". And indeed they had.

What a pity that there had not been any television cameras around to record those soaring sixty minutes. The rest of the innings belonged to Pollock and he proceeded, in the same classic vein, to chalk up one record after the other.

Ironically enough, this was Graeme Pollock's first century at Kingsmead, which had been a "hoodoo" ground for him over ten years of first-class cricket.

At 210, he reached his personal highest first-class score; at 233 he beat Dudley Nourse's record against Australia and an on-drive off Keith Stackpole which took him to 258 saw him past Jackie McGlew's all-time record of 255 for a Springbok batsman in tests. It seemed that he was just not going to stop and that for once and all he was going to allay his late father's fear that he couldn't really pile them on when a lazy, weary forward defensive prod, not quite to the pitch of the ball, presented Keith Stackpole with a simple return catch.

Graeme's 274 had been out of a total of 558 and he had also shared in a century partnership with Tiger Lance. The Springboks finally finished at 622 for nine wickets when Ali Bacher, mercifully, decided to declare.

Eddie Barlow is not the type to allow himself to be left out of the action and after having had to succumb in the limelight stakes to Richards and Pollock, he could hardly wait to make his own impact on the game. The Aussies had made a fair start to their innings and were 44 for no wickets. Ten balls later they were in dire trouble, for Eddie hatched, matched and despatched Lawry, Chappell and Walters and with Goddard dismissing Stackpole at the other end, 44 for none became 48 for four. It was then 79 for six, 114 for eight and finally all out for 157, with Paul Sheahan's 62 being by far the biggest contribution.

This time Bacher had no hestiation in enforcing the follow-on, what with two-and-a-half days' play remaining. It was all over late on the fourth afternoon, though Doug Walters, Ian Redpath and Keith Stackpole, each with seventies, had boosted the second innings total to a fair 336.

The third test at the Wanderers, though finally finishing with a 307-run Springbok victory, did have its more competitive moments, especially in the first two-and-a-half days when there was a certain amount of controversy over excessive bumpers from Mike Procter and I. The Wanderers pitch I have always found to be most helpful to fast bowlers — not that it aids in terms of movement off the pitch, but because of its bounce.

It gives quickies the opportunity of sorting out those players who are perhaps too inclined to play off the front foot and also those whose courage against the ball flying around their ears is not quite what it should be.

The Sunday papers made quite an issue of the bumpers because between Mike and I we did bowl more than our fair share in this match. But, once again, the explanation probably lies in

ROBERT GRAEME POLLOCK

Let us stick to the facts and not go overboard on Robert Graeme Pollock. Let us simply say that this blonde left-hander from Port Elizabeth is the most exciting, most devastating batsman in cricket today.

We are on safe ground there. Even the experts agree with us. We will also admit that the West Indies' great Garfield Sobers is a better all-round cricketer than Pollock but for sheer batting virtuosity the Springbok stands supreme.

What is it that makes Graeme Pollock's batting so much more memorable than the performances of his contemporaries — several of them no less successful when the cold figures are compared?

I think it is the spontaneity of his batting more than anything else which lifts Graeme Pollock head-and-shoulders above mediocrity. There is nothing fettered about his style. It is as if the bat becomes an extension of himself and the impulses of his brain guide it as naturally to the ball as it would guide his hand to scratch his head. There is never any constraint or awkwardness and even when he misses the ball altogether it is only when you see his rueful face through the binoculars that you realise that it was not after all a premeditated act of mercy on the bowler.

But that is not all. Without fallibility, there cannot be sustained excitement in a performance — and Graeme is always exciting. There is no mechanical perfection in his batting. He is a flesh and blood hero, subject to the same weaknesses we are all heir to and that is why there is so much buzzing excitement when he is in action. The spectators can identify themselves with him. They become part of him as he plays those glorious strokes but they are also constantly aware that the beautiful dream could end, suddenly and dramatically.

That is the essence of a Graeme Pollock innings — spontaneous, packed with power, grace and drama but also so human.

I went to see Graeme Pollock two days after his magnificent 209 against Bobby Simpson's Australians in the New Year Test at Newlands. I had to wait outside the dress-ingroom while he was receiving massage and treatment for the hamstring injury which troubled him throughout the match.

When it was over and he came out to talk to me his thigh looked as if the masseur had used sandpaper in the process. He was limping slightly as he led me to the players' dining room where we hoped to find some privacy for the interview. Graeme's older brother, Peter and David Pithey were fighting their last ditch stand against the Aussie bowlers but from where we sat we could not see the game at all. Peter was batting beautifully and I asked Graeme whether he would not like to watch his brother's innings.

"No," he smiled. "It is one of our little superstitions not to watch our team-mates bat."

"I'm not really superstitious," he added quickly, "but I haven't watched this morning and perhaps I'd better not take the chance now! It all started at Trent Bridge in

Graeme Pollock and Eddie Barlow relaxing after the first day's play in the first test against Bill Lawry's Australians. Barlow was not out overnight and went on to score his fifth test century

1965. Peter did not see me bat at all there and I scored 125 and 59. In the first test against the Aussies in Johannesburg he thought he would buck the superstition and watch me in the first innings. Well, I didn't make any runs and now all of them huddle in a corner of the dressingroom when I walk to the wicket."

Graeme Pollock is a well built young man whose lean 6 ft. 1 in. frame will probably one day have to carry considerably more weight than his present 185 lbs. At the age of 22, his features under the short, very blonde hair are very young and smooth. His eyes are blue and clear. I asked him if his sight is abnormally sharp.

"Not really," he answered. "My eyes were tested when I did my A.C.F. training and also before every overseas tour but my sight seems to be no better than normal."

To go out to bat in a test match is one of the loneliest tasks in sport and Graeme, whose temperament has been described as "ideal", is no stranger to the anxieties which gnaw at the international cricketer's insides as he waits his turn.

"It's grim, you know," he explains in his frank manner.

"I suppose I am a calm, complacent type though, and I do manage to control my feelings. Many people think that I take things easy and that I never have a care in the world — but don't you believe it. I have as many worries as anybody else and when I am waiting to walk out to the wicket I am pretty nervous. Usually I manage to bottle up my nervousness and just sit still but figuratively I am chewing my nails all the time.

"The moment the wicket falls and I know that the time has come, the nervousness passes. As I walk to the wicket I always try to look at the sun for a second to get my eyes accustomed to the sharp light. After that I pick out a subject about the 22 yards of a pitch's length away and then focus consciously on it for a few seconds.

"I prefer to play against fast stuff at the beginning of the innings. I'm perfectly happy against spinners because there are lots of runs to be picked off them but at the start of an innings I like the quickies.

"I've learnt not to worry about the state of the game. I can honestly say that it is all the same to me whether the score is 12 for two or 212 for two. Every test cricketer realises his responsibilities anyway and usually there is a word or two from our skipper as well to drive home the point. When I got my double century against the Aussies for example I was always conscious that the position was bad and I was trying to get as many runs as I could.

"It's a funny thing. As you face up everything seems to recede except the bowler pounding down on you. You don't hear a thing and you think of nothing else. Between overs and when I am not taking strike I often hear and enjoy the light banter between some of the fielders. Gamesmanship never worries me and I refuse to get annoyed or rattled. When you're angry you cannot survive in test cricket.

"To get a century in a test is a wonderful feeling. I cannot really describe it. When your score moves into the nineties, no matter how confident and in command you are, your nerves start tingling. But I am something of a fatalist in this respect and I will certainly never crawl into my shell only because I need a few more runs for another century."

That Graeme Pollock practices what he preaches is proved by the fact that he could easily have scored the fastest century of the season

Johnny Gleeson, the 'mystery bowler' who was never really collared by the Springboks in 1970

the fact that conditions at the Wanderers are certainly more conducive to this type of aggressive bowling than elsewhere in the country. And, maybe, we just wanted to enjoy ourselves!

The Springbok second innings, starting with a 77-run advantage, did at times threaten to become yet another run-spree. Barlow scored his second century of the series, Graeme Pollock added an 87 to his 52 in the first innings, Irvine made his second 70 of the game and finally we were all out for 408, leaving the Aussies with a most formidable challenge. Once again they failed miserably, especially when one considers that a last wicket stand of 52 between Brian Taber and Alan Connolly helped the total to limp up 178.

against Somerset during the Springbok tour of Britain in 1965. He had reached 94 in 68 minutes with three sixes and 15 fours when he tried to get his 100 with another six and was caught a yard from the boundary. If he had taken things easy at that stage he would certainly have won that prize for the fastest century of the season as the winning time eventually proved to be 102 minutes.

Graeme believes that a cricket ball is there to be hit. This attitude was drilled into him from the start by George Cox, the Sussex professional, who coached him at school.

Although Graeme gives Cox a great deal of credit for his development, his parents probably had as much, if not more, to do with his success. His father, Mr "Mac"Pollock (the editor of the *Eastern Province Herald*), was a provincial cricketer in his day and Graeme and his older brother Peter grew up in the right atmosphere. Their mother is as keen on the game and she often bowled to Peter and Graeme in backyard games — and even sometimes on the lounge carpet.

As a little boy, he admits, he did not have a very sporting attitude to cricket. He hated going out and his refusal to "walk" often meant the termination of the game and a summary dispatch to his room. His very earliest memories are of cricket and although he played rugby, hockey and tennis with fair success at school, cricket was the only game which really counted.

He played one of the first competititve matches of his career at the age of eight for the Grey Junior School under-11 team. And — wait for it — he scored 117 runs (seven sixes and 12 fours) and took 10 wickets for 25 runs! "You must remember it was on a concrete strip with short boundaries," he adds modestly.

Yes, as a schoolboy Graeme already served notice to test bowlers of the future. Playing against St. Aidans he once cracked 156 out of a total of 200 and it is in the cricket record books that he, on another occasion, hammered 111 out of a total of 120!

At the age of 16 Graeme was selected to play for Eastern Province and against Border in his first-ever provincial game he was run out for 54. He was 16 years and 355 days old when he notched his first provincial century, 102, against Transvaal B, thus becoming the youngest player in South African cricket history to score a hundred in first class cricket.

Twenty days after his 19th birthday Graeme scored 209 not out against Ron Roberts' Cavaliers to also become the youngest maker of a double century in South African history.

Still only 19, Graeme was playing test cricket against Australia and two months short of his 20th birthday, he scored his first test century — 122 magnificent runs which moved greats of the past like Don Bradman and Lindsay Hassett to pull out all stops in unqualified praise.

This was the innings which caused Australian writer and former first class cricketer Dick Whitington to write: " . . . it was this century of young Pollock's, in my opinion, that turned the whole trend of the series and possibly changed the whole character of South African batsmanship."

Prophetic words, because it is a fact that since that test, South African cricket has showed the aggressive self-confidence needed for victory in international sport.

In the fourth test just a few days later he hammered 18

Nearly 120 000 people had paid to watch this match but it finished on a rather sad note for the South African selectors had decided that Trevor Goddard, because he was not available for the planned 1970 tour of England — a tour that never took place — would be withdrawn from the final encounter at Port Elizabeth.

Trevor had been a very faithful and successful servant to South African cricket and I must admit that there were tears in the eyes of most of us in the changing-room when it was announced that he would not be playing. Everyone knew that it was his final series and his performances against Lawry's men had more that justified his retention for the fifth test.

I regarded it as a rather heartless move to omit him from being part, to the end, of what eventually turned out to be the most historic "grand-slam" triumph in South African cricketing history.

Trevor's only comment was: "I wouldn't be human if I did not say I was disappointed. But that's life". A typical remark from a typically warm and unassuming gentleman. As far as I am concerned it was no way to say thanks to a man who had been involved almost from the start in South Africa's rise to cricketing glory.

The final test followed the same sort of pattern as the rest — Bacher winning the toss, a first innings lead, piling on the pressure in the second and finally victory by an even bigger margin than at the Wanderers. This time 323 runs separated the two teams at the finish of a game which was totally free of controversy, except for Lawry's unwillingness to say a few words at its conclusion.

It was a great triumph for the three young cricketing musketeers, Mike Procter, Lee Irvine and Barry Richards. And these youngsters, whose promise was obvious in the mid 1960's, were now all three fully-fledged and brilliant test stars. Theirs would be the responsibility of forming Springbok cricket's new nucleus, or so we hoped. Little did we know than that the test match at Port Elizabeth was going to be the last and that Springbok cricket

---

fours and three sixes in his 175 which took him 283 minutes.

It is on record how some of Australia's most famous cricketers of all time rose in their seats to applaud this performance and in their forthright manner the Aussies hailed him then and there as one of the greatest batsmen of the century.

And how did Graeme, still only a teenager, react to all this praise?

"Did it give you a swollen head, Graeme?" I asked him.

"I should hope not!" he replied. "Cricket is a great leveller. The game itself cures you quickly enough of any tendencies to take yourself too seriously. I found out early in my career that in cricket you're a hero one day and the next day they're hollering for your head to roll!"

Not that he does not appreciate the many nice things said and written about him.

"I will always treasure the congratulations I have received from people like Sir Don Bradman, Denis Compton and Sir Len Hutton after various innings of mine," he confessed." Among other souvenirs I am keeping are three wickets and a bail as mementos from tests I have scored hundreds in."

There is not a bat among those souvenirs, you'll notice. The reason for this is that Graeme uses a bat he likes until it breaks and then he throws it away. (He uses a long handle weighing approximately 2 lbs 8 ounces and it carries his own autograph.)

Graeme also has his heroes and prominent among them are Neil Harvey, Ted Dexter and Gary Sobers. He refuses absolutely however to single out any particular bowler as the most difficult to handle.

"I treat every ball stricly on merit," he points out. "Any first class bowler can deliver one that can tumble your wicket and big reputations mean nothing to me on the field. When the ball leaves the bowler's hand I decide what I am going to do and the name and the fame of the bowler have nothing to do with my decision."

Individualism is part of his character and it did not surprise me much that, although he reads a lot about cricket, he does not follow the accepted dictums slavishly." I firmly believe that a cricketer should not cling too much to the basic techniques. Obviously you must respect the fundamentals but you should adapt them to suit you and not have it the other way around," he explains.

He admits that he favours the cover drive more than any other shot and, played by him, it is perhaps the loveliest stroke in cricket. His square and late cutting, gliding to leg and thunderous hooking are also magnificently executed however and satisfying to the most hidebound of purists. When he first played against the Australians they concentrated on his leg stump because they detected a weakness there but he soon overcame this and is now as good to the on as he is to the off.

"But it is not all peaches and cream, you know," Graeme points out. "As I have said before, cricket is a game you can never completely master. Remember my first three scores against the M.C.C in the 1964/65 season? I remember them all right — 0, 5 and 12! When I have a bad run like that my parents are invaluable. Their encouragement has helped me over many a rough patch.

Chris Greyvenstein
March 1967

Right: A photograph which proves that Mike Procter does not bowl off the wrong foot as many have claimed

Left: Barry Richards, in full stride, is one of the most magnificent sights in cricket

was about to be banished to the wilderness, at the mercy of the world's political agitators. Isolation was around the corner but it did not seem to us as we downed the bubbly at the conclusion of the series against Lawry's Australians.

In summing up this series, mention should be made of Ali Bacher, whose captaincy had much to do with the Springbok success. Modestly he has suggested that it was such a good team than anyone could have skippered it, but this is an over simplification. Sure enough he had the players but he used them to the best of their individual potential. He treated each player with an interest that was genuine and sincere and he had that capacity for working physically and mentally with his bowlers. Inspiring batsmen is not really that vital because it is the bowlers, who really win the matches. It's no good making hundreds and hundreds of runs if you have not got the men to bowl the other side out twice in five days.

Ali was always tactful and was never beyond accepting suggestions from team members. His job was that of collating ideas, sorting them out and applying the right tactics. His placing of the team before his own individual achievement couldn't have been better illustrated than at Kingsmead when he got himself out trying to help Barry Richards to his century before lunch.

In the final analysis, the averages told the whole story. Ian Redpath was the top Aussie scorer with an aggregate of 283 runs. The Springboks had four over 350, namely Pollock (517), Richards (508), Barlow (360) and Irvine (353). Seldom has any series seen such batting dominance. The best bowling average on the Aussie side was Connolly with 20 wickets at 26,10 a piece. The Springboks had seven bowlers under this average. And just to prove the old adage the fast bowlers are at their most effective when they hunt in pairs, Mike and I took 41 of the 75 wickets that fell to the Springbok bowlers.

Lawry summed up the series by complaining about the umpires and suggesting that it was time South Africa got this matter right. All the others paid tribute to what was generally accepted as the best side in the cricketing world.

"The world champions" was a phrase commonly bandied around and it was no doubt justified. But it was never to be put to the test. The glorious era that spanned thirty tests, had, through politics, been abruptly and unceremoniously ended.

Eleven tests had been won, four had been lost and half had been drawn, most well and truly in the Springbok's favour.

All that is left now are the memories, the nostalgia and a tremendous sadness. Yes, for indeed a great future appeared to lie ahead for South African cricket way back in 1970.

It seems like such a long time ago. •

Basil D'Oliveira — from rags to riches.

CHAPTER SIX

THE OTHER SIDE OF THE FENCE

The author's own introduction to black cricket was literally a case of climbing through a rusting corrugated iron fence to the other side. The cricket-mad young schoolboy had been playing on the banks of the Liesbeeck River in Observatory, Cape Town and, hearing the sweet sound of bat against ball followed by considerable applause, he quickly found an entry into what was then known as Mowbray Sports Ground and has since become the playing fields of St George's Grammar School. And there he found, to his amazement, a full-scale cricket game in progress, being played by coloured gentlemen.

A swift look around at his fellow spectators indicated that there were no other white people present but this was not important to a young lad whose first love was cricket. It turned out that this was a match in the programme of the Malay Barnato Trophy inter-provincial tournament and the white schoolboy was soon adding the names of "Dol" Freeman (always known as the Wally Hammond of Coloured cricket), "Tiney" Abed (the giant brother of the Lancashire League pro "Dik"), "Lobo" Abed (another brother in a famous cricketing family and probably the best black wicket-keeper produced in South Africa), "Marlie" Barnes (father of "Tiefie" Barnes and a prolific opening bat from Kimberley) and "Sharkey" Nackerdien, who led Western Province to Barnato Trophy honours that year, to the Huttons,Comptons, Lindwalls, Nourses and Rowans already held so enthusiastically in his memory.

The scene now moves forward in time to another match almost 25 years later, at the William Herbert Sportsground in Wynberg, Cape. The matting pitch has been laid over gravel, there are no sightscreens, and the outfield is sloping and irregular. And walking into bat is none other than the legendary West Indian, Rohan Kanhai to face up for his adopted Transvaal team against Western Province.

Again the white intruder looks at the sea of black faces around him. This time he eventually spies one other paler faced countenance, that of Gerald Mallinick, then the progressive president of Green Point Cricket Club, the first white club in the Cape to open its doors to black members, a move which was within the framework of the then existing legislation but in clear defiance of Government policy.

In an article in the late John Hetherington's fine *South African Cricketer* magazine, Mallinick recalled: " I wandered off to Newlands at about 3.30 p.m. to observe preparations for the S.A.B. Currie Cup match to begin the next day between Western Province and Transvaal. Umpires Craig and Kanjee (the first black umpire to stand in the Currie Cup) were busily measuring, inspecting and supervising the final preparations for the game. There I met a leading cricket administrator, a man who has devoted years of his life to serving cricket. He was amazed to hear that Kanhai had been batting down the road. Despite more than adequate press coverage, he was unaware that the Dadabhay Trophy match was taking place and that Kanhai was participating. When will we stop wearing blinkers?"

The Kanhai incident occurred four years after Barry Richards, Mike Procter and the Pollock brothers, amongst others, organised their cele-

Taliep Salie — Possibly South Africa's best black player between the Wars. Some critics considered him as good as Basil D'Oliveira.

Frank Roro — The "WG" of African cricket.

Mohammed Idris Yusuf — His 412 not out in Salisbury in 1936/37 is the highest recorded score in all Southern African cricket.

brated Newlands "walk-off" in support of the South African Cricket Association's application to the Government to allow the inclusion of "non-whites" in the team for the pending tour of Australia. Why must it always take so long for white South Africans to act? There has been amazing progress over the past few years but where were we when Freeman, the Abeds, Barnes and D'Oliveira were still playing on their mud-tracks whilst the cream of South Africa's white cricketers enjoyed only the best of facilities and opportunities? And what about the many fine black players who came before?

The story of black cricket in South Africa is as rich as it is varied. For many years there were frequent sharp divisions between the four main groups: Coloureds, Malays, Indians and Africans (the latter were known as Bantus until the 1960's) but there were also many bridges built which resulted ultimately in a "non-racial" inter-provincial tournament.

There are a few early references to Blacks playing some form of cricket during the last century but stories of "Kaffirs" playing the game with their farmer employers and events like the curious 1854 record of a contest between Hottentots and Africander (sic) Boers (the Hottentots won!) and "Kaffirs" playing club cricket in Queenstown in 1865 do not represent any real evidence of organised cricket amongst "Non-White" races.

The term "Non-White" has, incidentally, taken on connotations of representing some type of "Non-Person" and has by and large fallen into disuse in favour of the more explicit word "Black". A tongue-in-cheek suggestion was made some years back by a prominent member of Cape Town's Coloured community that the problem of what to call each other in South Africa would be solved by referring to the "Colourful" people (meaning of course the Africans, Coloureds and Indians) and the "Colourless" people. Needless to say the suggestion was not taken up.

The first truly organised black cricket in South Africa probably occurred with the formation of the South End Club in Port Elizabeth, although there is reference to some activity in Kimberley as early as 1876. Certainly the first major tournament of any kind took place in Cape Town in 1889/90 when Malay teams from Cape Town, Port Elizabeth and Johannesburg participated. A follow-up was staged in Kimberley in 1890/91 with three sides, all from the Cape Colony taking part.

Malays are the truly colourful people who live on the slopes of Signal Hill in Cape Town, the early home of Basil D'Oliveira. They came at first mainly from Malaya and were originally brought to the Cape as slaves by the Dutch East India Company, to be joined at a later date by many political exiles from their homeland.

To this community also fell the honour of providing the first-ever black South African side to take the field against an overseas touring eleven. The match was organised as an extra game for the benefit of the professionals in W.W. Read's England team in 1891/92 and was played over two days at Newlands, Cape Town.

Included in the Malay XVIII was the famous fast bowler "Krom" Hendricks whose omission from the 1894 South African team to England created such a furore. In M.W. Luckin's monumental *The History of South African Cricket* (which covers the years 1875 to 1915 in a mammoth 848 pages) a contemporary correspondent states that the proposed inclusion of the Malay player was considered by the selection committee "owing to the prominent way in which he (Hendricks) had performed against local and visiting teams". The writer goes on to say, "his inclusion was discussed publicly also", and continues: "The committee after due consideration decided that it would be *impolitic* to include him in the team" (author's italics). It has been recorded elsewhere that Hendricks was left out of the South African side "as a result of the greatest pressure by those in high authority in the Cape Colony" (the British ruled at the time). So politics in sport was as evident in 1894 as it is today. One can only wonder what the ultimate result might have been had an early precedent been set by the inclusion of a black player in South Africa's 1894 touring side.

The England Xl (without their amateurs — another indication of the class distinction prevalent at the time) easily beat the Malay XVlll but there were a couple of fine individual performances by some of the local side. "Krom" Hendricks himself claimed four wickets for 50 (including Frank Hearne's brother Alec) and, coming in at number six, L. Samoodien became one of only two South African batsmen to reach 50 against the tourists that summer, which was no mean feat against an attack which included Brockwell and the brothers Hearne.

Another early Malay player of note was the left-arm fast bowler C.J. Nicholls who so impressed Sir Pelham Warner that the England captain, having faced up to the Cape born player in the nets wrote: "One young Malay with a fast left-hand action hit my middle stump nearly every other ball and Denton began his South African career by being caught-and-bowled by the first three balls and clean bowled by the next three".

For his efforts Nicholls once earned as much as ten gold half-sovereigns in three afternoons bowling to Warner, Denton and company in the Newlands nets and "Charlie" Blythe, during a later tour, tried to persuade him to come to England and play for Kent. But the young aspirant's guardian refused consent and Nicholls continued to divide his time between Newlands and the nets at Diocesan College.

During the First World War he served in France and landed up as coach and cricket organiser for inter-division games thanks to the influence of Colonel van der Bijl, of the famous Western Province cricketing family. This put Nicholls in touch with cricket personalities from other lands and Herby "Horseshoe" Collins eagerly sought him out to do service as baggage-master and general factotum for the 1919 Australian Imperial Forces team. Always dead keen, the Malay cricketer continued to assist a number of subsequent touring sides in the twenties in a variety of roles: baggage-master, guide, coach and feared net bowler.

Nicholls was, of course, also very prominent in local club cricket amongst the Malays and was loyal to the well-known Roslyns Club for almost fifty years. The late Syd Reddy (without his efforts and those of popular Cape Town bar-waiter "Benny" Bansda there would be almost no records of South African Black cricket) once related a lovely tale about Nicholls's insatiable appetite for the game; the left-hander invariably opened the bowling and always displayed amazing stamina. His enthusiasm was wonderfully illustrated when he walked thirty-odd miles overnight to a match at Paarl, having lost his train ticket, and going straight onto the field after a very hurried breakfast, opened the bowling and took eight wickets for 50. The tail-end of the effort was not so positive though — the wicket-keeper was not competent enough to handle his express deliveries and no less than 65 byes meant a win for the opposition.

D.N. "Benny" Bansda was, incidentally, co-editor with Reddy of a series of "Non-European" cricket annuals in the fifties and sixties and was also the man mainly responsible for initiating the fund to send Basil D'Oliveira to England.

Another famous player from the Roslyns Club was a googly bowler called Taliep Salie, a protege of Nicholls, who was invited on numerous occasions to play in England. He always refused the temptation and a Roslyns member once told the author that his basic reason was the fear that he would be unable to find a Mosque close enough to the English grounds to enable him to properly observe the tenets of his Muslim faith. Syd Reddy records that the Malay spinner once claimed all ten wickets in a Malay Xl versus European Xl match, including those of such notables as Dave Nourse, Xenophon Balaskas and another Springbok, A.W. Palm.

He was frequently sought after as a net bowler by visiting English and Australian players. The great Australian Clarrie Grimmett reportedly stated that Salie was undoubtedly good enough to play at international level. Knowledgable critics have even rated Taliep Salie as having been superior to Basil D'Oliveira as an all-round cricketer. He was famous for his adept slip fielding and numerous fine batting performances included a mammoth 224 for Western Province versus Natal in the Barnato Tournament.

The ever enthusiastic Hadjie Salie retired from active play at the age of 64 years and died ten years later in 1969, to be greatly mourned by Cape Town's Malay community.

One of Salie's contemporaries, "Sakkie" Abrahams was known in his time as "Prince of the willow" and the names of the top players in the twenties and thirties give some clue to the genealogy of those who were top performers a couple of decades later: Matty Williams, "Toefy" Conrad, Hadjie Berhardien, Gamat Solomons, Cassim Meyer, Modien Hendricks and Henry Blanckenberg are a few of the names that will bring back memories for those who are still able to cast their minds back to such far off days.

Cricket thrived amongst the Malays in Cape Town during the early part of the century, but what of the rest of the country and the other racial groups? The strong Indian presence in Natal ensured the fostering of a game which some had learnt from the British in their country of origin (in 1922 a privately sponsored South African Indian team actually undertook a short tour in India). Indians were first brought to South Africa due to a labour shortage in the sugar plantations of Natal and the first indentured workers arrived in 1860. They have always been acknowledged as a forward-looking community who encourage and sponsor educational, cultural and sporting pursuits and have also been politically active over the years. The great Indian leader Mohandas K. Ghandi was, of course, very prominent in South Africa in the 1890's but was not known to have taken any interest in cricket.

A fully national South African Indian Cricket Union was only formed in 1940 (Syd Reddy's father was one of the founding vice-presidents) but Indians did participate in the early Barnato inter-provincial tournaments. Indian cricket personalities worthy of mention include the Rev. B.L.E. Sigamoney, a fine player in his day and an administrator who was one of the leading proponents of a totally non-racial cricket set-up, and B.D. "Bob" Pavadai, who was to become first president of the South African Cricket Board of Control or SACBOC. The much lamented Raschid Varachia, dedicated first president of the non-racial South African Cricket Union, was elected treasurer of the Indian Union as early as 1942.

An interesting game in aid of the Bengal Famine Relief Fund took place at the Old Wanderers ground in 1944. Sir Shafaat Ahmed Kahn, the High Commissioner for India, was one of the many spectators who observed some excellent play, on a rather slow pitch, between a Combined South African Indian XI and a Transvaal Cricket Union XI that included Springboks Syd Curnow, Len Brown and Xenophon Balaskas and was captained by the old Victoria and Worcestershire player Frank Warne.

The Indians' opening bowler, "Mac" Anthony, who was prominent in inter-provincial cricket for twenty-odd years, bowled with great accuracy and left-handed Dawood Hassan, nursing a finger which was split when catching Transvaal batsman Ronnie Somers-Vigne, batted with great resolution for 71 to earn his team an honourable draw.

Cricket amongst Indians was also very popular in the country then known as Southern Rhodesia and it was there that a truly remarkable performance was put up by the stocky, but very broad-shouldered, Mohammed Idris Yusuf, born in Durban and later to play for many years for Natal. At the age of twenty, he hit an incredible 412 not out for School's Cricket Club versus Star Cricket Club in Salisbury in 1936/37. It was no flash-in-the-pan for this prolific batsman who had two years earlier hit 240 off a Bantu XI attack in Johannesburg.

Several South African Indian doctors have featured well in India's Ranji Trophy Competition whilst studying in that country. Dr E.I. Bhorat of Stanger once hit a hundred for Western India and later played for Natal in the Christopher Cup and for S.A. Indians. Dr Aziz Kazee (who represented South African Indians in the SACBOC quadrangular in 1954/55) and Dr K.S. Naidoo of Maritzburg also played in India's premier competition.

A Transvaal Indian Cricket Union existed in 1896 and in the following year Sir David Harris, Chairman of De Beers Consolidated Mines Limited, presented a trophy in memory of the famous Barney Barnato to the Griqualand West Coloured Cricket Board which was situated in Kimberley and which represented the interests of Afri-

Jamaldien "Marlie" Barnes — prolific Malay batsman and father of "Tiefie" Barnes.

can, Coloured and Malay cricketers at the time.

In 1902 a full South African Coloured Cricket Board was created, it was also referred to as the "Barnato Board", and the Barnato Trophy tournaments provided the main incentive for black cricketers until 1926 when a splinter group formed the South African Independent Coloured Cricket Board, which also became the recipient of a trophy donated by Sir David Harris.

A period of dissent and disintegration had started and the end result was separate bodies controlling the different groups. It must be said that the original South African Coloured Cricket Board, like its eventual modern successors, SACBOC and the current South African Cricket Board, made no official distinctions based on colour or creed.

Mention should perhaps be made here of the efforts of the Johannesburg Inter Race Board which was formed as early as 1936 and which sponsored competitions involving teams from the various race groups with at one stage even a white team playing on a fairly regular basis.

Thus the South African Coloured Cricket Board, which later changed its name to the South African Malay Cricket Board, staged regular inter-provincial tourneys for the old Barnato Trophy; the "Independents" eventually reverted to calling themselves the South African Coloured Cricket Board and played regularly for the Sir David Harris Trophy.

As mentioned earlier, the South African Indian Cricket Union was founded in 1940, their members competing for the Christopher Cup; and, to complete the picture, a second dissident group had broken away from the original South African Coloured Cricket Board in 1932 to form the South African Bantu Cricket Board which competed yearly for the NRC Trophy, presented by the Chamber of Mines. All in all a dream situation in the eyes of any early proposer of the "apartheid" system!

There has, incidentally, been some reference to a "Native" cricket tournament in Port Elizabeth as early as 1890/91 and the nursery for cricket amongst the Africans was certainly a number of training colleges and other educational institutions, mainly in the Eastern Cape but it was the Witwatersrand Mines that provided the facilities to encourage the raising of the standard of play of South Africa's indigenous population.

Records of the early days are virtually non-existent but details of the feats of certain outstanding players have been carried forward by the time-honoured, and in most instances, surprisingly reliable word-of-mouth system.

Little is known for instance of the actual statistics of P.S.A. "Oom Piet" Gwele's exploits on the field of play. Suffice to say that he first appeared in 1916 and was still active as a player in 1941. "Oom Piet" is described in the *South African Non-European Cricket Annual* for 1954/55 as "a class player and an ace fielder", and in that year he was still extremely active as an organiser of the game.

There are, however, some written records of the "W.G." of African cricket, Frank Roro, a man of small physique but one who possessed a quick eye and a stroke for every ball on the oft unpredictable pitches prevailing in his time. Roro's scoring feats for his club, Crown Mines, included a century of hundreds in club cricket and a massive career best 304 versus Main Reef in 1942. He hit a number of double-hundreds against various opposition, including 228 versus a powerful Transvaal Coloured team and, at the

The South African Bantu Team 1953 — Noted personalities are: back row, third from left — fast bowler George Langa; back row extreme right — P.S.A. "Oom Piet" Gwele, second from right — Sam Ntshekisa, captain of the first official Black XI to play against a touring side; seated extreme left — Frank Roro.

The South African Malay Team 1953 — A. "Solly" Kirsten, a prolific batsman from Transvaal is in the back row, extreme left. Ace wicket-keeper Salie "Lobo" Abed is on his left. Off-spinner Eric Petersen who toured East Africa with such great success is fourth from the left in the back row and on his left is Gesant "Tiney" Abed. Extreme right, back row stands leg-spinner S. Bardien and seated amidst the officials are A.J. "Dol" Freeman, the captain (left) and Abdullah Rubidge (right) whilst J.M. "Marlie" Barnes is seated centre on the floor.

The historic first South African 'Non-White' XI at Hartleyvale Cape Town 1956: Standing: S. Bulbulia, S. Raziet, S. Abed, B. Malamba, C. Abrahams, E.I. Jeewa, H. Abrahams, Y. Lakay (12th man) Seated: M. Rashid Varachia (secretary), B.L. D'Oliveira (captain), A.M. Jassat (manager), A. Variawa, B.D. Pavadai (president), A. Bell.

age of 43, claimed the honour of compiling 116 in his first innings in the First National Tournament (in which representative sides from the Bantu, Coloured and Indian Boards competed as separate entities) played under the auspices of the newly-created SACBOC. His was also the only hundred registered in that inaugural competition.

An earlier reconciliation of the black groupings, with the exception initially of the Malay Barnato Board, had taken place in 1947 when SACBOC was first organised, with "Bob" Pavadai as president and Raschid Varachia as the first secretary. The initial tournament sponsored by the new organisation took place at Natalspruit, near Johannesburg in March 1951 and ended in a win for the Indian Union by virtue of an outright victory over the South African Coloureds after Roro's historic hundred had helped the Bantu Xl to a first innings win in the opening game.

The tall and pacy Gesant "Tiney" Abed (who would surely have challenged for Springbok colours if given the opportunity at the height of his career) was an important figure in the Indians' win over the much-fancied Coloured team with a match analysis of eight for 108. But the outstanding bowler of the week was the Coloured Xl captain Basil Waterwich, a tall off-spinner who totalled 21 wickets in two games at 7,33 runs apiece. This zealous player came from a long line of cricketers (his father and two brothers were also fine players) and the name Waterwich appears in cricket records dating back to 1898.

Other players to impress at Natalspruit were the Indian left-handed batsman Abbas Dinath, his team-mate I.A. Timol, a left-arm seamer whose brother A.I. Timol kept wicket competently, and the Coloured opening batsman "Chong" Meyer, who was to play for South Africa aginst the touring Kenya Asians in 1956.

The Bantu Xl back-up trio of Sam Ntshekisa, Ben Malamba and George Langa (who, together with Frank Roro and the more modern Edmund Nticinka and Edward Habane, comprise probably just about the best half-dozen African cricketers seen so far) were always in the picture and their team was unlucky not to defeat the Indians who ended 28 runs behind with but one wicket in hand.

To Samson Tyotyo Ntshekisa, after forty years as an active player, there eventually fell the honour at the age of 57 years of leading the first-ever "official" South African Black Xl against a touring side when he captained his team so proudly against the Derrick Robins Xl at Soweto in 1973/74. In a "friendly" match for S.A. Haque's combined Indian and African Xl against a strong white team in 1961 he achieved the distinction of displacing Johnny Waite's off-stump with the second ball he bowled to the Springbok. Waite's Xl contained such notables as Ali Bacher, Peter Carlstein, Russell Endean, Syd O'Linn, Mike Macaulay and Jackie Botten, all Springboks, and Haque's team won by 20 runs thanks to Ntshekisa's five for 27 and a century by Indian opener Armien Variawa.

After the historic Soweto encounter with the Robins' team, the veteran African all-rounder was quoted as saying: "When we played against the white side my fears were dispelled when I saw that, despite our crude-

Basil D'Oliveira's team at Dar-es-Salaam airport on arrival for their history making East African tour in 1958.

ness, we matched them here and there. These are people who get all the help to make outstanding players and the day they have us in their midst as players, and not as experiments, will be a wonderful day!". That day has to a certain extent now arrived, in Cape Town at least where a number of African teams are competing with fair success in the local third divison league.

Ben Malamba and George Langa for a long time opened the bowling for the South African Bantu teams, before the abolishment of racial groupings by SACBOC and the subsequent defection in 1968 to the non-racial but predominantly white South African Cricket Union by the South African Bantu Cricket Board, who felt that their players in certain areas in which the other black groups were not prominent, would be neglected under the new arrangement.

The giant but modest Malamba was a big-hitter and bowler of off-cutters who played with great flair for South Africa against the Kenya Asians but was troubled by injury when Basil D'Oliveira took the first official "Non-White" team to East Africa in 1958. The African was for some time a very valued member of the mainly Malay Roslyns Club together with the four talented Abed brothers, Gesant ("Tiney"), Salie ("Lobo"), Suleiman ("Dik"), the Enfield professional, and Goolam, who also played with success in the Lancashire Leagues, first as a pro for Rochdale and then for Castleton-Moor as an amateur. Ben Malamba is still very much involved with the game he loves and has become a much-loved figure amongst the up-and-coming young cricketers of Cape Town's African townships.

George Langa also toured East Africa in 1958 with some success. He bowled with a slinging almost round-arm action and was considered to be pretty quick by his contemporaries, which was probably very disconcerting on what Basil D'Oliveira once described as the "Burma Road" wickets prevailing in black cricket.

The next SACBOC inter-group tournament in 1952/53 saw the return of the Malay team to compete in a quadrangular event again held at Natalspruit. The strong Coloured team, with Basil D'Oliveira making his first appearance, experienced little difficulty in keeping well ahead. D'Oliveira and Meyer generally got them off to a good start and the seam bowling of future Milnrow and Radcliffe professional, Cecil Abrahams (father of Lancashire stand-in captain John Abrahams), and a lively left-hander from Port Elizabeth, Ralph Simon, usually proved too much for their opposition.

With their best performance a first-innings win over the Coloured team, the Malays also played with skill and veteran J.M. "Marlie" Barnes (father of A.L. "Tiefie" Barnes who played for the multi-racial South African team in 1975/76) batted with rare power for just over three hours to take 134 off the strong Coloured Xl bowlers. The newcomers' main attacker was the very tall 21 year-old Eric Petersen, who bowled off-breaks and right -arm medium pace with equal skill.

Another off-spinner to impress in this tournament was the Indians' Mohammed Garda who bowled off a longish run and was difficult to score off. But his team's batting was brittle, as was that of the S.A.Bantu side who failed dismally in every match.

A.J. "Dol" Freeman, who was almost a legend in his own time amongst Malay cricketers, played in his last major competition and batted with his customary authority to average 48,75 in five innings.

The SACBOC administration had tried without success to entice overseas teams to South Africa in the early 1950's. Negotiations with the Indian and later the Pakistani Boards fell through, in the first case because of lack of funds and possible disagreement by the Imperial Cricket Conference, and then because of Pakistan's own admittance to the ranks of the ICC.

So it was back to the local scene and another Dadabhay Trophy quadrangular tournament in 1954/55, again in Johannesburg, and which the Indians won by virtue of one outright and two first innings successes.

The outstanding event of the competition was the unprecedented feat by Indian all-rounder Walter Stephens when he claimed all ten Bantu team wickets in their second innings. For the S.A. Coloureds Basil D'Oliveira slammed a devastating 153 from the strong Malay attack and "Chong" Meyer played a three-figure innings against the Indians. Gesant Abed enjoyed a good all-round time for the Malays, whose best bowler was again Eric Petersen, but other than opening bat Jap Mahanjana no-one really impressed for the Bantu Xl, who missed the services of an injured George Langa and unavailable Ben Malamba.

Two setbacks in 1955 did not deter the SACBOC administration in their efforts to provide some meaningful opposition for its players. An application for admission as a full member of the ICC had been put aside with the proviso that a reconsideration would be entertained if two sponsors could be found amongst existing members and proof of the ability to conduct tours could be supplied. The white South African Cricket Association then refused a request for the inclusion of a SACBOC match in the itinerary of the 1956/57 MCC team, with the excuse that the fixture list had already been finalised.

But a trip to Kenya by the enterprising Messrs Pavadai and Varachia resulted in the arrival in South Africa in November 1956 of a highly competent looking team under the name "Kenya Asians". One of the tourists, Shakoor Ahmed, a fine opening batsman and wicket-keeper, had toured England with the Pakistan team and several had played Ranji Trophy cricket in India.

Shakoor was to prove the mainstay of the Kenya Asians batting and B.L. "Blaze" D'Cunha, a puzzling googly merchant, gave the South African batsmen most trouble.The team was ably captained by all-rounder Chandrakant Patel, who had played in India, and included two highly-rated opening bowlers in J.R.Jabbar and G.B.Jhalla who had impressed against various touring teams in Kenya. Unfortunately both seamers suffered injuries which restricted their appearances in the three "Test Matches" arranged for the tourists.

For the first time a "National" South African Xl was chosen representing the four black groups. Basil D'Oliveira (then only 24) was elected captain and was joined by four other players from the Coloured team: opening bat "Chong" Meyer, Salmodien "Lam" Raziet, a sound right-hander who was to score most runs in the series, the all-rounder Cec Abrahams (another who would surely have merited Springbok colours if given the chance) and Transvaal opening bowler Alec Bell.

The Indian Union was represented by young batsmen S.Bulbulia and Armien Variawa and E.I. Jeewa, a leg-spin bowler, whilst the Malays provided Hassiem Abrahams, a middle-order batsman and Salie "Lobo" Abed, who had no rival as first choice wicket-keeper. The remaining place went to the sole Bantu team player to gain recognition in this historic eleven, the six- foot- three Ben Malamba.

The late Tom Reddick, who devoted a large portion of his life to coaching in the Cape, rated Malamba as the most diffcult of the South African bowlers to get away and the big African certainly justified his selection by taking eight wickets in the first "test" which was played, strangely enough, on a soccer ground in Cape Town.

Hartleyvale was once the home of the now defunct Cape Town City professional soccer side and for many years it has been the centre of Cape Town's white soccer fraternity. Unable to obtain permission to stage the Kenya Asians match at Newlands or any similarly suitable "white" ground, the SACBOC committee had to opt for a matting wicket stretched over a newly-prepared gravel pitch on the Hartleyvale football ground so that they could at least provide some sort of stand accommodation for the spectators, who flocked in to, at long last, witness their players taking part in some sort of test encounter.

It is rather interesting to note that one of the main venues for the colourful "Coon Carnival" and for the famous Malay Choirs and Bands is Hartleyvale (the other has been traditionally Green Point). So the ground chosen for the first-ever international encounter involving a "non-white" South African team was not entirely unfamiliar to some of the participants, and certainly not for many of their supporters, albeit for a reason rather remote from the noble game of cricket.

Shakoor Ahmed saved his side on the first day with a dashing 101 in only 134 minutes after venemous bowling by Abrahams and Bell had levelled the Kenyans to 41 for three wickets. The former Pakistani player's contribution was remarkable in that it came out of a grand total of only 149. With D'Oliveira hitting top score of 70 and the later South African batsmen batting with great determination, the home side managed to build a lead of 109 and a second innings stand of 100 by the two Patels, Arvind and skipper Chandrakant, was insufficient to extend D'Oliveira. With due propriety the South African captain claimed the honour of hitting the winning run to set the seal on a six-wicket triumph.

Raziet and Variawa were promoted to open the innings for the second "test" at Natalspruit, Johannesburg and "Tiney" Abed and Abbas Dinath displaced Bulbulia and Meyer in the South African eleven. The new openers certainly celebrated their choice with a brisk stand of 50 in forty-seven minutes and, after Variawa's dismissal by the menacing D'Cunha, Raziet proceeded to compile the first South African century in two hours and forty-five minutes.

Hitting with great gusto the tall Abed cracked 54 in a quick second wicket stand which realised 123 in under two hours and the two unrelated Abrahams, Hassiem and Cecil proceeded to put the Kenyans bowlers to the sword with a rapid 96 fifth wicket partnership in 54 scintillating minutes. Then the South Africans twisted their

Above: John Neethling, South African all-rounder batting against Kenya Asians at Nairobi.

Right: The South Africans inspect the matting wicket at the Sikh Union Ground in Nairobi. Basil D'Oliveira is on the extreme right.

Below: Ben Malamba.

blade in the visitors' wound when Cecil Abrahams and Alec Bell claimed three wickets in the final twenty minutes.

Next morning Kenya lost two more wickets in quick succession but another magnificent offensive was launched by the free-scoring Shakoor Ahmed who thrashed the South African attack to the tune of 120 in two hours and thirty-five minutes. His fine effort could not, however, prevent the home team from gaining a first innings lead of 120 and, although South Africa failed against a determined Kenyan onslaught in their second innings, another heartening victory was achieved on the third day, this time by 39 runs.

Rain ruined the third "test", the only tour game to be played on a recognised first-class ground, Kingsmead in Durban. The first two days were a complete washout and South Africa claimed a narrow first innings lead after both teams had been dismissed for under a hundred in dreadful conditions.

New caps in the South African line-up were the up-and-coming Ahmed Deedat from Natal, who had hit 104 against Western Province a couple of years earlier whilst still a schoolboy, tall off-spinner Mohammed Garda and all-rounder A. George. They replaced D'Oliveira (injured), Dinath and Jeewa and Transvaal batsman Armien Variawa, century-making hero of the famous Haque's XI versus Waite's XI match, took over the captaincy.

Big Ben Malamba took his wicket tally for the series to 16 at 15,25 runs apiece, easily the best for South Africa. Cecil Abrahams came out with the best all-round figures and Basil D'Oliveira and "Lam" Raziet headed the batting averages. The unspectacular but quietly efficient wicket-keeping of Salie "Lobo" Abed was highly praised by all critics.

The dominating figure for Kenya Asians was Shakoor Ahmed with two centuries, and an aggregate of 251 in

"Tiney" Abed surrounded by enthusiastic spectators at Nairobi.

six innings. The tourists young left-arm seamer Rasik Patel hit a purple patch on the Kingsmead mud-track to take six for 34 and topped the bowling table.

Thus ended the first of the two successful attempts by SACBOC to broaden the experience of South Africa's black cricketers. Before the commencement of the second undertaking, however, there was a home tournament to take care of. And the 1957/58 quadrangular event proved to be the last competition staged with teams selected on the basis of race qualification. It was rather fitting therefore that the series should culminate with the South African Coloured team, led by Basil D'Oliveira, winning the Dadabhay Bros Trophy by completing their dismissal of the Malay eleven with the final ball of the last possible over of the tournament.

With the prospect of a tour to East Africa in the wind, on-the-field rivalry was at its sharpest and four centuries were added to the grand total of four scored in the previous three tournaments. D'Oliveira and the steady coloured opener Sydney Solomons secured their flights to Nairobi with hundreds against the Bantus and Indians respectively, Ahmed Deedat hit 100 not out off the Bantu attack, and Goolam Abed, later unlucky to miss a place in the South African team, scored a patient 102, also off the Bantus.

Although it may appear that the African bowlers provided cannon fodder for their opponents, one player in the S.A. Bantu Xl certainly gave notice of his credentials for the future. But, while Edmund Mthutuzeli Ntikinca was bowling with great energy on his debut to take five Coloured Xl wickets for 62, it is unlikely that his wildest imagining would have included the scenario of pitting his skill against that of such true masters of the willow as Springboks Barry Richards and Eddie Barlow or the Australian Chappell brothers. He was to miss the East African adventure but the miracle was ultimately to occur for this razor-keen player when he was chosen with schoolboy Edward Habane to participate in the first multi-national Datsun Double-Wicket Tournament at the Wanderers in 1973.

Veteran George Langa bowled well enough to gain a spot in the touring side whilst comparative new-comers John Neethling (medium pace) and Owen Williams (left-arm spin) also performed with enough skill to warrant selection. Neethling was to prove the next best all-rounder to D'Oliveira in East Africa and later signed as a professional for Colne in the Lancashire League. Williams, who was considered by D'Oliveira as of potential test-match class, was a pro with Radcliffe and played a highly succesful season for Warwickshire Second Xl before deciding to emigrate to the warmer climate of Australia. There he played with marked success in Adelaide and ended as Club Captain of Prospect C.C.

Malay seamer cum off-spinner, Eric Petersen who bagged 24 wickets at 10,80 apiece wrote his own ticket for the East African safari. "Tiney" Abed was also an automatic choice and other Cape players to gain inclusion were Cecil Abrahams, "Lam" Raziet, first 'keeper Salie Abed, Ben Malamba and wicket-keeper/batsman Basil Witten, who eventually withdrew because of employment problems and was replaced by the young Natal Indian Dawood Asmal.

Mohammed Bulbulia (Transvaal), another all-rounder, and Natal batsman Deedat and his leg-spinning team companion Essop Jeewa completed the team which thus consisted of ten players from Western Province (B.L. D'Oliveira (captain), G.T. Abed (vice-captain), S. Abed, C. Abrahams, B. Malamba, J.J. Neethling, E. Petersen, S. Raziet, S. Solomons, O. Williams), three from Natal (D.K. Asmal, A.I. Deedat, and E.I. Jeewa) and two from Transvaal (M. Bulbulia and G. Langa).The popular Mr B.D. Pavadai, one of the main architects of the tour, completed the party as team manager.

Considered unfortunate to miss selection were the talented Western Province stroke-player and leg-spinner Taliep Berhardien (yet another Roslyns player), Hassiem Abrahams, the Transvaal batsman who had performed well against the Kenya Asians team and the Natal seam bowler T. Parsuraman.

Basil D'Oliveira once stated that his 1958/59 "South African Non-European Touring Team" (as it is entitled in the 1958 *Kenya Cricketers' Almanac*) was the proudest team ever to leave the shores of South Africa. And, on their return nearly two months later, having ridden rough-shod over all and sundry who cared to place themselves in the path of D'Oliveira's highly talented cricketing machine, the first-ever official black South African combination to tour in another country had certainly provided sufficient justification for their feelings of high emotion.

The editor of *Kenya Cricketers' Almanac* wrote in his review of the tour: "Their names are unknown in the cricket world outside their own country, but they have proved themselves to be as strong a team as any that has visited us." No idle praise this from a country which had hosted a number of extremely powerful cricket teams over the previous couple of seasons. Typical of these visitors was the Pakistan Writers Cricket Club, led by none other than the "father of Pakistani cricket", A.H. Kardar and boasting an almost full-strength test match eleven including "the little master", Hanif Mohammed, and such early architects of Pakistani success in Imtiaz Ahmed, Alimuddin, Waqar Hassan and Zulfiqar Ahmed.

Then in 1957 the highly effective Indian Sunder C.C., captained by the flamboyant S. Mushtaq Ali and including players of the class of the legendary Vinoo Mankad, former Indian skipper Nari Contractor, all-rounders J.M. Ghorpade and Prakash Bhandari, off-spinner Jasu M. Patel (who took 9 for 69 in a single innings against Australia in 1959/60), Pankaj Roy (over 2000 test runs) and wicket-keeper N.S. Tamhane, who played 21 tests for India, played three games in Nairobi against mixed sides captained by D.W. Dawson, brother of old Springbok Ossie Dawson.

In 1958 there followed a tour by a powerful MCC side led by Freddy Brown and managed by S. C. Griffith. The Kenya Kongonis Club actually beat Brown's Xl by seven wickets despite the presence of such notables as Peter Richardson, Mike Smith (who captained the MCC in South Africa in 1964/65) and former England pace bowler John Warr. Teams from the Southern part of Africa like the Natal Crickets and Rhodesian Stragglers had also been frequent visitors, particularly to Kenya.

A number of East Africans had put up particularly impressive performances against these sides. Dawson himself was always in the game, as a stubborn batsman who could hit hard when necessary and as a leg-break bowler. He had scores of 52, 37 and 39, all not out, against the Pakistanis plus a fine 83 against Sunder C.C. to prove his ability as a run-getter and had the knack of claiming a wicket when most needed.

Ramandbhai Patel, who toured South Africa in 1956, made runs consistently and attractively and the fast bowler G.B. Jhalla included a feat of 7 for 95 against the Pakistanis (including Hanif bowled for 0) in his register of achievements. Of the white players new to the South Africans P.R. Prodger had been the key performer in the Kongonis win over MCC with stylish innings of 52 and 115 after having hit 121 in the annual "Officials versus Settlers" match at Nairobi Club.

Thus the East African players were accustomed to mixing it with opposition of the highest ability and the South Africans' performances can be judged accordingly. Although the South Africans lost their first match against a strong Kenya Asians Xl, which was not surprising as they had come straight out of a home winter and had no recent match practice, they soon found their feet and never looked back. In a fifteen game programme they eventually ran out winners in eleven (the last ten in a row), drew three encounters and suffered that lone defeat in the opening clash.

They played two "mini-tests" against Kenya and another major game against a combined East African team at the Sikh Union Club in Nairobi, which match, together with that against the powerful Kenya Kongonis Club at Nairobi Club, should have been the South Africans' sternest trial. This was, however, not to be the case for, after the initial setback in their warm-up game, no opposition was able to match the all-round power of D'Oliveira and his eager company.

After a cheap dismissal in their first innings against Kenya Asians (D'Oliveira hit 59 out of 131) fine seam bowling on the familiar matting wicket by John Neethling (six for 56) restricted the home eleven's lead to 69 runs. The South Africans performed stoutly at their second attempt against their old enemies "Blaze" D'Cunha and Rasik Patel.

A resolute Sydney Solomons, one of D'Oliveira's main pillars of strength on this tour, carried his bat through the innings for 90 not out and might have gained his coveted hundred if he had not played so devotedly for his team, ahead of his own personal ambitions. Ahmed Deedat hit a sparkling 75 and Cecil Abrahams also batted with great determination but the Asians made light of their 172 run target, which total was reached for the loss of five wickets.

There followed a run-in to the first "test" against Kenya of matches either won outright with consummate ease or in which rain, as in the case of the game against Tanganyika at Dar-es-Salaam, left no time to force a decision but with the South Africans invariably well on top of things.

Fine individual performances flowed from the bats of D'Oliveira, Raziet, "Tiney" Abed, Solomons and Deedat and the deadly bowling combination of Petersen, Abrahams, Neethling, Langa and Abed swept all resistance aside. The best individual bowling performances to that stage was George Langa's 5 for 19 against Tanga and 5 for 21 versus Tanganyika and Abed's 8 for 23 which decimated the Zanzibar Xl. Ben Malamba broke a finger during the second match at Moshi and was an onlooker for the remainder of the stay in East Africa.

Up to the start of South Africa's second innings in the first big match against Kenya at the Sikh Union Club at Nairobi, there seemed to be little difference between the sides opposing one another. Batting first D'Oliveira's men had struggled against Jhalla, Rasik Patel and D'Cunha and only determined late-order resistance from Neethling, Abrahams and Gesant Abed had carried the total to 196. In contrast four of the first five Kenyan batsmen scored thirty or more but a later collapse against the cutters of Eric Petersen (six for 51) brought the South Africans a slender six-run advantage.

The pattern of the match, and of the whole tour, now changed dramatically. After the shock of seeing Raziet and Solomons back in the pavilion with only 4 runs on the board had worn off, Basil D'Oliveira threw aside any inhibitions he may have had regarding his ability to cope with good-class bowling and proceeded to decimate the previously menacing swing attack of Jhalla and Daljit Singh who had put the two

South African openers back in the hut.

Ahmed Deedat, as he was to do on a number of occasions, matched his skipper stroke for stroke in a 112 run third wicket stand to be followed by John Neethling who gave D'Oliveira splendid assistance in a breakneck 141 partnership for the fourth wicket. The South African captain strode majestically to 139 before he was caught off the hard-working Jhalla (who bowled over sixty overs in the match for eight wickets) and Cecil Abrahams slammed his way to 50 not out before lunch on the third day to give his side an overall lead of 320.

This target was far beyond the immediate capabilities of Dennis Dawson and his men who succumbed to the four-pronged devil of Petersen, Neethling, Langa and D'Oliveira and the South African XI were conquerers by the handsome margin of 165 runs.

Disposing of their next four opponents in short order the proud men from south of the Limpopo confirmed their class with a resounding win over the much-fancied Kenya Kongonis Club. This was a prelude to their best achievement of the tour, the comprehensive thrashing of a combined East African XI, once again at the Sikh Union ground in Nairobi.

A determined if rather strokeless 88 by East African opener Mehboob Ali (he was dropped twice on the way) helped the composite side reach 213 but the old firm of Deedat (66) and D'Oliveira (96), this time in a 149 run fourth-wicket spree, followed by some big hitting from Abrahams (77) and Neethling (53 not out) saw the ball despatched to all corners of the congenial home ground of the Kenya Asian Sports Association. D'Oliveira declared with seven wickets down and a lead of 137 under his belt and then helped his vice-captain "Tiney" Abed to bowl the hapless East Africans out for another low score. The South Africans were thus left with 72 runs to win, which task was accomplished for the loss of three wickets.

If the Kenyan hosts had reached the opinion that Basil D'Oliveira and his merry band had by now moved into top gear they must have been totally devastated by the result of the final game of the tour, the second "test" against Kenya, this time at the Mombasa Sports Club field.

The ubiquitous G.B. Jhalla was again very much on the scene when South Africa took first strike. Two quick wickets were added to his considerable inventory for the season and the tragic run out of D'Oliveira by Vinoo Patel brought confident smiles to the faces of the Kenyans for the first time in many weary days in the field. But the obdurate Sydney Solomons, aided by John Neethling, perhaps the most valuable member of the South African team after Basil D'Oliveira himself, saw the score taken to a respectable but disappointing 193.

The mango trees that circled the Mombasa ground were just beginning to cast shadows across the pitch when the Kenyans came in to face Cecil Abrahams and Eric Petersen shortly after 5 p.m. After three overs of his normal over-the-wicket cutters at a gentle medium pace Petersen, sensing that the pitch would take spin, reverted to bowling his tantalising off-breaks from around the wicket with five men crowding in on the leg-side. Eight balls later he had taken three wickets to make the score a staggering 10 for 4, Abrahams having chipped in his share by getting Halim Mohammed caught behind by "Lobo" Abed and then himself taking two brilliant short-leg catches off Petersen's pin-point accurate bowling.

D'Oliveira brought on left-hander Owen Williams to bowl the final over of the day and he responded with a wicket to put the Kenyans in a frightful position at close of play. Next day the bout continued and Kenya were all out for 49 with Abrahams claiming the figures 11-3-20-4 and Petersen 9,4-6-14-5. Williams only bowled a single over to take one for 5.

Jhalla then put in another of his super-human bowling spells (28-4-59-3) and the Kenyan captain Chandrakant Patel did his best to restrict South Africa's scoring rate. D'Oliveira played rather uncharacteristically for two hours for his 50 but the lead was slowly extended to 327, a goal which was to prove an impossible task for the host eleven.

Abrahams and Petersen again bowled virtually unchanged and the entrapped Kenyans stumbled along to another disastrous conclusion in their second innings.The winning margin this time was a massive 255 runs and Basil D'Oliveira and his men could feel justifiably proud of their achievements on this historic tour.

One further game was played on the way home, at Salisbury against a Rhodesian Indian XI which was patently too weak to warrant a legitimate entry in the tour records but which did provide the occasion for a highly entertaining 225 run partnership between Sydney Solomons and Cecil Abrahams.

Politics was now beginning to become the name of the game on South African sportsfields. And the attitude of some black administrators which led to the cancellation of a proposed tour of South Africa by a West Indies team captained by none other than Sir Frank Worrell disillusioned even Basil D'Oliveira, one of the keenest cricketers ever to walk in to bat. South Africa's greatest black player was soon to be lost to his own land but, in an incredible rags-to-riches story, rivalled perhaps only by that of the legendary Sir Leary Constantine, he was to attain the highest possible peak of achievement for his adopted country, England.

The Worrell tour was opposed by a number of black political organisations with no sporting links, on the grounds that it would effectively create a situation which represented condonation of the South African Government's apartheid policy. It had, of course, been planned that the West Indian team would only play against teams affiliated to SACBOC, which ruled out possibility of contact with white South African cricketers, a rather ludicrous situation from any point of view when one considers the proposed composition of Worrell's party.

Included in that rather eminent list were the names of Garfield Sobers, Conrad Hunte, Lester King, Sonny Ramadhin, Alfred Valentine, "Collie" Smith, Tom Dewdney, Andy Ganteaume, Ralph Legall and Ivan Madray, all test players and, excepting their lack of fast bowling support for Dewdney, probably a stronger combination than Lawrence Rowe's 1983 team. One shudders to think what they might have accomplished against the then current "white" South African XI, let alone Basil D'Oliveira's talented and keen, but very inexperienced squad.

So, with the aid of the subscribers to the fund initiated by Benny Bansda, D'Oliveira set sail for new shores to end a rather glorious era in the history of black cricket in South Africa. He was soon to be followed by others who were inspired by the great player's success in the Lancashire League.

First of these disciples was the ebullient Cecil Abrahams, black cricket's answer to Eddie Barlow, who had performed with such all-round excellence against the Kenya Asians and then on the tour of East Africa. He was to play for a phenomenal fifteen seasons in the Lancashire league, first for Milnrow on D'Oliveira's recommendation, and later for Radcliffe and Oldham. His son John, a sound left-hand bat and useful off-spinner, is now Lancashire's stand-by captain in the absence of Clive Lloyd.

Another long-lived Lancashire League performer was Suleiman "Dik" Abed (like Abrahams a no-nonsense hard hitting bat and accurate medium pace seamer) who boasts the unusual record of ten successive seasons with one Lancashire League club, Enfield.

In *The Cricketer Winter Annual* for 1976 the following tribute is paid to the South African: "For the better part of ten years Abed has contributed much to Lancashire League cricket and his departure will be regretted by all who have watched a talented player go about his business of collecting wickets and runs and at the same time providing cricket entertainment of the highest order". Abed was one of the two black cricketers whom Jack Cheetham, then president of the South African Cricket Association, suggested as additions to South Africa's team for the 1971/72 Australian tour that never was.

The other "choice" as an additional player, in a move which in retrospect can only be regarded as one of expediency by SACA in a desperate bid to save the Australian tour, was the left-arm spinner Owen Williams, considered by many as worthy of inclusion in the South African team on his own merits alone. His main attack was orthodox but, like Peter de Vaal who was chosen for the aborted Australian venture, he could bowl a passable "chinaman" when required. Williams eventually did make it "down-under", but at his own expense, and he ended a distinguished career as Club Captain of the well-known Adelaide club, Prospect.

One of D'Oliveira's main helpers on the East African safari was John Neethling (another in the Abrahams/

S.A. Haque's Team takes the field against John Waite's XI in 1961. The four players in front are (from the left) A.L. 'Tiefie' Barnes, Abdul Bhamjee, Solly Chothia and the captain, Abdullah Rubidge.

Rohan Kanhai in action for Transvaal SACBOC on a 'Burma Road' wicket in Cape Town. The bowler is Cecil Abrahams.

Schoolboy Edward Habane in action during the Datsun Double-Wicket Tournament at Wanderers. Mike Procter is fielding at slip.

Abed mould as an all-rounder) who had a couple of successful seasons for Colne before becoming home-sick and returning to give staunch support to the SACBOC Western Province team. Yet another all-rounder of similar style was Desmond February who had one excellent season for Werneth but then lost touch and was not re-engaged.

Another Abed, Goolam, went to England in 1961 as a rugby professional but reverted to cricket in the Lancashire League with great success, first as a professional and later as an amateur. He was a gritty opening bat who was very difficult to dislodge.

There was a veritable exodus of South African black players to England in the sixties, mainly from Cape Town and, in addition to those already mentioned, Rushdi Majiet (a useful fast bowler and very hard-hitting bat who is still very active in Cape cricket) played for Todmorden and Ivan D'Oliveira (Basil's younger brother who in 1961/62 took part in a record Dadabhay Trophy partnership of 283 with Gerald Jardine for Western Province against Griqualand West) had a trial with Leicestershire whilst Transvaal's Ismail Garda, who later played for Transvaal "B" (SACU) in the Castle Bowl Competition, had one very good season for Nottinghamshire 2nd XI.

Interestingly enough the bulk of the players who followed the first pioneers to the green pastures of England almost to a man became involved in SACU sponsored multi-racial cricket in the 1970's. First of these was Sedick "Dickie" Conrad the opening batsman from Cape Town who was banned by Mr Hassan Howa's SACBOC committee for committing the crime of actually watching a non-SACBOC match at Newlands.

The then 30 years-old former Western Province captain, who had scored prolifically in inter-provincial cricket, became known as "the cricketer who was sacked for watching cricket" when his registration as a SACBOC affiliated player was cancelled because he had been observed as a spectator at Newlands! One wonders how Mr Howa, whose unwavering stance on certain issues does deserves full admiration, can reconcile this decision with his own admittance that he watched the 1983 West Indians play (albeit only through the medium of television) because of his "love for the game"?

Conrad actually challenged the SACBOC ruling in the Supreme Court and won his case. But he never again played under the auspices of Mr Howa's board, accepting instead an invitation from Gerald Mallinick to join Green Point Cricket Club. "Tiney" Abed, now past the first flush of youth, was already a member and played for Green Point thirds but Conrad went straight into Green Point's premier side to become the first black player to participate in the "white" Western Province first division league. But this plucky player's greatest moment had come during the previous season when he was included in the South African President's XI to play Derrick Robins XI, alongside the players he had gone to watch on his previous fateful visit to Newlands.

Two Natal players, Yacoob Omar and Ismail "Babu" Ebrahim also tried their luck in England but without any great success. Omar, a sound batsman who has scored heavily in Dadabhay tournaments, had a couple of seasons with Natal "B"(SACU) but has since returned to the SACBOC fold. Ebrahim, on the other hand still plays for

Natal "B" and has had the occasional outing in Mike Procter's Currie Cup side but has not quite reached the performance level he demonstrated on his debut in first-class cricket.

Also playing in this match was a young fast-medium bowler, Howie Bergins, one of the major wicket-takers in SACBOC tournaments over the two previous seasons, who also tried a spell in the UK and was another Green Point member.

The latest black South African recruit to the professional cricketing circuit of England holds the unique distinction of having earned a genuine international cricket cap. Omar Henry, a leading player in the SACU Western Province Xl, and certainly a contender for inclusion in any current Springbok touring side, represented Scotland against the Australians in 1981.

He is an accurate left-arm spinner, a brilliant close fielder, and a crowd-pleasing batsman who enjoys hitting sixes. He already has one first-class hundred to his credit for Western Province "B" but the batting performance which perhaps has given him most pleasure was put up in a league match for Micklehurst versus Newton Heath in 1979 when the left-hander smacked 23 sixes in his mammoth 243. Henry has also from time to time collared the bowling of South Africa's current number one spinner Alan Kourie and his appearance at the top of the pavilion steps at Newlands is always greeted with delight by spectators old and young.

Henry at one time featured prominently for Western Province under the SACBOC administration which continued to hold fairly regular competitions through the 1960's. Participation was now purely on a provincial basis with no colour distinctions but still no white players took part. It was not until after the merging of the then existing SACBOC under Rashid Varachia with the virtually all-white SACA and the South African *African* Cricket Board to form the non-racial South African Cricket Union (SACU) in 1976, and the subsequent formation by Mr Howa and his supporters of the South African Cricket Board (SACB), that a single white player, Denis Compton's son Richard, took part. 1 Richard Compton first appeared for Natal in a SACB Howa Bowl match and took 52 off Transvaal on his debut in 1978/79.

Abdulatief "Tiefie" Barnes batting against the International Wanderers.

Five Dadabhay Trophy single venue tournaments were staged between 1961 and 1971 at successively Johannesburg, Port Elizabeth, Durban, Cape Town and Kimberley and the powerful Western Province team dominated most of the time.

Sedick Conrad developed into SACBOC's foremost batsman during this period with Ismail "Morris" Garda hard on his heels. Garda was eventually to play for Transvaal 'B' (SACU) together with his team-mates all-rounder Solly Chothia and the talented "Tiefie" Barnes. It was indeed unfortunate that the SACA/SACBOC amalgamation came a bit too late in their careers for these fine players to do full justice to their undoubted talent. One of the most remarkable achievements during this period was the posting of a new record individual score by the South Western Districts captain A. Coericius who in 1963/64 hit 230 against Border.

Whilst SACBOC continued on its determined way, the African cricketer came out of the wilderness with the assistance of, initially the all-white SACA, and then the newly-constituted SACU, which embraced the old SACA, SACBOC and SAACB under one administration.

The African Board had first obtained assistance from the white SACA in 1968 and the three leading African administrators of that time, Messrs L.

Mlonzi, H. Butshingi and A.A. Dunjwa, in contrast to the intransigent stand taken by Mr Hassan Howa and his colleagues, welcomed all the assistance they could aquire. Andre Odendaal in his invaluable study of the politics of cricket, *Cricket in Isolation* quotes Mr Dunjwa as stating: "We do not want to be unrealistic. We are sensitive to what is going on in this country . . . but let us remember this Government might be in power for the next 25 years and we are not going to fold our arms and not play cricket".

The first fruits of co-operation with the helping hand of SACA was the provision of funds to organise an African schools' tournament which has become known as the John Passmore week, in honour of the SACA official who was mainly instrumental in getting the scheme off the ground.

A number of very promising players have been unearthed through this yearly competition, including Edward Zanele Habane, who partnered a man almost twice his age, the mustard keen veteran Edmund Ntikinca, in what was a special breakthrough for black players in South Africa, participation in the international Datsun Double-Wicket Competition at the Wanderers, Johannesburg in 1973. The two black players started off in astounding fashion by beating the New Zealand test pair Bev Congdon and Bruce Taylor and, although they were unable to repeat their success against the other combinations, their exuberant relish for the game made them popular with opponents and spectators alike.

Young Habane was to endear himself to an enthusiastic Newlands crowd in 1975 when he played under Eddie Barlow for the President's XI against the Derrick Robins XI. The young Xhosa excelled in the field (he brilliantly caught opposing skipper Brian Close at silly short leg) and brought proceedings to a close when he cleanbowled the visitors' last batsman, Australian Terry Jenner, to be carried off shoulder-high by his new-found fans.

Only a few weeks after the Datsun tournament another breakthrough occurred for African cricket when an official South African African XI, captained by veteran Sam Ntshekisa, squared up to the Derrick Robins XI at Soweto. Ntikinca took three wickets, including that of century maker John Edrich, and Habane hit 32 before being caught and bowled by mystery spinner Johnny Gleeson. Although the Africans lost by a big margin the experience of playing against such illustrious opponents had been the event of a lifetime.

Another "grand old man" of African cricket to bow out in this historic match was the venerable George Langa, well into his fifties but still capable enough a bowler to take the wickets of Younis Ahmed (clean bowled) and Graham Roope, the second Robins century maker.

Meanwhile SACBOC was still alive and well, and thanks to sponsorship was arranging more competitions than ever before. To the Dadabhay Trophy competition (which was played as one-day games for a season but then reverted to three-day games) was added a limited overs contest on an inter-provincial basis, "B" section and Under-19 tournaments, and a fixture between North and South elevens entitled a "Mini-Test". One of the sponsorships, from the Stellenbosch Farmers Winery caused a furore amongst many of the Muslim players, some of whom refused outright to take part in any game funded by a liquor company.

There was also trouble in connection with various overseas coaches brought to South Africa during this period, even Rohan Kanhai becoming the centre of a controversy when he refused to play on a patently dangerous pitch. The others involved were the little known West Indians, Keith Barker, an extrovert who appeared to make a habit of upsetting pompous officials, and John Holder, who actually lost his place in the Western Province side because of lack of playing success.

However, the period 1971 to 1976 saw the development of a new batch of highly competent local performers. "Tiefie" Barnes, "Dickie" Conrad, Neville Francis (the only man to hit two centuries in a SACBOC inter-provincial game), Ismail Garda and Yacoob Omar continued to hit hundreds with regularity whilst "Lefty" Adams and "Babu" Ebrahim vied for the spot of top wicket taker. A number of new pace bowlers appeared on the scene in the shape of Saait Majiet and Jock Mahoney of Western Province (the latter was another to later represent Western Province "B" (SACU)), Abdul Manack of Transvaal and the left-handed Jeff Frans of Eastern Province, who for a while 'defected' to SACU and played in the Currie Cup competition.

During this period Western Province continued to reign supreme and won virtually everything in sight. Howie Bergins was their leading wicket-taker when he decided to accept the invitation to appear against the International Wanderers and he is now, of course, a regular member of Eddie Barlow's enthusiastic young Boland brigade.

Other new names appeared on the score-sheets, including two more defectors to the Currie Cup scene in Eastern Province's left-hander Devdas Govinjee and all-rounder Imran Hendricks. Like Jeff Frans they both eventually returned to Mr Howa's SACB fold.

Rohan Kanhai came and saw and conquered, and then beat a hasty retreat when the conditions of play became too dangerous for his liking. It would appear that SACBOC were either loathe to spend much money on improving their grounds and pitches or perhaps just did not have sufficient funds to do the job properly. They were handicapped though by the fact that most of the fields they played on belonged to some local government or provincial authority.

Ignoring the criticism and calumny heaped upon his greying head, the, in many ways, totally admirable Mr Hassan Howa (whose slogan "no normal sport in an abnormal society" certainly has a highly moralistic ring about it) refused to abide by the majority decision of SACBOC to work together with SACU in the interests of unity in South African cricket and was one of the instrumental figures responsible for the formation of the South African Cricket Board in 1977.

Difficulty was now experienced in obtaining immediate and adequate sponsorship and it was a struggle to keep the various competitions going but, surprisingly enough, there was an immediate bonus in terms of playing strength through the almost immediate re-defection to the SACB from SACU

Difficulty was now experienced in obtaining immediate and adequate sponsorship and it was a struggle to keep the various competitions going but, surprisingly enough, there was an immediate bonus in terms of playing strength through the almost immediate re-defection to the SACB from SACU by a number of top players who prob-

Ben Malamba (left) exchanges his bat for a shovel whilst helping to prepare practice wickets at the Cape African township of Langa.

ably found it difficult to make the transition in mid-career.

The return of Govindjee, Hendricks and Frans certainly strengthened Eastern Province. Kaya Majola, who had played for Derrick Robins in England, also made himself available and Easterns became a strength in the land. Transvaal suffered most when the majority of their clubs went along with Mr Varachia but there has been a complete turnabout in recent times and the SACB appears to be gaining some ground in the north.

Many Western Province black players are now totally involved in the non-racial SACU leagues and there has been a resultant decline in the strength of that province with regards to competitions organised by the SACB, although "Lefty" Adams and the Majiet brothers remained active and a few new stars like opening bat Rashid Musson, fast bowler Vincent Barnes and all-rounder Michael Doman have appeared on the horizon.

The new young Western Province all-rounder's father, Ted Doman, editor of the *Cape Herald*, once organised a non-racial game in Cape Town in honour of that great character Freddy Trueman who was on a promotional visit to the city. There were a number of hilarious scenes during the match but none as illustrative of the humour ever-present amongst Cape Town's Cinderella people as when the great man lumbered in to bowl the first ball of the day. "Bowler's name?" came the cry, in chorus. Poor Fred Trueman was completely thrown and his first delivery landed in the centre of the mat to fly high over the batsman's head for nearly *six* byes.

If only some humour could be brought back into the situation we may see some sort of rapprochement between Mr Howa's Board and Mr Joe Pamensky and company. Hassan Howa has stated that he would be prepared to collaborate if only SACU would admit that the South African society is "abnormal" and has been quoted as saying "if they say that and ask us for help and ask us to play sport on the understanding that it is abnormal and they are working to normalise it, they would find us co-operative".

The SACB sponsorship situation has now improved but there has undoubtedly been some decline in the standard of play. The staggering success of Lawrence Rowe's West Indian team in drawing capacity crowds from all races will possibly result in some kind of swing to SACU affiliated unions and clubs. It can only be hoped that SACU and SACB will soon see their way clear to work together so that this attempt at relating some of the highlights of the story of Black cricket in South Africa may be the final record of a divided history. •

Dennis Lillee, who was regarded in the mid-seventies as the best fast bowler in the world, sorely tested Pollock, Richards & Co.

CHAPTER SEVEN

CRICKET IN THE WILDERNESS

South African cricket was effectively forced out into the cold in 1968 following the politically expedient statement at a Bloemfontein Nationalist Congress by the then Prime Minister Mr B J Vorster that Cape Town's Basil D'Oliveira would not be welcome in his homeland as a member of the MCC touring party.

The late Geoffrey Chettle's comment in his 'South African Cricket Annual' echoed the views of genuine cricket-lovers throughout the world:

"Can we subscribe to the view that the 2000 odd hysterically cheering people who acclaimed the fateful pronouncement constitute the 'voice' of genuine sportsmen and sportswomen in this country. We would like to know what percentage of that audience would have been sufficiently interested to attend an England/South Africa Test series ?"

In his autobiography, *Time to Declare*, the ever modest Basil D'Oliveira, central figure in this sad episode in South Africa's sporting and political history, describes his own reaction of shocked disbelief that such a fuss could have been generated on his account. He then realized that the political aspect of the matter was the prime motivation of Mr Vorster's action:

"I understand Vorster was facing a revolt within his Nationalist Party from the right-wing anti-liberal element and he clearly felt he had to clamp down to assert his authority. The game of cricket gave him that opportunity."

Other events were contributory to the state of affairs. The transactions surrounding the actual selection of the MCC touring party created a climate of instability and uncertainty. A string of prominent politicians and sporting officials became involved, from Britain's Sports Minister Denis Howell and former PM Sir Alec Douglas-Home, to South Africa's then Minister of the Interior, Piet le Roux and Prime Minister Vorster and from former MCC President Lord Cobham, MCC Secretary S.C. Griffith and even the Reverend David Sheppard to South Africa's Jack Cheetham and Arthur Coy.

D'Oliveira was also clandestinely approached by a certain Mr Tienie Oosthuizen, apparently on behalf of a South African business group, with an offer of a lucrative ten-year contract if he would declare his unavailabilty for the tour.

The cancellation of the tour was a body-blow to those South Africans who put sport ahead of politics but there can be little honest doubt that the current non-racial cricket administration of the South African Cricket Union would probably not have become such an early reality were it not for the shock engendered by the turn of events which commenced in the late 1960's and now carries forward into the 1980's with, alas, little sign of a settlement. Worth quoting here is the comment by Graeme Pollock, probably South Africa's greatest cricketer of all time, as recorded in a recent interview for an Australian cricket magazine :

"Unfortunately I think it is a situation where rules were laid down some years ago relating to South Africa's re-entry to test cricket but every year something gets added and the way it's going now on the political side it certainly looks as if we will not be brought back into the fold again until we have some sort of one-man-one-vote scene in South Africa."

South Africa's problems on the

cricket field had of course commenced much earlier. In 1958 a warning had already been sounded that the pending elevation of the West Indies, Pakistan, India and New Zealand to full membership of the Imperial Cricket Conference could spell future trouble and in 1961 South Africa was expelled from the world body. Other predominantly white sporting organisations were also starting to feel the effects of the concerted efforts made by local and external opponents to fully isolate South Africa in all international competition. Prominent in the anti-Springbok campaign was the 'non-racial' South African Sports Association who bombarded various world controlling groups with requests for South Africa's excommunication.

Various requests for re-admission to the ICC (the initials now stand for the re-named 'International' Cricket Conference) were met with polite refusals and the current SACU administration, the result of the joining of forces of the predominently black SACBOC led by Mr Raschid Varachia and the former white South African Cricket Association together with the former South African African Cricket Board, has been forced to pursue its unorthodox policies so that South Africa's cricket-starved players and public may have some glimpse of international standards.

To quote former Springbok captain Dr Ali Bacher, one of the prime motivators behind the 1983 West Indies 'Calypso Cavaliers' tour:

"The fact that our cricket is non-racial has had an influence on South African society as a whole. The very fact that laws have changed as a result of what has happened in sport is a vivid illustration of the powerful influence of sport."

Raschid Varachia — hard working first president of the South African Cricket Union.

The list of negative episodes involving South African cricket during the seventies has been chronicled *ad nauseum* in many books and journals. A proposed tour of England by South Africa in 1970 was eventually called off following frequent adjustments to the itinerary, which in its final truncated form would have seen the Springboks doing battle behind barbed-wire barricades on only some half dozen grounds which could be best protected from the ever increasing militancy of the anti-apartheid activists.

This was a bitter disappointment for South Africa's top players who had done so well against the two Australian teams in 1966/67 and 1969/70. It must have been particularly frustrating for players like Eastern Province opening bat Arthur Short and Transvaal fast bowler "Chaka" Watson who were still to win a Springbok test cap. The full team chosen for this aborted tour is worthy of recording: A. Bacher (captain), E.J. Barlow (vice-captain), B.A. Richards, R.G. Pollock, B.L. Irvine, D. Lindsay, H.R. Lance, M.J. Procter, P. MacL.Pollock, P.H.J. Trimborn, A.J. Traicos, A.M. Short, G.L.G. Watson and G.A. Chevalier. Of the fourteen only Traicos has since been accepted in England as an offficial tour party member, representing his home country Zimbabwe in the 1983 World Cup Tournament.

More heartache was to follow when the Australian Board of Control cancelled the South African visit to Australia in 1971/72, again after the Springbok team had been chosen.

South Africa's rugby players had with official protection defied the demonstrators in England and Australia but it was considered that it would be impossible to adequately police a game of cricket stretching over four or five days.

Phil Tresidder's sad lament in a special 'Exit South Africa' edition of 'Australian Cricket' aptly recorded one of the most important issues relating to the proposed tour:

"Whatever one's moral views, there can be no doubt among cricket lovers: the tour that wasn't might have been the greatest tour of them all."

The cancellation of this tour was undoubtedly a triumph for the type of illegality practiced then by a few and which is now so rampant and known simply as "terrorism" in many parts of the world. The fear of physical violence and the inability to cope with it over an extended period was obviuosly one of the major considerations in mind when the Australian Board made its fateful decision. Cricket lovers were thus robbed of the opportunity to watch the greatest team ever produced by South Africa and possibly one of the most competent combinations of all time from any country. Yes, it would certainly have been a great tour if it were not for the power of the minority who will always threaten violence if their views are not acceded to by the majority.

During the pre-tour trial match at Newlands, Cape Town where Currie Cup victors Transvaal faced up to a Rest of South Africa Xl in a match played as part of the Republic Festival celebrations, the top South African players staged a walk-off in support of their union's belated effort to save the tour by gaining permission from the South African Government to include a couple of what must have appeared to the outside world token black players in the final line-up.

The two players mentioned were Gesant "Tiney" Abed, who later caused a stir when he joined the all-white Green Point C.C., and Owen Williams, who eventually emigrated to Australia and wound up as Club Captain of Prospect C.C. in Adelaide.

The Republic Festival match produced, incidentally, centuries in contrasting style from South Africa's two acknowledged world class batsmen. In an uncharacteristically dour six-hour stint Barry Richards led off with 140 on the first day against a formidable attack of Procter, Peter Pollock, van der Bijl, Trimborn and Chevalier and, coming in towards the end of the second day, Graeme Pollock, wearing spectacles for the first time, hit a delightful 146.

The South Africans chosen for the ill-fated Australian venture were: A. Bacher (captain), E.J. Barlow (vice-captain), H.M. Ackerman, A.L. Biggs, G.A. Chevalier, P.D. de Vaal, B.L. Irvine, D. Lindsay, P. MacL.Pollock, R.G. Pollock, M.J. Procter, C.E.B. Rice, B.A. Richards, P.H.J.Trimborn, and V.A.P. van der Bijl. Barlow withdrew for business reasons before the tour call-off to be replaced by A.M.Short, the vice-captaincy being awarded to Graeme Pollock.

An attempt by Colin Cowdrey to organise a privately-sponsored team, including Basil D'Oliveira,to visit South Africa in 1972 also fell through and South African cricket was thrust well and truly into the wilderness.

Starting in 1975 SACBOC now made a number of efforts to gain recognition from the ICC as South Africa's sole cricket representative but there was no way that the group then dominated by Mr Hassan Howa, could prove that it represented the majority of South Africa's cricketers of all races. Another attempt was made in 1983 by Mr Howa's South African Cricket Board, probably with even less justification than eight years previously, taking into acount the enormous strides to 'normalise' cricket in South Africa that had been made by SACU under the successive presidencies of the much respected Raschid Varachia and the determined Joe Pamensky.

From 1976, in face of a disapproving government attitude, Messrs Varachia, Pamensky and company, actively encouraged the principle of mixed clubs and threw open the leagues under SACU jurisdiction to unrestricted participation by all race groups. It must be admitted that some ground has since been lost mainly in the Transvaal and Eastern Province through the influence of Mr Howa's SACB but the success of all-race cricket in the Western Province has been particularly notable.

Some fine black players have made their way into the various Western Province and Boland elevens and several black schoolboys from these and other provinces have attained Nuffield schools competition honours in recent years. A couple of 'famous sons of famous fathers' could well appear in the persons of Shukri Conrad and Salieg Nackerdien who played with success for the 'secret' South African Schools' "Albatros Xl" in England in June and July 1983.

British industrialist and avid cricket enthusiast Derrick Robins did much to keep South African spirits going during the 'isolation' years. Starting in 1972/73 the Derrick Robins' Xl tours became a welcome addition to the normal domestic Currie Cup programme, which, incidentally, remains one of the toughest home competitions in the world in spite of South Africa's being cut off from international stimulus.

Culminating in a match against a test strength South African Invitation Xl at Wanderers, the first Derrick Robins tour proved popular, although the visiting combination was nowhere near international class. The Johannesburg game saw the South Africans wipe out some of their frustrations with a massive innings and 117 run win. Barry Richards hit a sparkling hundred and good batting came from Lee Irvine and 'new-boy' Andre Bruyns who hit 97 and shared a grand 111-run partnership with a youthful Kenny McEwan.

1973/74 brought the second Robins' team which arrived soon after another innovation had served to re-instil some enthusiasm and hope for the game in South Africa. Sponsored by the Datsun motor company an international double-wicket competition at the Wanderers, Johannesburg in 1972 drew entrants from Australia, England and New Zealand, including the mighty Chappell brothers and erstwhile South African Tony Greig.

In addition the African pair of Edward Habane and Edmund Nticinka made a brilliant start to their 'international' involvement and Datsun's first cricket sponsorship developed into a venture which captured the imagination of the public and players alike. The one sad note was the the refusal to participate by SACBOC and Mr Howa's succesful blockage of a bid to get Basil D'Oliveira to partner Greig in the competition.

The Robins Xl included Younis Ahmed of Pakistan and John Shepherd from the West Indies, the first two

Left: Ismail 'Baboo' Ebrahim whose hour of glory came at Kingsmead against Greg Chappell's International Wanderers.
Below: John Shepherd — the first West Indian to play in the Currie Cup since 1931 when the West Indies captain, G.C. 'Jackie' Grant turned out for Rhodesia.

black players to officially tour South Africa, and also broke new ground by playing against Sam Ntshekisa's S.A.African Xl at the Jabuva Stadium in Moroko,Soweto. They faced a full South Africa side in three matches at Cape Town, Durban and Johannesburg, the first two were drawn but the South Africans claimed the 'rubber' by virtue of another big innings win at the Wanderers.

Barry Richards was in fine fettle at Cape Town and Durban with succesive scores of 61,54 and 180 and he added a well-played 59 in the third match. But the show at Wanderers was well stolen by the ebullient Eddie Barlow who survived a very confident appeal for caught behind when 65 to carry on to a massive 211 in a total of 528 for 8 wickets declared. The value of his innings was, however, somewhat diminished by the fact that the tourists' two main bowlers, John Snow and Johnny Gleeson were unavailable through injury.

1974/75 saw yet another Robins' tour plus a Datsun double-wicket competition which was notable for the inclusion of teams from Pakistan and the West Indies in the presence of Younis and "Billy" Ibadullah for the former and Geoffrey Greenidge and Shepherd from the Carribean. Public interest in the Derrick Robins teams was starting to wane. There was clearly a need for competition of a higher calibre and scratch teams thrown together with players from various countries just did not have the appeal which a fully-fledged national combination would have engendered.

Some history was made though with the inclusion of black players "Dicky" Conrad and Edward Habane alongside Barlow, Pollock, Richards and company in a South African President's Xl at Newlands. Conrad actually came into the side after first being chosen as twelfth-man when an administration bungle led to the withdrawal of original invitee "Tiefie" Barnes who heard of his selection second hand without ever receiving any sort of official notification.

History of a lasting variety was initiated the following season with the formation of a nine-man committee representing the South African Cricket Association, the South African Cricket Board of Control and the South African African Cricket Board, under the chairmanship of Mr Raschid Varachia and this time with the full approval of the South African Government via the offices of the Minister of Sport, Dr Piet Koornhof.

This move resulted ultimately in the birth of the still thriving all-race South African Cricket Union but a large number of former SACBOC members lined up behind Mr Hassan Howa to bring into existence the South African Cricket Board and so continued to maintain the distressing rift for so long inherent in South African cricket administration.

Before the final steps were taken to form SACU, a visit from a strong 'International Wanderers' team in 1975/76 gave some indication of the current strength of South African cricket. Other than in a pipe-opener at Soweto against an all-African Xl the Wanderers were opposed by multi-racial teams in every match. Under the captaincy of Greg Chappell and including his brother Ian, Dennis Lillee, Ashley Mallett, Gary Gilmour, Alan Hurst and Max Walker (Australia), Mike Denness, Bob Taylor, Phil Edmonds and Derek Underwood (England), Glenn Turner and John Morrison (New Zealand) and John Shepherd (West Indies) the fifteen-strong party was the most formidable to arrive in South Africa since Bill Lawry's 1969/70 Australians.

Chappell's team had the best of their first match against a very under-strength S.A.Invitation Xl at Newlands and, with Barry Richards, Graeme Pollock and Lee Irvine side-lined after a dispute over match payment terms, the composite international team had

Greg Chappell, one of the Australian greats of the seventies

little difficulty in gaining a 185 run victory.

The game was notable for a fine 97 from Clive Rice who was one of the few South Africans able to counter the unaccustomed sharpness of Alan Hurst and Gary Gilmour. In a brave attack, although suffering with a badly injured shoulder, the bustling left-hander Gilmour placed his personal seal on the match with a violent 80 not out after coming in at number eleven in the Wanderers' second innings. Batting one-handed he hit three sixes and 11 fours in a 96-run last-wicket spree with Derek Underwood in just 64 minutes.

At St George's Park, Port Elizabeth a young President's Xl held the tourists to a draw thanks to a grand hundred from their skipper Lorrie Wilmot (an Eastern Province contemporary of Graeme Pollock who must have played for South Africa were it not for isolation) and a brave 88 not out by 18 year-old Kepler Wessels.

A return to the fold by Richards, Pollock and Irvine brought some stiffening to the South Africans' order for the next match at Johannesburg but the simultaneous arrival of the fiery Dennis Lillee nearly heralded total disaster for the local line-up who struggled to a second innings 91 for eight wickets, with the great Australian coming out with figures of 7 for 27. Graeme Pollock and another Australian, Martin Kent, graced this match with powerful hundreds and, all in all, the home crowd was at last treated to some really top-class cricket.

The black players in the South African team were still finding their feet al-

An early shot of Clive Rice, one of the unluckiest of South Africa's top players — a potential great who was bowled out by politics.

though Barnes did play with great determination for 30 in the first innings and young Howie Bergins showed improved variety and direction as a fast-medium bowler.

Kingsmead, Durban then became the site for a demonstration of spinning magic by the little Indian left-hander Ismail "Baboo" Ebrahim who forced himself into recognition as a player who would stand a fair chance of inclusion in a full Springbok Xl purely on merit. For a long time the leading wicket-taker in SACBOC competitions, Ebrahim was appearing in his debut first-class match, which makes his performance all the more remarkable.

South African Xl captain Eddie Barlow did not even use the Durban born player in the first innings when another 'banana-boy' big Vintcent van der Bijl, with help from Clive Rice and Barlow himself saw the illustrious touring team back in the pavilion for just 99 runs after a dismal home first-effort of 178. Determined batting by Richards and Pollock against the menacing Lillee and Hurst built up a 348 run lead and Ebrahim then took over.

Although Mike Denness and Greg Chappell batted with their customary skill they were at no time totally comfortable against the SACBOC spinner who eventually claimed both their wickets (Denness to a superb gulley catch by substitute fieldsman Henry Fotheringham) and ended with the fine anlysis of 29,1-12-66-6.

Packer was the name on most cricket followers' lips during the following year and a number of South Africa's leading protagonists of the game jetted east to the Antipodes to try their skill against the best talent the world could offer. Over the next couple of seasons Barry Richards and Mike Procter confirmed their station in cricket's heirarchy whilst Clive Rice and Garth le Roux performed with skill and success. Kepler Wessels was also prominent for Australia prior to a four-year residential wait for full test honours. Graeme Pollock and Denys Hobson were invited to play but their participation was blocked by the politicos who differentiated between those South Africans who played as full-time professionals and the amateurs who were looking for an opportunity to display their skills in higher company.

South Africa's hopes of a remission of sentence were raised when the ICC sent a 'fact-finding mission' to their land in 1979 to report on progress made towards fully integrated cricket. Their report was not made public, probably because it was perhaps too favourable to find acceptance amongst South Africa's critics. Mr Varachia obtained a copy "by devious means" and it was quoted that the delegation were "greatly impressed by the progress made towards non-racial cricket and the amount of non-racial cricket being played . . . There is no hindrance to any non-white cricketer playing at the very highest level of the game in South Africa for any other reason than cricket ability."

The report went on to say that, although it did not recommend actual resumption of representative cricket involving South Africa, it did suggest that a strong unofficial team be sent out to play "a series of matches at the highest level." As stated earlier the report was never published and nothing was done about any of the recommendations.

It is perhaps appropriate to quote here the late Denys Heesom who in his typically clear and concise manner echoed the thoughts of many right thinking people around the world when he wrote:

"This sort of double standard is bad enough. It is made worse by the fact that probably in no country has the cricketing authority stood up so nobly and with as much success to 'Government Policy' as has the SACU in South Africa. Now we are told that international contacts between South Africa and other countries at cricket, or South Africa and France at rugby, may lead to boycotts at the 1980 Olympic Games in Moscow — described aptly by Michael Melford as 'that archetypal haven of freedom' — or by the Black African states, or by somebody else somewhere; the list of those who have axes to grind seems to be endless. This is nothing short of blackmail and to give in to it takes us back to the days of 'Appeasement' of 1938. It did not work then and it ought not to work now."

So it was back into the desert for another couple of seasons, with interest kept alive by an energetic administration and an action-filled domestic programme of Currie Cup and Datsun Shield matches (to replace the old Gillette Cup competition) plus a long list of new one-day competitions to keep the turnstiles moving: Computer Sciences Triangular Tournament, Protea Challenge Match, Hunt's Challenge Cup, S.A.B.C. Double-Wicket Competition and the popular night cricket presented by Benson and Hedges. Added to this are the many competitions at School and University level and the Country Districts' tournaments to prove conclusively that cricket was (and is) still alive and well and living in South Africa. •

1982/83 Springbok captain, Peter Kirsten.

CHAPTER EIGHT

THE REBEL TOURS

For most South Africans the first revelation that an international cricket tour by a team of English test players was imminent, came during the South African TV news programme on the evening of Sunday 28 February 1982. The sudden appearance of seven England stalwarts, led off the plane by none other than the almost legendary Geoff Boycott, one of the prime instigators of the shock arrangement, was more than welcome to a cricket-starved South African public fed up with the double-standards of 'official' cricketdom.

And, at first sight it looked as if South Africa would be provided with some fairly stiff opposition. It was sad that the absence of a genuine fast bowler or two and a brittle middle batting order soon became apparent, although it must be accepted that the run-in to the first 'Test' match was hardly adequate in international terms. The wretched weather encountered towards the end of the visit also contributed to what started out as a big bang but ended as a bit of a damp squib.

The subsequent three-year test ban imposed on this enterprising group of men by their home authorities after numerous appeals were made for them to abort the tour, severely weakened the strength of the current England eleven who will hopefully be happy to welcome the return of players such as Graham Gooch and John Emburey when their banning period is over.

Lord Chalfont, a former Foreign Affairs Minister and President of 'Freedom in Sport', came out strongly against the arbitrary bannings and, although he was very strong in his condemnation of South African government policy, abhorred the developing situation in which other countries were making attempts to dictate the composition of England teams by refusing to participate in matches with players who had been in South Africa.

In October 1981 then England captain Mike Brearley wrote an article for *Cricketer International* in which he put forward the idea that the time was possibly ripe for a tour of South Africa by a composite international side as an alternative to continued total exclusion. In retrospect it seems a pity that no action was taken at that time. Tommie Campbell of the 'Freedom in Sport' organisation was another who campaigned (and continues to do so) for a more realistic approach to the 'South African question'. He is a particularly strong opponent of the iniquitous 'Black List' put out by the United Nations Organisation which condemns sports people with South African connections to bannings and blacklisting with absolutely no recourse available to any kind of democratic process of appeal.

Masterminds of the tour were two Britishers, Peter Cooke, managing director of a Johannesburg company, and the well-known SABC TV sports personality, Martin Locke, who combined their efforts with the more than adequate resources of the mammoth South African Breweries group (the team was called the SAB England XI) to put together a package attractive enough to lure the Englishmen to South Africa. Obviously the South African Cricket Union was involved from the start but arrangements were kept severely secret whilst the visit was

Stephen Jefferies who is rapidly becoming South Africa's top strike bowler.

planned over almost a full year and the arrival of Boycott, Gooch and their men came as a profound shock to South Africa's critics, both local and overseas. Negotiations with the English players actually began in the West Indies in 1981 and Boycott continued recruitment throughout the following English summer.

Final plans were outlined in India where the proposed itinerary was referred to by the chosen participants as 'chess matches'. On their return from the Asian sub-continent a meeting was called in London and at the homes of some of the players and, when officials of the Test and County Cricket Board got wind of the project, efforts were made to persuade Boycott and his group to reconsider their decision. The die was cast, however, and no alterations were made to their travel arrangements.

Reaction to the news of the tour was widely varied, from "They are selling themselves for blood-covered kruger rands" (Gerald Kaufman — Shadow Environment Secretary) to Mrs Margaret Thatcher's comment: "We do not have the power to prevent our sportsmen and sportswomen visiting South Africa, or anywhere else. If we did we would no longer be a free country" .

The players themselves were firm about their reasons for coming. Graham Gooch, appointed by the English team as their skipper for the tour, was quoted early on as saying:

"We stand by our decision to come and play here. We want to encourage multi-racial sport in South Africa" .

Some of them apparently carried their defiance over into the subsequent English season when Sunil Gavaskar's touring Indian team was repeatedly greeted at the English County grounds by left-over stickers advertising the rebel South African tour placed strategically in their dressing rooms.

The Indians had been upset earlier by the fact that the whole affair was arranged whilst some half dozen of the Englishmen were guests in their country, Boycott having only been accepted as a tourist in India, following his earlier South African connections, after intervention by the Indian Prime Minister Mrs Nehru herself.

It was sad that another personality of Indian birth, the dedicated Raschid Varachia, first President of the 'multi-racial' South African Cricket Union passed away two months prior to what would have been a crowning achievement in his long career in cricket adminstration. The former SACBOC president, who was born in Bombay, worked untiringly for cricket and for the removal of racial discrimination in South Africa for over thirty years. He was first secretary of SACBOC when it was formed in the early 1950's to bring together the Malay, Coloured, Indian and Bantu administrations under one roof, and in January 1976, always a controlled and charming diplomat, he moved with ease into the chairmanship of the commitee of nine set up by SACBOC, SACA and SAACB.

Another man with an 'Indian' connection turned down the offer to join 'Gooch's Rebels' (as they soon came to be known). Northamptonshire captain Geoff Cook had, because of his previous playing connection with Eastern Province, become, with Boycott, the

Garth le Roux had great success in the Packer 'circus'.

centre of a controversy concerning his entry into India with the England touring team. Mrs Nehru saved the day for England, and Cook, in the hope that he may be on the brink of a lengthy international career, decided not to come to South Africa.

In his editorial in *The Cricketer International Spring Annual* of 1982 Christopher Martin-Jenkins led off with the words: "It was the timing of the unofficial England tour of South Africa, rather than the tour itself, which took everyone by surprise" and went on to comment that because of the frustration of 12 years of isolation, and with the resources available in South Africa, "this kind of 'pirate' tour was likely unless cricket officials got together to take some initiative themselves".

The editor of the oldest surviving cricket publication also goes on to say that it was unfortunate that no action was taken regarding the recommendations in 1979 by the ICC fact-finding mission that a team of international strength be sent to South Africa.

It was a severe disappointment to players and public alike that the standard of cricket during this ice-breaking tour did not reach anywhere close to the heights that had been hoped for at the start of the venture.

A serious injury to John Emburey, the only class spin bowler in the side, during the third match against Western Province at Newlands seriously upset the balance of Gooch's attack. Emburey had caused some headaches for the strong Western Province line-up, which included Peter Kirsten, Kenny McEwan and Adrian Kuiper, and his absence for the rest of the tour must have affected the overall performance of his team.

The most entertaining match was the one-day international played at St George's Park, Port Elizabeth. Batting first, Gooch got his team off to a thunderous start with a power-packed 114, hitting 14 fours and 4 sixes. Dennis Amiss (71) gave grand support in a 138-run third wicket stand and the English XI looked to be in a good position with 240 for five wickets off their alloted 50 overs.

Les Taylor, the Leicestershire fast bowler who had been playing for Natal, then caused the raising of eyebrows with a lively opening spell but Barry Richards, as calm and elegant as ever and Jimmy Cook, technically and temperamentally the best of South Africa's new generation of batsmen, stood fast, and then put on the pressure once they had settled in. The first wicket went at 125 and, when Peter Kirsten departed quickly, the great Graeme Pollock strode to the wicket to play an innings full of majesty and power.

One pull shot into the stand off Taylor left the English bowler shaking his head in disbelief. Gooch had asked Pollock how he felt before the match and had been given the reply: "not in very good nick" . The question now for the Englishmen was that, if Pollock's performance was not his best, whatever would they do to contain him when he did strike top form ?

As it turned out though, the visitors only once again experienced the full fury of the South African left-hander when he hit 64 not out in the first 'Test' at the Wanderers after Richards,

Cook (114 in his debut international innings) and Kirsten had raised the total to 278 for 2 wickets. South Africa won this game by eight wickets after a fighting hundred by Gooch had extended the England XI's follow-on sufficiently to force the home side to bat again.

Apart from the four top batsmen the South African player who stood out head and shoulders above his colleagues (literally and figuratively) was giant Vince van der Bijl who tirelessly spear-headed a four-man attack to end with the figures of 10 wickets for 104 off fifty-four overs.

The South Africans, who received full Springbok colours for this series, were captained by Mike Procter but the magnificent all-rounder was past his best and sorely troubled by a knee injury which side-lined him completely after the second one-day bash at his home ground, Kingsmead in Durban.

All the South Africans made runs in this game and the English XI were swept away by the local attack aided and abetted by their quick-silver wicket-keeper Ray Jennings who pouched three fine catches and stumped a bewildered Arnie Sidebottom off the left-arm spinner Alan Kourie. Along with Cook as a batsman, Jennings and Kourie, as an all-rounder, were emerging as personalities of the future.

A very wet Newlands was the scene for the second 'Test' and painfuly slow batting ruined any prospect of a result. Gooch hit his wicket while trying to cut Kourie after top-scoring with 83 in the England XI first innings 223 and Peter Kirsten continued his run of good scores against the tourists with a slow but faultless 114. Gooch, Wayne Larkins and Amiss livened up the final day but there was no question of there being sufficient time to force a win and Gooch allowed his men to bat well into the day to gain some much needed practice.

South Africa won the third one-day encounter, at the Wanderers, by virtue of a quicker run-scoring rate when rain halted proceedings after only 23 overs had been completed in the English innings and the final four-day 'Test' was ruined once more by rain after Gooch's team had gained a first-innings lead thanks to a patient century from Bob Woolmer.

So the SAB England XI went home to face the music provided by the TCCB and sundry other organisations and individuals and South Africa's cricket organisers went back into a huddle to see what they could cook up for their public and players the following season.

And again the first news most people received of another sensational South African cricket coup was provided by television news coverage of the arrival of a party of, for the most part, tiny Sri Lankans who were to play under the title 'Arosa Sri Lankans' (after the initials of their manager/organiser Tony Opatha) and who became known by some sections of the local press as the 'Red Lions'.

If it were not for the fact that this rather lack-lustre tour was to pave the way for the acceptance of terms by Lawrence Rowe's West Indians to venture to the land of apartheid, it would have been written off as a mistake of some proportion. Financially it proved to be a total disaster when it became obvious to the South African public that the strength of the team was little ahead of their own 'B' section provinces. SACU was unable to find a sponsor and, as with the later West Indian venture, were loathe to accept any form of Government funding for fear of compromise of their autonomy regarding non-racial principles and practices.

Anyone with minimal knowledge of current Sri Lankan cricket would have experienced immediate misgivings when the composition of the touring party was published. Only five of the players had appeared in an 'official' test match, with little or no record of success at that level.

The captain, Bandula Warnapura, for all his keeness, had averaged only 12 in eight test innings and of the four only Anura Ranasinghe had reached 50 in an international game. The three test bowlers, Ranasinghe, Ajit de Silva and Lalith Kaluperuma had captured but 8 test wickets between them at nearly 70 runs apiece and only wicket-keeper Mahes Gunatilleke would have been assured of a place in a contemporary Sri Lankan team.

The 'Red Lions' flattered to deceive with a resounding win in their first 'knock-about' against Nicky Oppenheimer's scratch XI (their only success of the tour) but thereafter almost a complete roster of failure was recorded against all opposition placed in their pathway.

Even Eddie Barlows's Boland team drew blood, thanks to the incisive off-spin of "Pine" Anker, and the 'international' matches fast developed into farcical exhibitions with players like Graeme Pollock and Barry Richards batting as if they were playing with their kids in the local park.

There were some moments when a few of the Sri Lankans rose to the occasion with outstanding individual performances but too much was expected from the handful of players who did not possess the skill and temperament to square up to their seemingly all-powerful opponents. Ranasinghe, a dashing right-hander, sparkled with a century in the one-day 'test' at Port Elizabeth and hit a couple of quick and entertaining fifties in other games but the only batsman to put forward any claim as being of international class was the diminuitive Bernard Perera, who had toured India and Pakistan without ever playing in a first-class or test match and was probably quite justified in his disillusionment with his country's cricket bosses.

Perera's skill and fortitude brought a ray of sunlight during the rather gloomy closing days of the tour when he hit a fine hundred at Newlands in the second four-day clash with the full might of South Africa. This came after the Springboks had battered their way to a gargantuan 663 for 6 wickets declared which included 112 by Jimmy Cook (his fourth three-figure innings in six knocks against the Sri Lankans), a breath-taking 197 from Graeme Pollock who at one point carted off-spinner Lalith Kaluperuma for four successive sixes, and a blistering 188 from new opener Lawrence Seeff who had a week earlier hit 141 on his South African debut in the limited overs game at Port Elizabeth. Needless to say South Africa won the Newlands game by an innings and plenty and they achieved a similar result in the first international at the Wanderers, although with slightly less imposing statistics.

Cook was top scorer at the Wanderers with 169 and in all matches against the Sri Lankans he totalled 556 at 92.66. Bandual de Silva and Gerry Woutersz batted with some character in the Sri Lanka first innings and the tall (for a Sri Lankan) Flavian Aponso

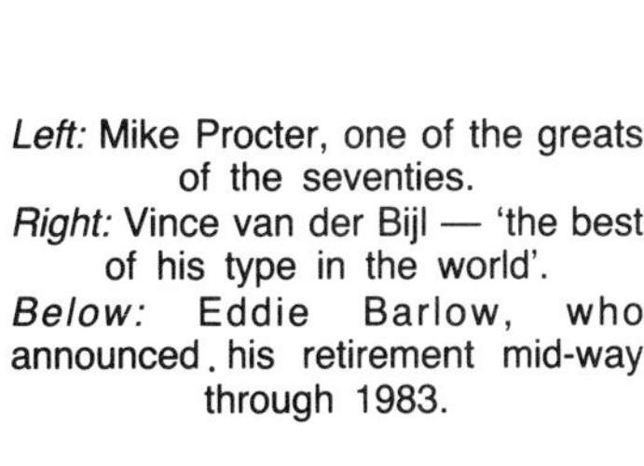

Left: Mike Procter, one of the greats of the seventies.
Right: Vince van der Bijl — 'the best of his type in the world'.
Below: Eddie Barlow, who announced his retirement mid-way through 1983.

Jimmy Cook — a century on his international debut. He has become a batsman of world class.

showed skill and grit in the follow-on (he also impressed at Cape Town with 81 in the first innings).

It was the Sri Lankans bowling which really let them down. Not one of the members of their attack was anywhere near to being labelled a penetrative bowler. In all matches only the manager Tony Opatha took in excess of ten first-class wickets, bowling at a brisk military medium-pace.

Biggest failure was the much-fancied left-arm spinner Ajit de Silva who had some record of success against eminent overseas opposition on his own home grounds but who would not even have qualified as a regular net bowler on his performances in South Africa. This likeable player's problem was a psychological one which must have caused some considerable depression in the tourists' dressing room.

For their troubles, and for a financial reward that for some must have seemed a small fortune, the hapless Sri Lankans were hit with a staggering 25 year ban by their country's cricket authorities. There have been reports of some softening of the excessively hardline attitude taken by the powers-that-be in Colombo towards Warnapura's brave little band of trail-blazers and it will be a shame if young players of the calibre of Perera, Ranasinghe and Gunatilleke are forever destined to sit on the sidelines in their home country. Sri Lanka, considering its international record so far, can surely not afford to have a fair number of leading players left idle for any lengthy period of time.

Whilst the 'Arosa Sri Lankans' were doing battle with the Springboks, the official Sri Lankan side were finding the going tough in Zimbabwe where Duncan Fletcher's well-drilled side, many of whom had received their cricket education in the gruelling atmosphere of the Currie Cup tournament, looked by far the superior combination, notwithstanding Sri Lanka's test status.

The number thirteen is an unlucky set of digits for most people but to South Africa's determined former cricket captain turned administrator, Dr Aaron "Ali" Bacher, it must surely now be a symbol of considerable good fortune for exactly thirteen seasons after his resounding success as South Africa's skipper in a 4-0 whitewash of Bill Lawry's Australians, he was one of those instrumental in arranging the unbelievable, a tour of South Africa by a team of West Indian players.

South Africa's most successful test captain was first inspired to try for the big one after discussions with Transvaal pro Alvin Kallicharran during their early morning jogging efforts in the Johannesburg suburb in which both reside.

When he visited England in July 1982, as a member of the SACU delegation which again failed to get any sort of hearing by the Imperial Cricket Conference, Bacher approached a number of West Indians but with no tangible results.

A few days after the arrival of Lawrence Rowe's party in January 1982 the *Sunday Times*, Johannesburg, broke the full story of the almost chance events which did eventually lead up to the final amazing coup by the South African Cricket Union. It had all started when Bacher, then director of the Transvaal Cricket Council, together with SACU president Mr Joe Pamensky, approached Barbados and Surrey fast bowler Sylvester Clarke to

Sylvester Clarke — too fast for many South African batsmen.

partner Vincent van der Bijl in opening the bowling for Transvaal in the ensuing season.

In September Don Mackay-Coghill (a former Transvaal left-arm fast bowler who would surely have played for South Africa were it not for isolation) and TCC vice-chairman Raymond White (Cambridge Blue" and Currie Cup batsman of note) delivered the contract to Clarke. The West Indian declined but kept Raymond White's business card which he then passed on to fellow-Barbadian Gregory Armstrong.

It was Armstrong, himself an ex-Barbados Shell Shield pace bowler of note, who developed the idea to put together a full West Indian party to visit South Africa. Some journals and newspapers have used this item as a post-tour "revelation" but the fact of Armstrong's instigation of the idea was well-publicised at the start of the playing side of the venture.

After he had sounded out a number of possibles during a series of night matches in Barbados during October, Armstrong visited Johannesburg as a guest of Messrs Pamensky and Bacher whilst the first 'international' was in progress against the Sri Lankans in November, 1982 but did not risk a trip to the Wanderers ground for fear of recognition. Code-names were allocated to the various players concerned and Ali Bacher became involved in a seemingly endless round of trans-world telephone conversations, sometimes to pre-arranged callboxes in the Caribbean to avoid detection.

There have been reports that when the West Indian authorities got wind of a tour attempt there was some resort to suspected particapants' telephones being tapped and embassies staked out to detect players applying for visas but much of this 'cloak-and-dagger' stuff has been subsequently denied. It is however a fact that several players, notably the captain Lawrence Rowe, were forced to make public denial of their involvement in order to save the tour.

Then, due to an unforgivable leak by a still un-named official to an Australian journalist, SACU announced the cancellation of the venture in what was actually a clever bid to save matters. Air tickets were swiftly re-validated using alternative routes to confuse the opposition and on January 12th, 1983 a beaming Joe Pamensky announced finally that the team was on its way.

On Thursday, January 13th the arrival at Jan Smuts airport, Johannesburg of an advance guard consisting of Jamaican batsmen Richard Austin and Everton Mattis, both former West Indies test players, put aside all doubts that the impossible had been accomplished and that South African spectators would soon thrill to the sight of Clarke, Colin Croft and company hurling down their thunderbolts at the likes of Pollock, Richards, Kirsten and Cook.

A shocked reaction of the much-respected West Indian Cricket Board chairman and former test opener of note, Mr Alan Rae, summed up the fears and hopes of his colleagues:

"It is no longer rumour. I fear it is fact. It will be a blow to world cricket and West Indian cricket, but we will get over it."

The first portion of Mr Rae's statement is certainly true but whether world and West Indian cricket *will* ever

The ungainly action of West Indian Franklyn Stephenson who became a favourite with South African crowds.

quite be the same again is open to question. After a long battle for support in his aspirations the West Indian cricket chief has now at last reached success in his efforts to obtain a better deal for Caribbean players, but it has all come a little too late for tears.

South African response to the cricketing coup of the century was one of euphoria. Mr Pamensky summed it all up when he said, "this is a dream come true and with few exceptions people feel that this is a good thing for the country, a good thing for sport".

When booking opened for the first scheduled match of the tour at Newlands, Cape Town the thousands of fans of all races who besieged the ticket office, found the unprepared officials caught flat-footed by the unprecedented demand and the occasion soon turned into a chaotic sell-out.

Meanwhile opponents of the tour enjoyed a field day in the local and overseas press. Mr Hassan Howa was accorded the prominence which behoves his accredited position as chief spokesman for some thousands of cricketers who play outside the auspices of SACU, preferring to follow the banner of the SACB and its firm dictum of 'no normal sport in an abnormal society'. Claiming that the SACU officials were "strangers to the truth" his view on the matter was aptly clarified in the statement:

"It hasn't dawned on them that what the international sporting world wants before associating with South Africa is not normal sport as Mr Pamensky or anybody sees it, but a normal society."

West Indies tour Manager Albert Padmore, who had captained Barbados the previous season, sent a letter to the Barbados Cricket association on behalf of the players in the team from that island outlining their reasons for taking the plunge and accepting the South African contract. It was made clear that the economic consideration involved was the prime motivation for the presence of the West Indian cricketers in South Africa but there was certainly no endorsement of the overall South African situation if the following paragraph is any guide to the attitude of the players:

"We, and each of us, loathe apartheid as vehemently as, if not more than, the loudest and strongest other opponents of that inhuman practice. But we do not subscribe to the view that by playing South Africa we will make the situation any worse for coloureds and blacks there."

The pragmatic attitude adopted by most of the West Indians is perhaps best summed up in the simple statement accredited to opening bat Richard Austin at the beginning of the tour: "I cannot feed myself or my family on principles . . . cricket is all I know and I am a professional. All I am doing is earning my living".

The leading Pakistani cricket magazine, *The Cricketer*, which is edited by the legendary high scoring Hanif Mohammed, headlined an article on the South African development "Caribbean Catastrophe" and proceeded to highlight Padmore's letter and the comments of incumbent West Indies captain Clive Lloyd who affirmed that "Caribbean cricketers who play in South Africa do not understand the damage they can do to cricket in the Third World as well as to people fighting apartheid".

Mr Sam Ramsamy, Chairman of SANROC (the South African Non-racial Olympic Committee) and an implacable opponent of the SACU administration, pointed out that as apartheid permeates all aspects of life in South Africa the tour by the west Indians could be considered as "normal cricket — but only for a day!".

In *The Cricket Player*, New Zealand's cricket mouthpiece, editor Richard Becht in an editorial discussing the dramatic step taken by Lawrence Rowe and his men commented that the situation "obviously creates a ticklish double standards slant to the case of those fighting against international cricket being played in South Africa, and the progress in the whole matter from now on should be fascinating for those who keenly follow the political intricacies involved in this ever-more-complex cricketing sore".

As John Bishop so aptly put it in an article entitled "West Indians 'Resurrected' South African cricket" in *Wisden Cricket Monthly*: "One could not but wonder what John Vorster thought about it all!"

Lawrence Rowe stated firmly on his arrival in South Africa that his happy band were professionals who had come to do a job but from all reports it was not all work and no recreation and in the little free time available to them the West Indians certainly had themselves a ball. This was especially evident in Cape Town, a city long known for its warm-hearted hospitality. Richard Austin was even reported to have made contact with some long-lost cousins — the progeny of a sea-faring uncle who had jumped ship in Table Bay Harbour and settled at the Cape.

First focus from a playing angle was projected in the direction of the much-vaunted West Indies fast bowlers. Even though Colin Croft arrived with a fitness question mark over his head and Ezra Moseley's recent discarding of a plaster cast used to correct a stress fracture in one of his vertebrae must have caused some concern, it was thought that Malcolm Marshall (possibly the quickest of contemporary West Indian bowlers) would still be joining the side. With Sylvester Clarke and the gangling Franklyn Stephenson in trim and raring to go it was felt that South Africa's batsmen were in for something of a bombardment.

Although Marshall decided after all to opt out in favour of a season in the West Indies and an assured continuation of his test career, the artillery left available to skipper Lawrence Rowe proved more than adequate for the task ahead. Croft, as it happened, hardly appeared but young Moseley of the long arm and awesome lift was an instant success as a foil to the magnificent Sylvester Clarke who must have bowled on this short tour as fast and as well as ever in his distinguished career.

Franklyn Stephenson, of course, found immediate approval from South African fans of all ages who thrilled to his rumbustious hitting, super-athletic fielding and whirling-windmill bowling action which epitomised all that is best in the typical West Indian approach to the grand old game of cricket.

It was the batting which remained suspect throughout. Unfortunate was the non-appearance of high-scoring opener Desmond Haynes who went the way of Marshall and whose presence in the team may have made just that bit of difference between failure and success in a couple of the one-day internationals.

The burly Alan Kourie another 'international class' Springbok. Here he is in conversation with provincial team-mate Alvin Kallicharran.

Lawrence Rowe, the popular captain and attractive run-maker of the West Indian tourists.

Collis King who made a big impression in South Africa with his hard hitting approach.

As it turned out the run-getting capabilty revolved around three players, the elegant Lawrence Rowe (who failed miserably in the four-day 'tests'), a normally sparkling but on this tour rather subdued Alvin Kallicharran, and the outrageously aggressive Collis King who did most to get things moving at the start with a series of almost brutal attacks on South African provincial bowlers in the run-in to the first four-day match at Cape Town. His carnival batting in the 'test' at the Wanderers brought back memories of Lindsay's slaughter of the Australians in 1966/67 and was the perfect complement to Sylvester Clarke's superb fast bowling in this match.

Wicket-keeper David Murray arrived from Australia under the double cloud of leaving an expecting wife in Adelaide and the prospect of refusal of re-entry to his adopted home. His agony showed during the first big game at Newlands but the safe birth of a daughter and a softening of the previously insensitive and almost inhuman attitude of the Australian Government, saw him settle down to some very useful cricket in the remaining games.

Another extremely handy member of Rowe's team was the off-spinner Derick Parry who proved the next most successful bowler to Clarke in the two internationals against South Africa and batted and fielded with concentration and application.

The total failure as a batsman of Everton Mattis, one of the tallest in a team of tall men and a leading Shell Shield scorer who had made a useful test debut against England a few years previously, thrust an even greater load on the shoulders of the main scoring trio. Richard Austin, who made the catch to win the match in the first game of the tour against Western Province when he leaped high in the air to dismiss England 'rebel' Graham Gooch, played only one innings of any note and his opening partner, Alvin Greenidge, one of nine Barbadians in the party, only found form under adverse circumstances in partnership with Collis King at the Wanderers.

The top-order batsmen frequently expressed their surprise and displeasure at some of the leg-before-wicket decisions adjudged against them and the local umpires came in for heavy criticism from players and press alike. It was generally agreed that this was a department of South African cricket which needed some attention but it was also acknowledged that until more ex first-class players donned the white coat of official adjudication, there would be a problem in finding umpires of sufficient experience to handle the game at the highest level. Over the years only 28 former players have taken up umpiring and of these only one man, W.W. Billy Wade, actually played test cricket for South Africa.

Late recruit Herbert Chang, a left-hander from Jamaica, had little chance to find his feet and another Jamaican to join the party after the start of the tour was Ray Wynter who went straight into the eleven for the Johannesburg 'test' and was then side-lined until the Clive Rice/Barry Richards benefit thrash at Welkom was added on at the end of the official itinerary.

Emmerson Trotman, "ET" to his fans, was a glorious boundary fieldsman who doubled as reserve wicket-keeper but received few opportunities to demonstrate his stroke-making ability as a middle-order batsman. Lastly, Bernard Julien, the lone Trinidadian in a party dominated by players from Barbados, bowled his left-arm seamers with skill and direction in the one-day games but, judging by his performance with the willow on this short tour, it was hard to picture him as a batsman who had once hit a century for the West Indies in a test match.

South Africa's batting was dominated by the "Golden Oldies", Graeme Pollock and Barry Richards. Pollock batted with his customary flair and responsibility in both four-day matches, hitting a fine hundred at Newlands, and certainly gave Sylvester Clarke the 'treatment' in the limited overs 'test' on his former home ground at Port Elizabeth. The burly Clarke, who possesses the build of a prize-fighter, was left more than a little punch-drunk when the Springbok left-hander supreme pummelled him for four successive fours in the final over of the South African innings.

Richards made a classic hundred in the Port Elizabeth one-day game and his first hour in the Newlands international was pure magic as he unleashed a series of sweetly timed hooks, drives and cuts in almost indolent fashion.

Jimmy Cook batted with fortitude at Newlands and always looked the part of a fully-fledged Springbok opener but seemed to have run out of steam to a certain extent after his high-scoring antics against Gooch's XI and the Sri Lankans. South Africa's batting hopes in the next few years still rest with the phlegmatic Transvaaler who, together with Peter Kirsten and Kenny McEwan, will probably form the nucleus of his country's batting line-up into the mid-1980's.

The burden of captaincy probably affected Kirsten's concentration but, having successfully crossed his first international leadership hurdle, he should settle down to his accustomed pattern of consistent scoring.

Coming into the side after Clive Rice and Kevin McKenzie had failed in the 'tests', Kenny McEwan demonstrated in no uncertain terms why the West Indians were amazed at his omission from South Africa's initial eleven. This world-class player certainly justified his late selection with a series of highly professional stroke-play exhibitions in the limited overs games.

It was sad to see that grand player Clive Rice battling to find form. He is really one of the most unfortunate latter-day Springboks (having been chosen for the cancelled Australian tour in his late teens when so brimful of promise) and the 'rebel' tours came when a neck injury prevented him from bowling. There is no doubt that at the height of his career Rice ranked in skill and performance with the great Springbok all-rounders of the past.

Two all-rounders of contrasting style, Alan Kourie and Stephen Jefferies emerged as possible king-pins of the South African 'test' combination for the next couple of seasons. Kourie has developed into one of the characters of the game and his never-say-die attitude is carried forward into all three departments of the game. He has no peer as a left-arm spinner with a particularly devastating arm ball, a possible legacy of his days as one of South Africa's premier baseball players, and his reputation of never dropping a catch at his usual first-slip position has earned him the sobriquet "Fly-trap". Kourie is also an effective, if rather ungainly batsman, who makes a habit of playing match-saving innings when most needed.

The Western Province left-arm seam bowler Stephen Jefferies must have had envious eyes cast in his direction by the England selectors when he made a few appearances for Lancashire in the season following the West Indians' tour. This tireless performer has quickly developed into South Africa's main strike bowler and he wielded the willow to such good effect against Rowe's men at the Wanderers that there were visions of a South African win until the young Springbok was run out by a dazzling direct throw.

Big Vince van der Bijl bowled with his customary competence and was always a problem and Garth le Roux, although now much slower than when he played Packer cricket in Australia, provided an able fourth prong to a reasonably well-balanced Springbok attack.

Effervescent Ray Jennings, possibly the most heavily sponsored South African player in history, kept up a non-stop dialogue with his burly pal Kourie in between pouching a series of brilliant catches and effecting some quick-silver stumpings. He lets little through and deserves to be ranked in the class of Waite, Sherwell, Cameron and Dennis Lindsay.

Left-handed all-rounder Robbie Armitage moved smoothly into the side for the one-day games which also saw the introduction of pace bowlers Kenny Watson and Rupert Hanley, both of whom performed very adequately. Hanley's great day of success came when he claimed a hat-trick after coming into the Springbok XI as a late replacement for le Roux at the Wanderers.

Although South Africa won the first international at Cape Town by five wickets after leading the way for most of the encounter, there was enough drama on the final day to ensure a record crowd for the second match at Johannesburg.

Pollock's double of 100 and 43 not out and Kourie's gritty all-round excellence were the main success factors at Newlands where the West Indies XI was best served by Austin, Stephenson and Kallicharran, in contrasting styles, with the bat and by the tantalising and accurate off-spin of Parry.

There was a calypso carnival atmosphere during four blazing hot days at the Wanderers and a record-breaking Saturday crowd in excess of 30 000 were moved to chant "blow them away Windies" as big-hearted Sylvester Clarke scythed his way through the South African line-up after a sparkling

A moment of mirth as Sylvester Clarke is assisted to his feet by Lawrence Rowe after slipping during his bowling run-up.

stand by Pollock and Kirsten had brought the home team back from the brink of a disastrous beginning.

South Africa's first three batsmen had all failed to score and all this heady excitement had followed on the spectacle of Collis King putting the South African attack to the sword on the first day in a typical West Indies innings, lacking somewhat in purist technique but all wonderful eye and timing.

A fiery burst from young Stephen Jefferies had the Windies tottering at 70 for seven in their second knock but a last-ditch stand of 71 by the West Indies walking wounded, Alvin Greenidge (suffering from migraine and double vision) and King (severe leg cramps) edged the visitors' lead past 200.

With Richards and Cook seemingly in command it looked as if the Springboks would walk it on the final day. But they had reckoned without the amazing Clarke. The big Barbadian bowled his heart out in an almost non-stop performance and a series of blistering deliveries threatened to blow the home team onto the rocks until Jefferies swung lustily and frequently to engineer a change of direction.

Then came the one high spot of the tour for Everton Mattis who ran Jefferies out with a bullet-like throw when the South African backed up too enthusiastically. Clarke soon put a final end to the proceedings by bowling van der Bijl neck-and-crop to bring his personal tally for the match to a career best international performance of 12 wickets for exactly 100 runs.

This grand match, won by the West Indies XI by just 29 runs, inspired a Johannesburg attorney, Keith Lister, and his "North Stand Googly Band" to immortalise the proceedings by producing a gramaphone record of excerpts from the radio ball-by-ball commentary by the doyen of South African cricket broadcasters Charles Fortune and his 'back-up' for many seasons, Chick Henderson, plus a specially composed calypso entitled "The Windies blew my Springboks clean away".

A series of six one-day limited overs internationals, including the first-ever 'night' game of this stature in South Africa, continued to draw capacity crowds at Port Elizabeth, Cape Town, Pretoria (a record attendance for any match in this city), Johannesburg and, finally, Durban where Lawrence Rowe's XI completed their adventure with a crushing 84 run win during which South Africa's favourite young West Indian, Franklyn Stephenson fittingly claimed six wickets for 9 runs and the 'man-of-the match' award.

The tour had revitalised South African cricket and on every street corner and every available vacant plot the kids were out with their tin cans for stumps and their make-shift bats, something that has not been so enthusiastically pursued since Bobby Simpson's team toured in 1966/67. Cricket fever had taken over, especially in the coloured and black townships, and the spin-off for South African cricket could well become evident in a new generation of Pollocks and Richards, Kallicharans, Kings and Clarkes! •

CHAPTER NINE

WHERE DO WE GO FROM HERE?

Lawrence Rowe's 1983 calypso cavalier band went home to face the music and were pleasantly surprised to find that not all people in the islands were out to hang, draw and quarter the recalcitrant West Indians cricketers.

The captain himself decided to take up residence in England whilst some of the others spread out to various corners of the globe. Emmerson Trotman, for instance, is married to a Dutch woman and plays professional cricket in Haarlem, Holland and Manager Albert Padmore and fast bowler Colin Croft (a commercial pilot) joined their families in the USA.

About half the party jetted back with not a little trepidation to their homes in Jamaica and Barbados but, after an initial press bombardment, appear to have settled down without too much difficulty. In Jamaica, for instance, radio "call-in" programmes reflected a fair measure of support for the rebels as sportsmen pursuing their profession.

Everton Mattis told a television interviewer that although he was no supporter of apartheid he saw things which he did not expect to see and added, "I think our tour will have a good effect". Unfortunately his cricket in Jamaica is now limited to street corner knock-ups following expulsion from his Kingston club.

Colin Croft, who missed most of the playing side of the South African tour through injury, came out strongly in favour of maintaining contacts with South Africa. He, more than the others, had the opportunity to see something of the country and meet some of its people.

In an interview published in *Wisden Cricket Monthly* he was quoted thus: "I doubt I can convince people back home of what I've seen. People have their set ideas. They may not want to hear what I tell them."

In Barbados where cricket is a way of life, almost a religion, Collis King was quoted as saying that the trip had been "extraordinary" and that it had done "a great deal for relationships between whites and blacks in South Africa". Barbados Cricket Association President, Mr Peter Short, passed the tour players as eligible for club cricket but upheld the West Indies Board lifetime ban from test and inter-island games.

Back in South Africa the post tour situation reflected all the symptoms of a cricket hangover on the one hand (there had been a surfeit of domestic cricket, including a much-debated decision to stage a Currie Cup final, to add to the Sri Lankan and West Indies XI programmes) but, on the positive side, there was an air of expectancy relating to the forthcoming 1983/84 season and much evidence of a new-found interest in the game amongst the various black population groups, whose main recreation before had always been "king" soccer.

Cricket has always been popular by and large amongst the Coloured and Indian groups but the majority of the blacks have had little exposure to the game, other than those living close to the big cities. Even so, soccer has always reigned supreme and is played virtually twelve months of the year in places like Soweto near Johannesburg and amongst the Zulus in Natal. If South Africa were given immediate international recognition in this latter sport there is little doubt that the

Mr Joe Pamensky, the energetic president of the South African Cricket Union.

National Xl would consist primarily of black players, and would give a pretty good account of itself against most opposition.

It would, however, be many years before a black is likely to make it into a Springbok cricket team purely on merit. Until recent years (and thanks to such dedicated men as John Passmore, whose annual cricket week for black schoolboys has created a nursery for the future) the facilities and opportunities available to black players has made it impossible for any budding Clarke's or Collis King's to emerge. Even the more well equipped Coloured and Asian groups can provide, at this stage, few players who would challenge for places in the Castle Currie Cup Competition, let alone for international honours. Basil D'Oliveira was indeed unique — a giant of the game in relation to his contemporaries. Like Bradman, Sobers or Graeme Pollock he was just so far ahead of his colleagues that comparison with lesser mortals (in a cricketing sense) would be futile.

Thus for anyone to conclude that a more open society in South Africa would immediately produce a Springbok cricket eleven including some black players would be a demonstration of naivety in the extreme. The single contemporary player who may have such a chance is the Western Province left-arm spinner Omar Henry, probably the best of his type in the country after Alan Kourie.

To bring about change in South Africa there can be no alternative to controlled constitutional reform in an orderly fashion, implemented as quickly as is practical. Anything else would probably result in no cricket at all (or any other worthwhile activity) for a long period of time.

Prophets of doom abound in this day and age but South Africans, by and large, appear to have become inured to the prospective dangers put forth in the various prognostic scenarios about their land which seem to alter on an almost daily basis as they pour forth from the mouths and pens of the country's critics.

Some events connected with the noble game of cricket have illustrated a shift from the ridiculous to the sublime in what could be almost described as an hilarious fashion if it were not for the fact that in the end result it is all so depressingly tragic.

The unbelievable cancellation by the West Indies powers-that-be of a proposed one-month tour to the Caribbean by the England women's cricket team simply because a number of the players had, a few years previously, in all innocence and as private individuals played some cricket in South Africa, was ridiculous in the extreme.

Now there is the prospect of the cancellation of a West Indies tour to England because the authorities in the islands are fearful that their players may become contaminated by playing against men who have some connection with South Africa. At the latest count, some 30-odd per cent of the players presently contracted to England's seventeen counties have either played or coached in South Africa or, horror of horrors, were actually born in that unspeakable land!

And, whilst the famed MCC was agonising over its South African tour ballot at Lord's, a fully representative South African Schools cricket team was happily touring Britain, right under the noses of the usually vigilant SANROC and the Anti-Apartheid Movement. What fun!

Perhaps too much fuss was made of the MCC referendum. It is doubtful that a party capable of exciting South African fans could have been raised by that august club in any event and anything short of test or near-test class would have been a grave financial risk.

Tory MP John Carlisle and his supporters deserve an accolade for their worthy try (it was good to see the old heroés Denis Compton and Bill Edrich so prominent in the ranks) but MCC secretary Jack Bailey may have been close to the mark when he stated that the referendum did provide an outlet for those members who were impatient at the hypocritical attitudes towards South Africa but "of itself it will achieve nothing save lasting damage to the game and to the club." There had of course been gloomy threats of Lord's being in future by-passed as a test match venue, a situation which would have been poignantly distressing to even the most hardened supporter of the South African cause.

There appears to be, strangely enough, a more abundant fund of goodwill directed towards South Africa from the most unlikely sources than has hitherto been acknowledged. One of the most improbable recent sympathisers with the stoic efforts of the South African Cricket Union to have laws amended within their country to permit a freer expression on the cricket field, has been none other than the much-respected West Indies cricket chief, Mr Alan Rae.

The former West Indian test opening bat has been quoted as saying: "I feel- and this is my private view — a fair deal of sympathy for the SACU and what they are doing to sustain cricket in their country". He does , however, strongly assert that the 'rebel tour' road is counter-productive and is in fact playing into the hands of the "apartheid government".

Mr Rae's argument is that the luring of international cricketers clandestinely to South Africa will, in effect, slow the process of change which he feels (as do so many others within and without South Africa's borders) "that must be forced (sic) on South Africa if it is to have a democratic future". The comment that could be added here is that, almost without exception, wherever 'force' has been the catalyst for change on the African continent, and elsewhere, the chances of any kind of 'democratic' process to follow has declined with almost indecent rapidity!

But it must be accepted that Mr Rae is an honourable man with goodwill in his heart towards South Africa and its peoples. Now is the time for bridge-building, however awesome the chasm ahead may appear, and it is with open-hearted men such as Mr Rae that our administrators should be in communication, if they are not already.

One of the major keys to a change of attitude towards cricket in South Africa could well rest in the pocket of Mr Hassan Howa, that implacable foe of apartheid whose intransigence over the years has certainly played a major role in motivating white administrators to make an effort to bring about an alteration of the original pattern of control and conduct of the game.

Mr Howa's major objection to a closer co-operation with Mr Joe Pamensky's SACU has been clearly documented in an earlier chapter of this work but the essence of this last presumably major stumbling block to the formation of a single controlling body for cricket in South Africa, certainly warrants repeating.

"All" Mr Howa asks is that the SACU officials admit that South African society is in fact "abnormal" and that SACU is working towards an acceptable normalisation. Then, if they request the South African Cricket Board's assistance, he and his colleagues would be duly co-operative.

Mention must be made here of the efforts being made at a much higher administrative level to found a new constitution for South Africa and the valiant efforts of Prime Minister P.W.Botha have even been lauded by that life-time liberal opponent of segregation, world famous author Alan Paton.

Perhaps Mr Howa is after all carrying his intransigence too far and should now give credit where it is due and take hold of the hand which has been offered to him on many occasions over the years. By all reports time is short and those who have the love of South Africa and South African cricket truly in their hearts must surely be able to locate enough goodwill in their souls to give them the spur to come together in common purpose.

Hassan Howa, the tough boss of the South African Cricket Board.

Spectacles like the BBC televison debate between Ahmed Mangera of the SACB and Geoff Dakin of SACU only serve to widen the rift between the two organisations whose only slim hope of recognition by the International Cricket Conference would be based on a united front truly representative of *all* cricketers in South Africa.

And then, of course, there is the probability that even if Messrs Howa and Pamensky and their respective cohorts do manage to reach some form of accomodation and then present themselves in London as one homogeneous alliance, the politicians and their pals will really take over and quicken the beat on their "one-man-one-vote" drum.

In a "can't win" situation expedience will perforce remain the name of the game. The prognostication is therefore that, whatever happens, SACU will continue on the rebel road and do whatever they can to brighten the cricket season for South Africa's players and spectators. And this will be to the acknowledged detriment of the game in most overseas countries whose players will be regarded as 'fair game' for SACU's recruiting agents.

With the doors of the ICC firmly shut to Mr Pamensky and his SACU, the likely prospects for South Africa's cricketers and their ever-loyal supporters revolves around the spectacle of further tours by teams as near as possible representative of their respective countries, with the odd composite XI or two thrown in, and the intriguing possiblity of some kind of "Mini World Cup" to really enliven the proceedings.

Perhaps David Frith of *Wisden Cricket Monthly* is correct when he says that "South Africa's cause has been set back years by the events of the past few weeks", referring to the MCC resolution and the refusal by the ICC to hear the case of either the SACU or Hassan Howa's SACB — which body Mr Frith labels as "less undiscriminating"! Maybe Mr Howa can give us a definition of that one? After reading recently the 'definitions' of the terms 'multi-racial', 'multi-national', 'non-racial' and even 'anti-racial' in a South African cricket publication the author, who dearly would like to get on with the *game*, confesses a state of total confusion relating to the 'descriptive' tags which plague sport in general and cricket in particular.

Christopher Martin-Jenkins of *The Cricketer International* has stated that the ICC "must grasp the nettle" and questions whether the interests of particularly the black and coloured sportsmen would be best served through isolation. His attitude is in sharp contrast to some journalists who find it so simple to condemn "that accursed land" (and presumably it's many peoples) from the comfort of their London homes with few ever making the effort to go and check the facts at first hand.

One fact is unmistakeably certain. Until some indication becomes apparent of a softening of the ICC's attitude to South Africa and, at the very least, an opportunity is presented for an official hearing, the present South African cricket administration will continue along the rebel road with the energy and entrepreneurial ability which has already been so dramatically demonstrated over the past eighteen months. •

BIBLIOGRAPHY

Altham, H.S.& Swanton, E.W. — A History of Cricket
Australian Cricket (various editions)

Bansda, D.N.& Reddy, S.J. — The S.African Non-European Cricket Almanack 1953/54
Bansda, D.N.& Reddy, S.J. — The S.African Non-European Cricket Almanack 1954/55
Bansda, D.N.& Reddy, S.J. — South African Cricket Almanack 1969
Bassano, Brian — South Africa in International Cricket
Beldham, G.W.& Fry, C.B. — Great Batsmen — their methods at a glance
Beldham, G.W.& Fry, C.B. — Great Bowlers and Fielders — their methods at a glance
Bowen, Rowland — Cricket : A History of its Growth and Development
Bradman, Sir D.G. — Farewell to Cricket

Cheetham, Jack — Caught by the Springboks
Cheetham, Jack — I Declare
Chettle, G.A.(ed) — South African Cricket Annual 1951/52 to 1975
Cozier, Tony — Benson & Hedges West Indies Cricket Annual 1982
Cricketer (Australia) (various editions)
Cricketer International, The (various editions)
Cricketer, The (Pakistan) — (ed. Hanif Mohammed) July 1982 and February 1983
Cricketer Quarterly (various editions)
Crowley, Brian — The Springbok and the Kangaroo
Crowley, Brian — Currie Cup Story
Crowley, Brian — Calypso Cavaliers , the story of the 1983 tour

D'Oliveira, Basil — An Autobiography
D'Oliveira, Basil — The D'Oliveira Affair
D'Oliveira, Basil — Time to Declare
Duffus, Louis — South African Cricket 1927/1947
Duffus, Louis — Play Abandoned
Duffus, Louis — Cricketers of the Veld

Faulkner, G.A. — Cricket, Can it be Taught?
Fortune, Charles — Cricket Overthrown
Frindall, Bill — The Wisden Book of Test Cricket, 1876/77 to 1977/78
Fry, C.B.& Beldham, G.W. — Great Batsmen — their methods at a glance
Fry, C.B.& Beldham, G.W. — Great Bowlers and Fielders — their methods at a glance

Giants of South African Cricket (various — publisher/editor Don Nelson)

Heesom, Denys — Protea Cricket Annual of S.Africa 1976/79(with Peter Sichel)
Hetherington, John — South African Cricketer Nov 1974 to Dec 1977

Litchfield, E. — Protea Cricket Annual of S.Africa 1982 (with Peter Sichel)
Luckin, M.W. — History of South African Cricket (1880/1915)
Luckin, M.W. — South African Cricket 1919/1927
Luker, W.J.& West, S.E.L. — Century at Newlands 1864/1964

Moyes, A.G. — Australian Cricket, A History

Nourse, A.D. — Cricket in the blood

Odendaal, Andre — God's Forgotten Cricketers
Odendaal, Andre — Cricket in Isolation
Owen-Smith, M. — Protea Cricket Annual of S.Africa 1980/81(with Peter Sichel)
Peerbhai, Adam — Cricket Coach
Playfair Cricket Monthly (various editions)
Pollard, Jack — Australian Cricket — the Game and the Players
Pollock, Peter — The Thirty Tests
Porter, J.L. — The Kenya Cricketers' Almanack 1958

Reddick, Tom — Never a Cross Bat
Reddy, S.J — Cricket Annual 73/74
Reddy, S.J. — Cricket Annual 76/77
Reddy, S.J. — The South African Cricketer Vol 1 No 1
Reddy, S.J.& Bansda, D.N. — The S.African Non-European Cricket Almanack 1953/54
Reddy, S.J.& Bansda, D.N. — The S.African Non-European Cricket Almanack 1954/55
Reddy, S.J.& Bansda, D.N. — South African Cricket Almanack 1969

Sichel, Peter — Protea Cricket Annual of South Africa 1976/82
Sunderasan, P.N. — Forty Five Years of Ranji Trophy
Swanton, E.W. — Best Cricket Stories
Swanton, E.W.& Altham, H.S. — A History of Cricket
Swanton, E.W.& Woodcock, J. — Barclay's World of Cricket

The Cricketer (Pakistan) — (ed.Hanif Mohammed) July 1982 and February 1983
The Cricketer International (various editions)

Warner, Sir P.F. — MCC in South Africa (1905/06)
West, S.E.L.& Luker, W.J. — Century at Newlands 1864/1964
Wisden Cricketers' Almanack (various editors) 1891 to 1983
Wisden Cricket Monthly (various editions)
Woodcock, J.& Swanton, E.W. — Barclay's World of Cricket

TEST RESULTS

1888/89 SOUTH AFRICA vs ENGLAND
Ist Test, Port Elizabeth — England won by eight wickets
2nd Test, Cape Town — England won by an innings and 202 runs

1891/92 SOUTH AFRICA vs ENGLAND
Only Test, Cape Town — England won by an innings and 189 runs

1895/96 SOUTH AFRICA vs ENGLAND
1st Test, Port Elizabeth — England won by 288 runs
2nd Test, Johannesburg — England won by an innings and 197 runs
3rd Test, Cape Town — England won by an innings and 33 runs

1898/99 SOUTH AFRICA vs ENGLAND
1st Test, Johannesburg — England won by 32 runs
2nd Test, Cape Town — England won by 210 runs

1902/03 SOUTH AFRICA vs AUSTRALIA
1st Test, Johannesburg — Match Drawn
2nd Test, Johannesburg — Australia won by 159 runs
3rd Test, Cape Town — Australia won by ten wickets

1905/06 SOUTH AFRICA vs ENGLAND
1st Test, Johannesburg — South Africa won by one wicket
2nd Test, Johannesburg — South Africa won by nine wickets
3rd Test, Johannesburg — South Africa won by 243 runs
4th Test, Cape Town — England won by four wickets
5th Test, Cape Town — South Africa won by an innings and 16 runs

1907 ENGLAND vs SOUTH AFRICA
1st Test, Lord's — Match Drawn
2nd Test, Headingley — England won by 53 runs
3rd Test, The Oval — Match Drawn

1909/10 SOUTH AFRICA vs ENGLAND
1st Test, Johannesburg — South Africa won by 19 runs
2nd Test, Durban — South Africa won by 95 runs
3rd Test, Johannesburg — England won by three wickets
4th Test, Cape Town — South Africa won by four wickets
5th Test, Cape Town — England won by nine wickets

1910/11 AUSTRALIA vs SOUTH AFRICA
1st Test, Sydney — Australia won by an innings and 112 runs
2nd Test, Melbourne — Australia won by 89 runs
3rd Test, Adelaide — South Africa won by 38 runs
4th Test, Melbourne — Australia won by 530 runs
5th Test, Sydney — Australia won by seven wickets

1912 TRIANGULAR TOURNAMENT in ENGLAND
vs Australia, Old Trafford — Australia won by an innings and 88 runs
vs England, Lord's — England won by an innings and 62 runs
vs England, Headingley- England won by 174 runs
vs Australia, Lord's — Australia won by ten wickets
vs Australia- Trent Bridge — Match Drawn
vs England, The Oval — England won by ten wickets

1913/14 SOUTH AFRICA vs ENGLAND
1st Test, Durban — England won by an innings and 157 runs
2nd Test, Johannesburg — England won by an innings and 12 runs
3rd Test, Johannesburg — England won by 91 runs
4th Test, Durban — Match Drawn
5th Test, Port Elizabeth, England won by ten wickets

1921/22 SOUTH AFRICA vs AUSTRALIA
1st Test, Durban — Match Drawn
2nd Test, Johannesburg — Match Drawn
3rd Test, Cape Town — Australia won by ten wickets

1922/23 SOUTH AFRICA vs ENGLAND
1st Test, Johannesburg — South Africa won by 168 runs
2nd Test, Cape Town — England won by one wicket
3rd Test, Durban — Match Drawn
4th Test, Johannesburg — Match Drawn
5th Test, Durban — England won by 109 runs

1924 ENGLAND vs SOUTH AFRICA
1st Test, Edgbaston — England won by an innings and 18 runs
2nd Test, Lord's — England won by an innings and 18 runs
3rd Test, Headingley — England won by nine wickets
4th Test, Old Trafford — Match Drawn
5th Test, The Oval — Match Drawn

1927/28 SOUTH AFRICA vs ENGLAND
1st Test, Johannesburg — England won by ten wickets
2nd Test, Cape Town — England won by 87 runs
3rd Test, Durban — Match Drawn
4th Test, Johannesburg — South Africa won by four wickets
5th Test, Durban — South Africa won by eight wickets

1929 ENGLAND vs SOUTH AFRICA
1st Test, Edgbaston — Match Drawn
2nd Test, Lord's — Match Drawn
3rd Test, Headingley — England won by five wickets
4th Test, Manchester, England won by an innings and 32 runs
5th Test, The Oval — Match Drawn

1930/31 SOUTH AFRICA vs ENGLAND
1st Test, Johannesburg — South Africa won by 28 runs
2nd Test, Cape Town — Match Drawn
3rd Test, Durban — Match Drawn
4th Test, Johannesburg — Match Drawn
5th Test, Durban — Match Drawn

1931/32 AUSTRALIA vs SOUTH AFRICA
1st Test, Brisbane — Australia won by an innings and 163 runs
2nd Test, Sydney — Australia won by an innings and 155 runs
3rd Test, Melbourne — Australia won by 169 runs
4th Test, Adelaide — Australia won by ten wickets
5th Test, Melbourne — Australia won by an innings and 72 runs

1931/32 NEW ZEALAND vs SOUTH AFRICA
1st Test, Christchurch — South Africa won by an innings and 12 runs
2nd Test, Wellington — South Africa won by eight wickets

1935 ENGLAND vs SOUTH AFRICA
1st Test, Trent Bridge — Match Drawn
2nd Test, Lord's, South Africa won by 157 runs
3rd Test, Leeds — Match Drawn
4th Test, Old Trafford — Match Drawn
5th Test, The Oval — Match Drawn

1935/36 SOUTH AFRICA vs AUSTRALIA
1st Test, Durban — Australia won by nine wickets
2nd Test, Johannesburg — Match Drawn
3rd Test, Cape Town — Australia won by an innings and 78 runs
4th Test, Johannesburg — Australia won by an innings and 184 runs
5th Test, Durban — Australia won by an innings and 6 runs

1938/39 SOUTH AFRICA vs ENGLAND
1st Test, Johannesburg — Match Drawn
2nd Test, Cape Town — Match Drawn
3rd Test, Durban — England won by an innings and 13 runs
4th Test, Johannesburg — Match Drawn
5th Test, Durban — Match Drawn

1947 ENGLAND vs SOUTH AFRICA
1st Test, Trent Bridge — Match Drawn
2nd Test, Lord's — England won by ten wickets
3rd Test, Old Trafford — England won by seven wickets
4th Test, Headingley — England won by ten wickets
5th Test, The Oval — Match Drawn

1948/49 SOUTH AFRICA vs ENGLAND
1st Test, Durban — England won by two wicket
2nd Test, Johannesburg, Match Drawn
3rd Test, Cape Town — Match Drawn
4th Test, Johannesburg — Match Drawn
5th Test, Port Elizabeth — England won by three wickets

1949/50 SOUTH AFRICA vs AUSTRALIA
1st Test, Johannesburg — Australia won by an innings and 85 runs
2nd Test, Cape Town — Australia won by eight wickets
3rd Test, Durban — Australia won by five wickets
4th Test, Johannesburg — Match Drawn
5th Test, Port Elizabeth — Australia won by an innings and 259 runs

1951 ENGLAND vs SOUTH AFRICA
1st Test, Trent Bridge — South Africa won by 71 runs
2nd Test, Lord's — England won by ten wickets
3rd Test, Old Trafford — England won by nine wickets
4th Test, Headingley — Match Drawn
5th Test, The Oval — England won by four wickets

1952/53 AUSTRALIA vs SOUTH AFRICA
1st Test, Brisbane — Australia won by 96 runs
2nd Test, Melbourne — South Africa won by 82 runs
3rd Test, Sydney — Australia won by an innings and 38 runs,
4th Test, Adelaide — Match Drawn
5th Test, Melbourne — South Africa won by six wickets

1952/53 NEW ZEALAND vs SOUTH AFRICA
1st Test, Wellington — South Africa won by an innings and 180 runs
2nd Test, Auckland — Match Drawn

1953/54 SOUTH AFRICA vs NEW ZEALAND
1st Test, Durban — South Africa won by an innings and 58 runs
2nd Test, Johannesburg — South Africa won by 132 runs
3rd Test, Cape Town — Match Drawn
4th Test, Johannesburg — South Africa won by nine wickets
5th Test, Port Elizabeth — South Africa won by five wickets

1955 ENGLAND vs SOUTH AFRICA
1st Test, Trent Bridge — England won by an innings and 5 runs
2nd Test, Lord's — England won by 71 runs
3rd Test, Old Trafford — South Africa won by three wickets
4th Test, Headingley — South Africa won by 224 runs
5th Test, The Oval — England won by 92 runs

1956/57 SOUTH AFRICA vs ENGLAND
1st Test, Johannesburg — England won by 131 runs
2nd Test, Cape Town — England won by 312 runs
3rd Test, Durban — Match Drawn
4th Test, Johannesburg — South Africa won by 17 runs
5th Test, Port Elizabeth — South Africa won by 58 runs

1957/58 SOUTH AFRICA vs AUSTRALIA
1st Test, Johannesburg — Match Drawn
2nd Test, Cape Town — Australia won by an innings and 141 runs
3rd Test, Durban — Match Drawn
4th Test, Johannesburg — Australia won by ten wickets
5th Test, Port Elizabeth — Australia won by eight wickets

1960 ENGLAND vs SOUTH AFRICA
1st Test, Edgbaston — England won by 100 runs
2nd Test, Lord's — England won by an innings and 73 runs
3rd Test, Trent Bridge — England won by eight wickets
4th Test, Old Trafford — Match Drawn
5th Test, The Oval — Match Drawn

1961/62 SOUTH AFRICA vs NEW ZEALAND
1st Test, Durban — South Africa won by 30 runs
2nd Test, Johannesburg — Match drawn
3rd Test, Cape Town — New Zealand won by 72 runs
4th Test, Johannesburg — South Africa won by an innings and 51 runs
5th Test, Port Elizabeth — New Zealand won by 40 runs

1963/64 AUSTRALIA vs SOUTH AFRICA
1st Test, Brisbane — Match drawn
2nd Test, Melbourne — Australia won by eight wickets
3rd Test, Sydney — Match drawn
4th Test, Adelaide — South Africa won by ten wickets
5th Test, Sydney — Match drawn

1963/64 NEW ZEALAND vs SOUTH AFRICA
1st Test, Wellington — Match drawn
2nd Test, Dunedin — Match drawn
3rd Test, Auckland — Match drawn

1964/65 SOUTH AFRICA vs ENGLAND
1st Test, Durban — England won by an innings and 104 runs
2nd Test, Johannesburg — Match drawn
3rd Test, Cape Town — Match drawn
4th Test, Johannesburg — Match drawn
5th Test, Port Elizabeth — Match drawn

1965 – ENGLAND vs SOUTH AFRICA
1st Test, Lord's — Match drawn
2nd Test, Trent Bridge — South Africa won by 94 runs
3rd Test, The Oval — Match drawn

1966/67 SOUTH AFRICA vs AUSTRALIA
1st Test, Johannesburg — South Africa won by 233 runs
2nd Test, Cape Town — Australia won by six wickets
3rd Test, Durban — South Africa won by eight wickets
4th Test, Johannesburg — Match drawn
5th Test, Port Elizabeth — South Africa won by seven wickets

1969/70 SOUTH AFRICA vs AUSTRALIA
1st Test, Cape Town — South Africa won by 170 runs
2nd Test, Durban — South Africa won by an innings and 129 runs
3rd Test, Johannesburg — South Africa won by 307 runs
4th Test, Port Elizabeth — South Africa won by 323 runs

RESULTS – THE INTERNATIONAL MATCHES 1981/82 and 1982/83

1981/82 SOUTH AFRICA versus SAB ENGLISH XI

*First Match at Johannesburg, March 12,13,14,*15 1982 — South Africa won by eight wickets

SOUTH AFRICA 400 for 7 wkts decl (B.A. Richards 66, S.J. Cook 114, P.N. Kirsten 88, R.G. Pollock 64 n.o) and 37 for two wkts
SAB ENGLISH XI 150 (D.L. Amiss 66 n.o., V.A.P. van der Bijl 5 for 25) and 283 (G.A. Gooch 109, van der Bijl 5 for 79, G.S. le Roux 4 for 44)

*Second Match at Cape Town, March 19,20,21,*22 1982 — Match Drawn

SAB ENGLISH XI 223 (G.A. Gooch 83, A.J. Kourie 4 for 52) and 249 for 3 wkts decl (Gooch 68, W. Larkins 95, D.L. Amiss 73 n.o.)
SOUTH AFRICA 235 (P.N. Kirsten 114, J.K. Lever 6 for 86) and 38 for 0 wkt

Third Match at Durban, March 26,27,28,29 — Match Drawn

SOUTH AFRICA 181 for 9 wkts decl (A.J. Kourie 50 n.o.,L.B. Taylor 5 for 61) and 143 for 2 wkts (S.J. Cook 50 n.o.)
SAB ENGLISH XI 311 for 8 wkts decl (D.L. Amiss 50, R.A. Woolmer 100, V.A.P. van der Bijl 5 for 97)

1982/83 SOUTH AFRICA versus AROSA SRI LANKA

*First Match at Johannesburg, Nov 19,20,22,*23 1982 — South Africa won by an innings and 24 runs

AROSA SRI LANKA 213 (P.B. De Silva 70, J.F. Woutersz 51, G.S. le Roux 6 for 55) and 141 (A.J. Kourie 5 for 54)
SOUTH AFRICA 378 (S.J. Cook 169, R.G. Pollock 79, L.W. Kaluperuma 5 for 123)

*Second Match at Cape Town, December 9,10,11,*13 1982 — South Africa won by an innings and 100 runs

AROSA SRI LANKA 282 (G.J.A.F. Aponso 81, A.N. Ranasinghe 54) and 281 (H. Devapriya 53, J.N.B. Perera 102)
SOUTH AFRICA 663 for 6 wickets declared (S.J. Cook 112, L. Seeff 188, R.G. Pollock 197, A.P. Kuiper 66)

1982/83 SOUTH AFRICA versus WEST INDIES XI

*First Match at Cape Town, January 21,22,24,*25 1983 — South Africa won by five wickets

SOUTH AFRICA 449 (S.J. Cook 73, R.G. Pollock 100, A.J. Kourie 69, D.R. Parry 5 for 117) and 108 for five wkts
WEST INDIES XI 246 (R.A. Austin 93, F. daC. Stephenson 56, V.A.P. van der Bijl 4 for 44) and 309 (A.I. Kallicharan 89, S.T. Jefferies 4 for 58)

Second Match at Johannesburg, January 28,29,31,February 1 1983 — West Indies XI won by 29 runs

WEST INDIES XI 267 (C.L. King 101, A.J. Kourie 6 for 55) and 176
SOUTH AFRICA 233 (P.N. Kirsten 56, R.G. Polock 73, S.T. Clarke 5 for 66) and 181 (B.A. Richards 59, Clarke 7 for 34)

RESULTS OF SACBOC TESTS

1956/57 SOUTH AFRICA versus KENYA ASIANS

First Match at Cape Town, Dec 7, 8, 10 1956 — South Africa won by 6 wickets

KENYA ASIANS 149 (Shakoor Ahmed 101, A. Bell 3 for 63, B. Malamba 4 for 41) and 218 (Arvind Patel 52, Chandrakant Patel 84, C. Abrahams 3 for 51, Bell 2 for 40, Malamba 4 for 73)

SOUTH AFRICA 258 (S. Raziet 36, B.L. D'Oliviera 70, A. Variawa 35, G.B. Jhalla 5 for 93, Rasik Patel 3 for 60) and 112 for 4 wickets (D'Oliveira 36 not out, B.L. D'Cunha 2 for 16)

Second Match at Johannesburg, Dec 15, 16, 17 1956 — South Africa won by 39 runs

SOUTH AFRICA 377 (S. Raziet 109, G. Abed 54, H. Abrahams 63, C. Abrahams 55, B.L. D'Cunha 5 for 109) and 165 (Raziet 40, B.L. D'Oliveira 44, Rasik Patel 3 for 16)

KENYA ASIANS 257/9 Shakoor Ahmed 120, Arvind Patel 36, V. Bhandari 34, C. Abrahams 3 for 19) and 246 (Ghafoor Ahmed 63, Bhandari 91, A. Bell 3 for 50, G.Abed 3 for 37)

Third Match at Durban, Dec 22, 23, 24 1956 — Match Drawn (Rain)

KENYA ASIANS 71 (G. Abed 4 for 9) and 111 for 8 wickets (Ramanbhai Patel 34, B. Malamba 4 for 34)

SOUTH AFRICA 88 (C. Abrahams 39, Rasik Patel 6 for 36)

1958/59 SOUTH AFRICANS IN EAST AFRICA

vs Kenya at Nairobi, Aug 23, 24, 25 1958 — South Africa won by 165 runs

SOUTH AFRICA 196 (A. I. Deedat 38, C. Abrahams 41, G. Abed 31, G. B. Jhalla 4 for 70, B.L. D'Cunha 3 for 23) and 314 for 7 wickets decl. (Deedat 59, B.L. D'Oliveira 139, J.J. Neethling 52, C. Abrahams 50 not out, Jhalla 4 for 97, Daljit Singh 3 for 83)

KENYA 190 (Mehboob Ali 37, P.R. Prodger 41, Halim Mohammed 36, Gursaran Singh 36, E. Petersen 6 for 51) and 155 (Ghafoor Ahmed 35, Neethling 3 for 23, D'Oliveira 3 for 24)

vs East Africa at Nairobi, Sept 13, 14, 15 1958 — South Africa won by 7 wickets

EAST AFRICA 213 (Mehboob Ali 88, Gursaran Singh 33, Bhanu Patel 34, E. Petersen 3 for 36, G. Abed 4 for 30) and 205 (Ghafoor Ahmed 72, Ramanbhai Patel 51, Abed 4 for 50)

SOUTH AFRICA 350 for 7 wickets decl. (A.I. Deedat 66, B.L. D'Oliveira 96, J.J. Neethling 53 not out, C. Abrahams 77, B.L. D'Cunha 4 for 78) and 72 for 3 wickets (Abrahams 31 not out, Ranjit Singh 2 for 10)

vs Kenya at Mombasa, Sept 21, 22, 23 1958 — South Africa won by 255 runs

SOUTH AFRICA 193 (S. Solomons 76, J.J. Neethling 57, G.B. Jhalla 3 for 31, B.L. D'Cunha 3 for 49) and 183 for 7 wickets decl. (B.L. D'Oliveira 50, G. Abed 34, Jhalla 3 for 59)

KENYA 49 (C. Abrahams 4 for 20, E. Petersen 5 for 14) and 72 (Abrahams 3 for 22, Petersen 4 for 29)

SOUTH AFRICAN TEST MATCH STATISTICS

RESULTS

versus	Played	Won	Lost	Drawn
ENGLAND	102	18	46	38
AUSTRALIA	53	11	29	13
NEW ZEALAND	17	9	2	6
Total	172	38	77	57

SOUTH AFRICAN TEST MATCH GROUNDS

Seven grounds have been used for test matches in South Africa. The full list is:

PORT ELIZABETH: St George's Park (or Crusaders)

JOHANNESBURG: Old Wanderers; Ellis Park; The Wanderers Stadium (since re-named the Wanderers Oval)

CAPE TOWN: Newlands
DURBAN: Lord's; Kingsmead

INDIVIDUAL RECORDS OFFICIAL TEST MATCHES

* = not out

	Tests	Runs	HS	Avrge	ct	st	Wkts	Avrge	Best
Adcock, N.A.T.	26	146	24	5.40	4	—	104	21.10	6-43
Anderson, J.H.	1	43	32	21.50	1	—			
Ashley, W.H.	1	1	1	0.50	—	—	7	13.57	7-95
Bacher, A.	12	679	73	32.33	10	—			
Balaskas, X.C.	9	174	122*	14.50	5	—	22	36.63	5-49
Barlow, E.J.	30	2516	201	45.74	35	—	40	34.05	5-85
Baumgartner, H.V.	1	19	16	9.50	1	—	2	49.50	2-99
Beaumont, R.	5	70	31	7.77	2	—			
Begbie, D.W.	5	138	48	19.71	2	—	1	130.00	1-38
Bell, A.J.	16	69	26*	6.27	6	—	48	32.64	6-99
Bisset, M.	3	103	35	25.75	2	—			
Bissett, G.F.	4	38	23	19.00	—	—	25	18.76	7-29
Blanckenberg, J.M.	18	455	59	19.78	9	—	60	30.28	6-76
Bland, K.C.	21	1669	144*	49.08	10	—	2	62.50	2-16
Bock, E.G.	1	11	9*	—	—	—			
Bond, G.E.	1	0	0	—	—	—			
Botten, J.T.	3	65	33	10.83	1	—	8	42.12	2-56
Brann, W.H.	3	71	50	14.20	2	—			
Briscoe, A.W.	2	33	16	11.00	1	—			
Bromfield, H.D.	9	59	21	11.80	13	—	17	35.23	5-88
Brown, L.S.	2	17	8	5.66	—	—	3	63.00	1-30
Burger, C.G.deV.	2	62	37*	20.66	1	—			
Burke, S.F.	2	42	20	14.00	—	—	11	23.36	6-128
Buys, I.D.	1	4	4*	4.00					
Cameron, H.B.	26	1239	90	30.21	39	12			
Campbell, T.	5	90	48	15.00	7	1			
Carlstein, P.R.	8	190	42	14.61	3	—			
Carter, C.P.	10	181	45	18.10	2	—	28	24.78	6-50
Catterall, R.H.	24	1555	120	37.92	12	—	7	23.14	3-15
Chapman, H.W.	2	39	17	13.00	1	—	1	104.00	1-51
Cheetham, J.E.	24	883	89	23.86	13	—			
Chevalier, G.A.	1	0	0*	0.00	1	—	5	20.00	3-68
Christy, J.A.J.	10	618	103	34.33	3	—	2	46.00	1-15
Chubb, G.W.A.	5	63	15*	10.50	—	—	21	27.47	6-51
Cochran, J.A.K.	1	4	4	4.00					

	Tests	Runs	HS	Avrge	ct	st	Wkts	Avrge	Best
Heine, P.S.	14	209	31	9.95	8	—	58	25.08	6-58
Hime, C.F.W.	1	8	8	4.00	—	—	1	31.00	1-20
Hutchinson, P.	2	14	11	3.50	3	—			
Innes, A.R.	2	14	13	3.50	2	—	5	17.80	5-43
Ironside, D.E.J.	3	37	13	18.50	1	—	15	18.33	5-51
Irvine, B.L.	4	353	102	50.42	2	—			
Johnson, C.L.	1	10	7	5.00	1	—			
Jones, P.S.T.	1	0	0	0.00	—	—			
Keith, H.J.	8	318	73	21.20	9	—			
Kempis, G.A.	1	0	0	0.00	—	—	4	19.00	3-53
Kotze, J.J.	3	2	2	0.40	3	—	6	40.50	3-64
Kuys, F.	1	26	26	13.00	—	—	2	15.50	2-31
Lance, H.R.	13	591	70	28.14	7	—	12	39.91	3-30
Langton, A.B.C.	15	298	73*	15.68	8	—	40	45.67	5-58
Lawrence, G.B.	5	141	43	17.62	2	—	28	18.28	8-53
Le Roux, F.L.	1	1	1	0.50	—				
Lewis, P.T.	1	0	0	0.00	—	—			
Lindsay, D.T.	19	1130	182	37.66	57	2			
Lindsay, J.D.	3	21	9*	7.00	4	1			
Lindsay, N.V.	1	35	29	17.50	1	—			
Ling, W.V.S.	6	168	38	16.80	1	—			
Llewellyn, G.C.B.	15	544	90	20.14	7	—	48	29.60	6-92
Lundie, E.B.	1	1	1	1.00	—	—	4	26.75	4-101
Macaulay, M.J.	1	33	21	16.50	—	—	2	36.50	1-10
McCarthy, C.N.	15	28	5	3.11	6	—	36	41.94	6-43
McGlew, D.J.	34	2440	255*	42.06	18	—			
McKinnon, A.H.	8	107	27	17.83	1	—	26	35.57	4-128
McLean, R.A.	40	2120	142	30.28	23	—			
McMillan, Q.	13	306	50*	18.00	8	—	36	34.52	5-66
Mann, N.B.F.	19	400	52	13.33	3	—	58	33.10	6-59
Mansell, P.N.F.	13	355	90	17.75	15	—	11	66.90	3-58
Markham, L.A.	1	20	20	20.00	—	—	1	72.00	1-34

Coen, S.K.	2	101	41*	50.50	1	—			
Commaille, J.M.M.	12	355	47	16.90	1	—			
Conyngham, D.P.	1	6	3*	—	—	1	—	2	51.50
1-40									
Cook, F.J.	1	7	7	3.50	—	—			
Cooper, A.H.C.	1	6	6	3.00	1	—			
Cox, J.L.	3	17	12*	3.40	1	—	4	61.25	2-74
Cripps, G.	1	21	18	10.50	—	—			
Crisp, R.J.	9	123	35	10.25	3	—	20	37.35	5-99
Curnow, S.H.	7	168	47	12.00	5	—			
Dalton, E.L.	15	698	117	31.72	5	—	12	40.83	4-59
Davies, E.Q.	5	9	3	1.80	—	—	7	68.71	4-75
Dawson, O.C.	9	293	55	20.92	10	—	10	57.80	2-57
Deane, H.G.	17	628	93	25.12	8	—			
Dixon, C.D.	1	0	0	0.00	1	—	3	39.33	2-62
Dower, R.R.	1	9	9	4.50	2	—			
Draper, R.G.	2	25	15	8.33	—	—			
Duckworth, C.A.R.	2	28	13	7.00	3	—			
Dumbrill, R.	5	153	36	15.30	3	—	9	37.33	4-30
Duminy, J.P.	3	30	12	5.00	2	—	1	39.00	1-17
Dunell., O.R.	2	42	26*	14.00	1	—			
Du Preez, J.H.	2	0	0	0.00	2	—	3	17.00	2-22
Du Toit, J.F.	1	2	2*	—	1	—	1	47.00	1-47
Dyer, D.V.	3	96	62	16.00	—	—			
Elgie, M.K.	3	75	56	12.50	4	—			
Endean, W.R.	28	1630	162*	33.95	41	—			
Farrer, W.S.	6	221	40	27.62	2	—			
Faulkner,G.A.	25	1754	204	40.79	20	—	82	26.58	7-84
Fellows-Smith, J.P.	4	166	35	27.66	2	—			
Fichardt,C.G.	2	15	10	3.75	2	—			
Finlason, C.E.	1	6	6	3.00	—	—			
Floquet, C.E.	1	12	11*	12.00	—	—			
Francis, H.H.	2	39	29	9.75	1	—			
Francois, C.M.	5	252	72	31.50	5	—	6	37.50	3-23
Frank, C.N.	3	236	152	39.33	—	—			
Fuller, E.R.H.	7	64	17	8.00	3	—	22	30.36	5-66
Fullerton, G.M.	7	325	88	25.00	10	2			
Funston, K.J.	18	824	92	25.75	7	—			
Gamsy, D.	2	39	30*	19.50	5	—			
Gleeson, R.A.	1	4	3	4.00	2	—			
Glover, G.K.	1	21	18*	21.00	—	—	1	28.00	1-28
Goddard, T.L.	41	2516	112	34.46	48	—	123	26.22	6-53
Gordon, N.	5	8	7*	2.00	1	—	20	40.35	5-103
Graham, R.	2	6	4	1.50	2	—	3	42.33	2-22
Grieveson, R.E.	2	114	75	57.00	7	3			
Griffin, G.M.	2	25	14	6.25	—	—	8	24.00	4-87
Hall, A.E.	7	11	5	1.83	4	—	40	22.15	7-63
Hall.G.G.	1	0	0	0.00	—	—	1	94.00	1-94
Halliwell, E.A.	8	188	57	12.53	9	2			
Halse, C.G.	3	30	19*	—	—	1	—	6	43.33
3-50									
Hands, P.A.M.	7	300	83	25.00	3	—			
Hands, R.H.M.	1	7	7	3.50	—	—			
Hanley, M.A.	1	0	0	0.00	—	—	1	88.00	1-57
Harris, T.A.	3	100	60	25.00	1	—			
Hartigan, G.P.D.	5	114	51	11.40	—	—	1	141.00	1-72
Harvey, R.L.	2	51	28	12.75	—	—			
Hathorn, C.M.H.	12	325	102	17.10	5	—			
Hearne, F.	4	121	30	15.12	2	—			
Hearne, G.A.L.	3	59	28	11.80	3	—	2	20.00	2-40

Marx, W.F.E.	3	125	36	20.83	—	—	4	36.00	3-85
Meintjies, D.J.	2	43	21	14.33	3	—	6	19.16	3-38
Melle, M.G.	7	68	17	8.50	4	—	26	32.73	6-71
Melville, A.	11	894	189	52.58	8	—			
Middleton, J.	6	52	22	7.42	1	—	24	18.41	5-51
Mills, C.	1	25	21	12.50	2	—	2	41.50	2-83
Milton, W.H.	3	68	21	11.33	1	—	2	24.00	1-5
Mitchell, B.	42	3471	189*	48.88	56	—	27	51.11	5-87
Mitchell, F.	3	28	12	4.66	—	—			
Morkel, D.P.B.	16	663	88	24.55	13	—	18	45.61	4-93
Murray, A.R.A.	10	289	109	22.33	3	—	18	39.44	4-169
Nel, J.D.	6	150	38	13.63	1	—			
Newberry, C.J.	4	62	16	7.75	3	—	11	24.36	4-72
Newson, E.S.	3	30	16	7.50	3	—	4	66.25	2-58
Nicholson, F.	4	76	29	10.85	3				
Nicholson, J.F.W.	3	179	78	35.80	—	—			
Norton, N.O.	1	9	7	4.50	—	—	4	11.75	4-47
Nourse, A.D.	34	2960	231	53.81	12	—			
Nourse, A.W.	45	2234	111	29.78	43	—	42	37.87	4-25
Nupen, E.P.	17	348	69	14.50	9	—	50	35.76	6-46
Osche, A.E.	2	16	8	4.00	—	—			
Osche, A.L.	3	11	4*	3.66	1	—	10	36.20	4-79
O'Linn, S.	7	297	98	27.00	4	—			
Owen-Smith, H.G.	5	252	129	42.00	4	—			
Palm, A.W.	1	15	13	7.50					
Parker, G.M.	2	3	2*	1.50	—	—	8	34.12	6-152
Parkin, D.C.	1	6	6	3.00	1	—	3	27.33	3-82
Partridge, J.T.	11	73	13*	10.42	6	—	44	31.20	7-91
Pearse, C.O.C.	3	55	31	9.16	1	—	3	35.33	3-56
Pegler, S.J.	16	356	35*	15.47	5	—	47	33.44	7-65
Pithey, A.J.	17	819	154	31.50	3	—			
Pithey, D.B.	8	138	55	12.54	6	—	12	48.08	6-58
Plimsoll, J.B.	1	16	8*	16.00	—	—	3	47.66	3-128
Pollock, P.MacL.	28	607	75*	21.67	9	—	116	24.18	6-38
Pollock, R.G.	23	2256	274	60.97	17	—	4	51.00	2-50
Poore, R.M.	3	76	20	12.66	3	—	1	4.00	1-4
Pothecary, J.E.	3	26	12	6.50	2	—	9	39.33	4-58
Powell, A.W.	1	16	11	8.00	2	—	1	10.00	1-10
Prince, C.F.H.	1	6	5	3.00	—	—			
Procter, M.J.	7	226	48	25.11	4	—	41	15.02	6-73
Promnitz, H.L.E.	2	14	5	3.50	2	—	8	20.12	5-58
Quinn, N.A.	12	90	28	6.00	1	—	35	32.71	6-92
Reid, N.	1	17	11	8.50	—	—	2	31.50	2-63
Richards, A.R.	1	6	6	3.00	—	—			
Richards, B.A.	4	508	140	72.57	3	—	1	26.00	1-12
Richards, W.H.M.	1	4	4	2.00	—	—			
Robertson, J.B.	3	51	17	10.20	2	—	6	53.50	3-143
Routledge, T.W.	4	72	24	9.00	2	—			
Rowan, A.M.B.	15	290	41	17.05	7	—	54	38.59	5-68
Rowan, E.A.B.	26	1965	236	34.66	14	—			
Rowe, G.A.	5	26	13*	4.33	4	—	15	30.40	5-115
Samuelson, S.V.	1	22	15	11.00	1	—			
Schwarz, R.O.	20	374	61	13.85	18	—	55	25.76	6-47
Seccull, A.W.	1	23	17*	23.00	1	—	2	18.50	2-37
Seymour, M.A.	7	84	36	12.00	2	—	9	65.33	3-80
Shalders, W.A.	12	355	42	16.13	3	—	1	6.00	1-6
Shepstone, G.H.	2	38	21	9.50	2	—			
Sherwell, P.W.	13	427	115	23.72	20	16			

Siedle, I.J.	18	977	141	28.73	7	—	1	7.00	1-7
Sinclair, J.H.	25	1069	106	23.23	9	—	63	31.68	6-26
Smith, C.J.E.	3	106	45	21.20	2	—			
Smith, F.W.	3	45	12	9.00	2	—			
Smith, V.I.	9	39	11*	3.90	3	—	12	64.08	4-143
Snooke, S.D.	1	0	0	0.00	2	—			
Snooke, S.J.	26	1008	103	22.40	24	—	35	20.05	8-70
Solomon, W.R.T.	4	2	2.00	1	—	—			
Stewart, R.B.	1	13	9	6.50	2	—			
Stricker, L.A.	13	342	48	14.25	3	—	1	105.00	1-36
Susskind, M.J.	5	268	65	33.50	1	—			
Taberer, H.M.	1	2	2	2.00	—	—	1	48.00	1-25
Tancred, A.B.	2	87	29	29.00	2	—			
Tancred, L.J.	14	530	97	21.20	3	—			
Tancred, V.M.	1	25	18	12.50	—	—			
Tapscott, L.E.	2	58	50*	29.00	—	—			
Tayfield, H.J.	37	862	75	16.90	26	—	170	25.91	9-113
Taylor, A.I.	1	18	12	9.00	—	—			
Taylor, D.	2	85	36	21.25	—	—			
Taylor, H.W.	42	2936	176	40.77	19	—	5	31.20	3-15
Theunissen, N.H.	1	2	2*	2.00	—	—			
Thornton, P.G.	1	1	1*	—	1	—	1	20.00	1-20
Tomlinson, D.S.	1	9	9	9.00	—	—			
Traicos, A.J.	3	8	5*	4.00	4	—	4	51.75	2-70
Trimborn, P.H.J.	4	13	11*	6.50	7	—	11	23.36	3-12
Tuckett, L.	9	131	40*	11.90	9	—	19	51.57	5-68
Tuckett, L.R.	1	0	0*	0.00	2	—			
Van der Bijl, P.G.V.	5	460	125	51.11	1	—			
V/d Merwe, E.A.	2	27	19	9.00	3	—			
V/d Merwe, P.L.	15	533	76	25.38	11	—	1	22.00	1-6
Van Ryneveld, C.B.	19	724	83	26.81	14	—	17	39.47	4-67
Varnals, G.D.	3	97	23	16.16	—	—			
Viljoen, K.G.	27	1365	124	28.43	5	—			
Vincent, C.L.	25	526	60	20.33	27	—	84	31.32	6-51
Vintcent, C.H.	3	26	9	4.33	1	—	4	48.25	3-88
Vogler, A.E.E.	15	340	65	17.00	20	—	64	22.73	7-94
Wade, H.F.	10	327	40*	20.43	4	—			
Wade, W.W.	11	511	125	28.38	15	2			
Waite, J.H.B.	50	2405	134	30.44	124	17			
Walter, K.A.	2	11	10	3.66	3	—	6	32.83	4-63
Ward, T.A.	23	459	64	13.90	19	13			
Watkins, J.C.	15	612	92	23.53	12	—	29	28.13	4-22
Wesley, C.J.	3	49	35	9.80	1	—			
Westcott, R.J.	5	166	62	18.44	—	—			
White, G.C.	17	872	147	30.06	10	—	9	33.44	4-47
Willoughby, J.T.	2	8	5	2.00	—	—	6	26.50	2-37
Wimble, C.S.	1	0	0	0.00	—	—			
Winslow, P.L.	5	186	108	20.66	1	—			
Wynne, O.E.	6	219	50	18.25	3	—			
Zulch, J.W.	16	985	150	32.83	4	—			

INDIVIDUAL RECORDS — The Seven 'International' matches played as a South African Team in 1981/82 and 1982/83 (vs SAB England XI, Arosa Sri Lanka and West Indies XI)

Played : 7
Won : 4
Lost : 1
Drawn : 2

Batting and Fielding

	Games	Inngs	NO	Total	H.S.	Avrge	100	50	ct	st
Cook, S.J.	7	11	1	582	169	58.20	3	2	4	0
Hobson, D.L.	2	1	0	2	2	2.00	—	—	1	-
Jefferies, S.T.	6	5	1	130	45	32.50	—	—	2	—
Jennings, R.V.	7	9	2	134	32	19.14	—	—	19	4
Kirsten, P.N.	7	11	1	355	114	35.50	1	2	2	—
Kourie, A.J.	7	8	2	196	69	32.66	—	2	11	—
Kuiper, A.P.	4	5	1	87	66	21.75	—	1	2	—
Le Roux, G.S.	6	6	1	44	30	8.80	—	—	—	—
McKenzie, K.A.	2	4	1	57	27	19.00	—	—	1	—
Pollock, R.G.	7	11	3	593	197	74.12	2	3	8	—
Procter, M.J.	1	1	0	1	1	1.00	—	—	1	—
Rice, C.E.B.	7	10	1	189	39*	21.00	—	—	3	—
Richards, B.A.	6	10	1	252	66	28.00	—	2	4	—
Seeff, L.	1	1	0	188	188	188.00	1	—	2	—
Van der Bijl, V.A.P.	6	6	3	21	10	7.00	—	—	—	—
Watson, W.K.	1	1	1	4	4*	—	—	—	—	—

Bowling

	Overs	Mdns	Runs	Wkts	Avrge	Best
Hobson, D.L.	102	21	298	5	59.60	3/87
Jefferies, S.T.	232,2	71	648	25	25.92	4/58
Kirsten, P.N.	28,3	9	96	4	24.00	1/5
Kourie, A.J.	214	52	523	24	22.16	6/55
Kuiper, A.P.	40	9	99	5	19.80	2/33
Le Roux, G.S.	184,5	36	569	25	22.76	6/55
Procter, M.J.	6	3	6	0	—	—
Van der Bijl, V.A.P.	257	82	576	29	19.86	5/25
Watson, W.K.	25,2	4	79	2	39.50	2/7

INDEX